THE LOST YEARS

Revealed here for the first time in stunning detail are the years that have long been shrouded in secrecy. Family insider Earl Greenwood traces the Presley clan back over one hundred years, and paints vivid and colorful portraits of Presley's parents: the charming and irresponsible Vernon Presley, whose scandalous criminal record haunted Elvis throughout his life . . . and Presley's alcoholic mother, Gladys, whose death in 1960 marked the beginning of Presley's long descent into drug-dependency and self-destruction. And then there are the early years of Elvis' career: the empty halls of brawl-prone dives . . . his first record contract with Sun Records . . . and Greenwood takes us behind the scenes of The King's many Hollywood movies, revealing Presley's affairs with leading ladies such as Ann-Margaret, Natalie Wood and Nancy Sinatra. Brimming with ''Elvis'' anecdotes and insider information, *The Boy Who Would Be King* is the definitive biography of one of the most fascinating and enigmatic legends of our times.

EARL GREENWOOD, a second cousin to the late Elvis Presley, was with Elvis in a personal and professional capacity—serving as his press agent for a time—throughout Presley's career. He lives in Los Angeles.

KATHLEEN TRACY is a writer who lives in California.

Earl Greenwood
and Kathleen Tracy

THE BOY WHO WOULD BE KING

A SIGNET BOOK

SIGNET
Published by the Penguin Group
Penguin Books USA Inc., 375 Hudson Street,
New York, New York 10014, U.S.A.
Penguin Books Ltd, 27 Wrights Lane,
London W8 5TZ, England
Penguin Books Australia Ltd, Ringwood,
Victoria, Australia
Penguin Books Canada Ltd, 2801 John Street,
Markham, Ontario, Canada L3R 1B4
Penguin Books (N.Z.) Ltd, 182–190 Wairau Road,
Auckland 10, New Zealand

Penguin Books Ltd, Registered Offices:
Harmondsworth, Middlesex, England

Published by SIGNET, an imprint of New American Library, a division of
Penguin Books USA Inc. Previously published in a Dutton edition.

First SIGNET Printing, August, 1991
10 9 8 7 6 5 4 3 2 1

Photo credits courtesy of Greenwood family in Memphis, Tennessee, and Tupelo, Mississippi, the Elvis Special Fan Club, Maria Columbus, Robin Rosaaen, and Susan Ragan.

Ⓟ REGISTERED TRADEMARK—MARCA REGISTRADA

PRINTED IN THE UNITED STATES OF AMERICA

A very special dedication to my family and some of Elvis's family in Tennessee and Mississippi who supplied early information on Elvis and especially my mother, Nora Greenwood, who was a tremendous help and encouraged me to continue with the book. To my agent, Denise Marcil, whose direction and advice made this book possible. To my good friends, Timothy Perez, his son, Timmy, his parents, Mr. & Mrs. Robert Perez, and his sister, Diane Hernandez, who are strong Elvis fans and never stopped supporting me on writing this book. To Todd McDurmot for his assistance. To Kathy Tracy for her excellent writing and to the following Elvis fan clubs and dedicated Elvis fans for their loyal support and assistance for which I will always be grateful: the Elvis Special Fan Club, King of Our Hearts Fan Club, Maria Columbus, Robin Rosaaen, Susan Ragan, and Irene Maleti.

This book is especially dedicated to all of Elvis's fans, hoping they will better understand a man we all loved.
—E.G.

To the one who has given me equal parts joy and gray hair.
—K.T.

ACKNOWLEDGMENTS

I'd like to thank my agent, Denise Marcil, for both her guidance and for accepting all those late-afternoon, panic-stricken calls from the West Coast. I would also like to express my heartfelt gratitude to Jill Evans for her suggestions, assistance, and comic relief during the rewriting phase. I figure about fifty more dinners will make us even . . .

—K.T.

INTRODUCTION

For years I debated whether or not to write a book about my cousin, Elvis Presley. On one hand, I simply wasn't sure I wanted to relive all the memories. The good moments we shared as children, teenagers, and young adults have turned bittersweet, shadowed by the painful knowledge that Elvis died far too young and far too unhappy. But on the other hand, it has always irked me that the majority of people writing books about Elvis either never knew him at all or only knew him for a certain part of his life. Too often, I'm afraid, what's been written is full of half-truths, supposition, or out-and-out falsehoods. Family, friend, and fan alike have urged me to write a book about the real Elvis—to share what I know about a man still beloved by millions of people the world over. It's taken me a while, but I've finally decided to accept the challenge.

This will be the first time a blood relative has spoken up, and there are several reasons for this. On the Presley side, there are not many relatives left, which is a shame. The ones who are left are not the type who would or could tell the family story. First of all, the Presleys as a clan weren't that close and second, after Elvis's family left Tupelo, they fell out of touch. Whether by choice or circumstance, Vernon, Gladys, and Elvis were closer to the Greenwoods than just about any other relatives. No one else, to my knowledge, was as close to Elvis in as many different ways as I was. I hope to use my personal insights and shared family background to paint a full-color picture of Elvis, from his boyhood in Tupelo to his adolescence in Memphis to his adult success. His relationship with Priscilla and the last seven years of his life have been covered extensively elsewhere, but I think his early development is especially important to know if you want to understand the man that Elvis became. We all know how his tragic story ends, now we're going to see the framework on which it was laid.

Nobody's life story can ever be complete unless you know about their beginnings and, up to now, Elvis's family history and early years have remained largely unexplored. Not because nobody was interested—quite to the contrary—but mostly because Elvis and Elvis's family chose not to talk about it to the strangers who approached them. Most people, southerners especially, simply don't trust outsiders. The friendliest farmers will abruptly clam up as soon as they suspect anyone is snooping around and asking questions they deem too personal to be proper. They're also afraid that they'll say one thing, only to be misquoted later in print. When in doubt, don't, are southern words to live by.

It's been different for me. Since it's my family, too, relatives have opened up and admitted to family skeletons they would have otherwise denied. This is the source of the family history I present in the first chapters, which is a composite of various relatives' memories and insights. Most of those who agreed to help did so on the condition I not name them—"I'll tell you, Earl, 'cause you're family, but don't go usin' my name." Nowhere is that old adage about blood being thicker than water truer than among southern families. And believe me, it's at once both our greatest strength and biggest weakness.

Both Elvis and I were born in the small rural community of Tupelo, Mississippi, located about one hundred miles southwest of Memphis, Tennessee. My grandfather, Tom Greenwood, married Elvis's aunt, Dixie Presley, making us second cousins. I was two years younger, but the age difference was of little concern to us, and we grew up the best of friends and as close as brothers. In fact, since Elvis was an only child, he often told me he *did* consider me his brother, and I took that responsibility quite seriously, knowing how important family was to Elvis.

Several years later, as Elvis and I approached our teens, our families moved to Memphis within months of one another. The closeness we had developed in Tupelo cemented itself in Memphis. We found ourselves plucked out of the Mississippi countryside and in a city with more people than we thought possible. We were the new kids on our respective blocks, and the culture shock we experienced caused us to cling to each other tighter than ever, although to be honest, the move was much more difficult for Elvis than it was for me.

After Elvis became famous, I fell into the role of his press agent, partly because he knew I was capable but mostly because he felt most comfortable having family around him. I was in the unique, and what I'll admit I occasionally considered cursed, position of being family, friend, confidant, and business associate all wrapped up in one. It was often fun and usually exciting, but believe me when I tell you it was also exhausting.

In the years since his death, there's been a lot written about Elvis, the majority of it negative and out of context. I hope to set the record straight with balance and insight. Not that I'll deny the truth of his drug abuse or excuse his sometimes abysmal treatment of women, but it's important for people to understand this: Elvis wasn't depraved and does not deserve to be written off as simply another self-indulgent star. He was lost and depressed and a victim of his background and upbringing. Yes, he was stubborn and pig-headed, but most of that was born from fear. He was thrust into the limelight totally unprepared, and the force of his popularity was eventually his downfall. He simply couldn't handle everything that had happened to him, good and bad, because he was basically a little boy who never grew up. He'd never been taught the tools of survival.

I want to contribute to his fans and do my best to answer a lot of questions that they have asked over the years. They deserve an answer. That's what Elvis would have done. A lot of people who have tried to capitalize on Elvis have never so much as been to Memphis, much less ever met or knew him. Then they make up some crazy, bizarre book, like the one claiming Elvis was alive. That kind of foolishness is just an insult to the man's memory. First and last, besides its just being preposterous—I've got copies of the autopsy reports and have spoken to several of the doctors who saw his body—Elvis would have never done something like that to his fans. It's that simple. He was a down-to-earth man who genuinely appreciated very much what the public had done for him, and he would never betray them. It wasn't in his makeup.

Our family is tired of people writing books like that and of strangers nobody has ever heard of saying terrible things about Elvis, without explaining what drove him to do some of the things he did. They are happy there is someone who has the knowledge, the background, and the love to come forward and tell it like it was, from day one to the grand finale. Good and bad.

I hope my honesty doesn't hurt or offend anyone. It is not my intention to hurt anybody, especially not Elvis. He'd be the last one I'd betray in any way. But I don't feel it would be fair to his fans to whitewash his life and leave out certain things just because it might not paint the prettiest picture. I don't want to lie to his fans and neither would Elvis. While I refuse to believe people only want to read sensational, negative things about celebrities, I also realize they don't want to be lied to, either. My cousin wasn't an angel, he wasn't blessed by the pope. He made mistakes, like all of us do, and had character flaws. He also had to overcome a lot of obstacles in his life and endured more than his share of humiliation and embarrassment, especially as a youth, because he was ahead of his time and considered different. Even as an adult, he spent most of his life feeling he was an outsider, and the accompanying loneliness drove him to do things he might have otherwise not done. Before anyone should judge Elvis, they've got to know who he was and how his background dogged him to the day he died.

As I might have expected, the one person who was particularly concerned by my decision to trace our family tree was my mother, who worried about what people would think once they got an earful about our relatives' shady background. Specifically, what they would think of her and me. When I told her that it would help people understand Elvis better, she just walked away, grumbling about the lack of modern proper behavior. Which brings up another southern truism: You're never too old for your mama to get on to.

While I didn't admit it to her, I had harbored the same doubts, wondering if I wasn't about to open up a hornet's nest. I searched my conscience and asked myself the same question I always asked when confronted with a problem that concerned Elvis—what would Elvis say? In my heart, I know he'd say, Earl, if you don't, I will, so you'd better do it.

Up to now, nobody has accused me of trying to capitalize on Elvis, although I'm sure that will come. No matter. What does matter is that I'm finally telling the story that Elvis's fans have been waiting to hear and ought to hear. It's to them that I dedicate this book.

Part I

FAMILY INFLUENCES

1

I got the phone call from my brother on the morning of August 16, 1977, telling me the news. Elvis was dead. I stood there clammy and numb as I listened to how he'd been found on the floor of his bathroom—then, for some bizarre reason, a sense of relief flooded over me, followed by a crushing sense of sadness. I prayed there was a heaven, and that he was with his brother and mama, and hoped he had finally found the peace he'd sought for so long.

I caught the first flight to Memphis out of Los Angeles and went directly to Graceland. The place was in absolute chaos. Mobs of people gathered at the front gate, some clutching photographs of a younger, thinner, smiling Elvis, many weeping uncontrollably, comforted by strangers who shared in their grief. Dozens of Memphis policemen attempted to keep the crowds clear of the driveway, but it still took several minutes for the taxi to get through the throng. Piles of roses littered the lawn near the gate, tossed there in tribute by the fans keeping vigil on the street.

Inside Graceland was almost as bad. Elvis's father and grandmother sat together in a corner, holding each other as they prayed with a minister. Relatives and family friends streamed in, bringing food and words of condolence, while off to the side members of Elvis's entourage argued among themselves in whispered but passionate tones. I'd find out later the dispute centered around the ownership of some jewelry; Elvis was

barely cold, and the vultures had already started cir-
cling his body.

The phone rang constantly—mostly journalists trying to get a scoop, with an occasional call from a
shocked friend or industry acquaintance hoping against
hope the news reports were wrong. I stood in the doorway of the music room, watching workers move out
the furniture. Like his mother before him, almost exactly twenty years to the day earlier, this is where Elvis would be laid out.

I went through the next few days in a haze, unable
to accept he was really gone. As I stared at him in his
copper-lined coffin, it occurred to me that Elvis would
have hated the way he looked—in a light-blue shirt
with a white suit and tie. He would have much rather
been buried in one of his favorite Vegas outfits. Or in
a plaid jacket with loud green pants.

The miserable weather heightened the sense of un-
reality that hung over Graceland and reached its peak
the day of the funeral. It was so hot and humid you
couldn't breathe, the heat shimmering off the streets
and sidewalks. The service and burial were a blur,
punctuated only by an occasional sharp wave of tin-
gling grief in my chest.

That night, I sat on the front steps of Graceland,
waiting for a breeze that never came, reminded of other
hot, humid, southern August nights. A childhood full
of them. Suddenly, I felt old for the first time in my
life, as I realized that I had buried a big part of my
childhood that afternoon. I sat by myself for a long
time and my thoughts took me back to Tupelo, Mississippi, the dusty town where Elvis and I grew up.
Memories flickered through my mind—Elvis and I
walking home and pointing out the different constellations to each other; listening to Elvis imitate the
black workers singing spirituals in the fields; trying to
help Elvis overcome his terrible shyness; defending
my skinny, tongue-tied, homely cousin from local bullies.

Who would have ever guessed that awkward boy would grow up to be the King?

One of my earliest memories of Elvis is sitting with him on the back steps of my Uncle Ben's home on a muggy Mississippi summer's day. I couldn't have been much older than five, which would have made Elvis almost seven. We were sipping lemonade, which was considered a special treat, and listening to Ben and my dad, B.G. Greenwood, tell the Tornado Story. Now, even at that young age, both Elvis and I had heard the story enough times that we could repeat it with firsthand accuracy—even though he had only been an infant and I a mere gleam in my parents' eyes when the catastrophe occurred. But we never got tired of hearing about that night of terror when half of Tupelo was destroyed, partly out of macabre, childish curiosity, but mostly because there was nothing else to do and we were bored to death. Any entertainment was deeply appreciated.

My dad and his brother took practiced turns telling the story, and each time it got a little more detailed and dramatic.

"It was a stormy day back in April of thirty-six," Ben would say, looking skyward. "There'd been thunder and lightning on and off all day, and the wind was blowing so hard you'd lose your hat if you didn't have the good sense to take it off."

My dad would pick up the story. "It rained into the night. But then along before midnight everything stopped, and it got deathly quiet outside."

Elvis would nudge me, his face a mask of intense anticipation, his eyes riveted on my dad.

"There was no wind, no rain, not even the crickets were calling. It was like the night was holding its breath waiting for something to happen. Then all of a sudden, a roar dropped out of the sky." Ben's voice rose, and even though we both knew it was coming, it never failed to make us jump. "It sounded like someone dropped a bomb."

"It was about eleven o'clock at night, but still, you could see a black cone, slithering like a snake, coming right at you across the fields. People were running out of their houses in their nightclothes and jumping into their storm cellars, knowing their lives depended on it."

"In their skivvies." Elvis giggled at the thought, then got serious again.

"Your daddy, Elvis, stood in front of his little house just watching the tornado hopscotch from one part of town to the other, while your mama had the better sense to get herself and you into the nearest storm cellar. Vernon's lucky to be alive."

"We're *all* lucky to be alive," my dad said.

Ben nodded agreement. "The thing I remember most was the noise."

My dad looked skyward as the story came to an end. "It was the sound of death."

Years later, my mother and Gladys would roll their eyes if the Tornado Story was brought up.

"Neither Ben, your dad, nor your Uncle Vernon would know what happened 'cause they were all too drunk to remember," my mom said.

"I had you in one arm and your daddy in the other, while your Aunt Nora grabbed the other two," Gladys told Elvis. "I was so mad at him I was tempted to just leave him and let him get blowed away."

"After we dragged them down to the cellar, they all passed out—slept through the whole thing." My mom and Gladys shook their heads in mutual disgust.

What made the tornado of 1936 stick in people's mind so strongly was that it was the deadliest anyone could remember. The storm killed over a hundred people and destroyed most of Tupelo, tearing down rows of sharecropper shacks and tearing up the land they doggedly worked to barely break even in the best of conditions. Fires lit the stormy night and scores of injured poured into local hospitals, which were little more than clinics and not equipped to deal with such an emergency. The overflow of injured were put up in the few business buildings left standing, including the courthouse.

Mind you, tornadoes are hardly a rare occurrence in Mississippi, which constantly gets horrible weather. All the way down the edge of the Mississippi River there's nothing like mountains or lakes to knock the storms away, so they come hard and often. There were many nights Elvis and I huddled together in the family storm cellar, waiting for the danger to pass. At first we enjoyed the excitement of possible disaster, but after that feeling wore off, the wait began to wear on us and our imaginations would run wild. The cellars were like caves built into the ground and were very spooky, especially at night. I would terrify myself and Elvis to death by imagining horrible thoughts.

"In school we read about these miners who were in a place just like this, and one of them sneezed, and they all got buried alive," I whispered to Elvis, who had been sniffing and sneezing constantly with a bad cold.

"I don't remember readin' nothin' like that," Elvis said. "You're makin' it up."

"I'm not. The dirt fell in on 'em and they choked to death. That's what could happen to us if you're not careful."

Gladys, with her supersonic hearing, grabbed my shoulder—hard. "You stop tryin' to scare Elvis—no such thing happened. He's got enough nightmares as it is."

But for as bad as they could be, storms were really the least of anybody's worries, because most of their lives were spent just trying to keep their heads above water. Except for the few big landowners, it seems that everybody in that part of Mississippi was a share-cropper at one time or another, a life filled with hard work and few rewards. The idea behind sharecropping was a good one until you put it into practice.

A landowner would give out plots of farmland to anyone willing to work it. The sharecropper would build a one- or two-room shanty and farm his corner of land, with the understanding that the landowner would share the harvest's profits at the end of the season. The only problem was that usually there were barely enough profits to go around. For most people, sharecropping was just a way to keep food on the table and a roof over your head with little hope of ever saving enough money to buy your own land.

My dad proved to be one of the lucky ones, whereas Vernon, Elvis's father, always seemed snake-bit. Part of the difference was due to circumstance, part had to do with the type of men they were. My dad was ambitious and had the advantage of having several children who could help him work his plot. I'm pleased to say that as the youngest I managed to miss being called for farm duty, as did my sister, being the oldest girl. But my four older brothers and my mother joined my father in the fields. The extra hands allowed my dad to save enough money to buy dairy cows, which in turn earned him enough money so that he was eventually able to buy his own land—one hundred acres.

Vernon had a tougher go of it. Elvis was the only child and too young to be of much use in the fields during the bleakest days of the Depression, and Gladys preferred to find work in the one or two local factories, or do whatever seamstress jobs she could find. Gladys never shied away from hard work, although she wasn't afraid to let her family know just how hard she toiled.

Vernon was another story. Amiable and personable, he was also terribly irresponsible, to Gladys's unending embarrassment and dismay. He lacked ambition and was often laid up with what he claimed to be a chronic bad back, but nobody ever knew what from. Elvis's family was always on the verge of going under and quite often needed to turn to relatives for financial help.

Gladys always accepted food or money gratefully, her voice steady but her eyes betraying the humiliation she felt. She knew better than to promise the loan would be repaid, so instead she offered to do sewing or other tasks as a form of payback. Gladys would walk back home with her head held high, but her stooped shoulders and shuffling walk gave away the heaviness of her heart, weighted down by poverty made worse by her husband's easygoing acceptance of it.

The crop of choice in our area was cotton, and it's been said that the mere thought of picking cotton is enough to give anybody an aching back. Late one afternoon during harvesting time, Elvis and I were perched above a field in our favorite climbing tree, watching the rows of hunched-over sharecroppers plucking the fuzzy bulbs off the bushes, the long cotton sacks dragging along the ground behind them. From this vantage point, you could see the workers' hands were bloodied and gnarled, and their bodies permanently bent.

"I don' ever wanna be no farmer," Elvis announced. Even as a child, his speech was distinctively indistinct.

"Mama says you jus' spend the day breakin' your back for someone else to get rich from. That's why she hates Orville Bean so bad."

"I *know* I don't want to be no farmer," I said with a touch of horror. "No, thank you."

We sat on the branch, our bare feet dangling down, trying to catch any breeze that might wisp by.

"Know what I want? A gas station," Elvis said, his face lighting up. "Pumpin' gas is a long sight easier than workin' the fields, and all day you jes' mess around with all sorts of cars. And I'd paint up a sign out front with my name on it, so ever'one would know it's mine."

"Maybe you can be a race-car driver—they make lots of money and get to travel all over."

"I don't need that much money—jes' enough for me and Mama to get by on," Elvis said.

"Not me—I want to be rich. I wanna be so rich that Orville Bean has to work for me."

Elvis laughed and gave me a shove that nearly sent

me flying from the tree. "Yeah—how you gonna make any money?"

I swung myself upright on the limb with as much dignity as I could muster, buying time for an answer.

"Maybe I'll go to Hollywood and become a movie star."

Elvis leaned back, laughing so hard *he* nearly went sprawling.

"Not with those ears."

"Stop pickin' on my ears—there's nothin' wrong with 'em."

"Nothin' a good croppin' wouldn't fix."

"Go ahead and laugh. My dad says there's nothin' you can't do if you want it bad enough. No reason why I couldn't be in movies when I get older."

"Okay, you be a movie star—then you can get me a station."

"I'll be so rich, I'll buy you *two.*"

Shows you how much either of us knew.

Elvis was right, of course, to be skeptical that either of us would amount to much. Our family had been farmers and ne'er-do-wells for as far back as anyone could remember, and there was no reason to think the future generations would be any different. Growing up in the Depression, simply having three meals a day was a goal seldom achieved. For someone like Elvis, whose family owned little more than the clothes on their backs, owning his own gas station was a fantasy that, at the time, seemed like an impossible dream.

Elvis and I were second cousins on his dad's side, and neither the Greenwood nor the Presley branch of the family tree gave any indication we would stray from our ancestry, which was ripe with con artists and other assorted shady characters who eked out a living as best they could. We seemed destined to carry the weight of two hundred years of struggle.

Tracing the family tree was difficult because so many of the Presleys were transients. They settled in some out-of-the-way little town and lived a quiet life. When they died, their line died with them and who would know? Today our every movement is tracked, especially by the IRS, but income tax is a relatively new curse. Record keeping, especially in the South, was haphazard at best, all the way into the twentieth century.

I've been able to trace Elvis's ancestry back about two hundred years, to his paternal great-great-great-great-grandfather, a Scotsman named Andrew Presley, Jr., who was born in 1754. His father, Andrew, Sr., had emigrated to North Carolina in 1745 and made his living as a blacksmith.

Just two weeks after the signing of the Declaration of Independence, when he was twenty-two, Andrew bought 150 acres of land in Lancaster County, South Carolina, where he intended to settle down with his new wife, a young Irish lass whose name has been lost to history. The War of Independence interrupted his plans and Andrew dutifully joined the fight, although he still managed to visit home often enough to father at least one war baby. He had great faith in his new country and was a willing soldier, if not a skilled one. Andrew was a private in the Continental Army, and family records indicate that he fought with George Washington during his long tour of duty in the Revolutionary War. According to documents attached to his pension records, Andrew also claimed to know General Lighthorse Harry Lee. The highlight of Andrew's service in the army occurred in 1781 at the battle of Etauw Springs, South Carolina, not far from where he and his wife had settled.

You'd have to scour a few history books to come up with that skirmish, but it figured quite highly with Andrew. His brigade fought troops led by General Cornwallis and the battle is said to have lasted an hour and forty-five minutes. The Continental Army's forces succeeded in driving back the British redcoats, who by this time in the conflict were probably fighting without much conviction. Casualties were light on both sides and the Americans took over five hundred prisoners.

There's an amusing historical footnote that comes to light in an officer's report that turned up, unexplained, in Andrew's personal papers. Since Andrew was illiterate, he could not have written, nor even read, the report, so why he kept it is a mystery. Perhaps it was meant as a memento of his greatest day in battle and the adventure that followed.

During the confrontation, Andrew's regiment overran a building the British were using as a base, forcing the redcoats to flee out the back into the woods. While searching for possible prisoners, the soldiers came across what must have been the officers' quarters—well stocked with quality liquor. As the battle raged outside, Andrew and his cohorts settled back in the safety of the building and drank themselves senseless. It was the beginning of a long-standing Presley tradition.

Andrew stayed in the service until the war ended in 1783. He was twenty-nine years old and needed to support his little family now that the army wasn't caring for him anymore. Following in his father's footsteps, he looked up the local blacksmith and offered to work for free to learn the trade. After his apprenticeship ended, Andrew set up his own shop, and lived out his life in quiet obscurity. He lived comfortably in retirement off the twenty-dollar-a-month pension he received from the government and died shortly before his hundred and first birthday.

One of Andrew's children was Dunnan Presley, the war baby born in 1780. Dunnan suffered from a severe case of wanderlust and spent half of his life roaming the countryside, although he never traveled more than 120 miles from his birthplace.

When he was twenty, Dunnan said goodbye to his parents and moved to North Carolina. I can only assume that the relationship between Andrew, a man who believed in duty and hard work, and his flighty son must have been strained. Whether Dunnan forfeited his share of Andrew's land by leaving or left because

Andrew had no intention of staking him to his own plot is anybody's guess.

In North Carolina, Dunnan earned a living any way he could, taking one odd job after another. He continued to move whenever the urge struck, seldom staying in any one place long enough to establish himself. He never had a penny to spare but did manage to support a family. By the time he was forty, Dunnan had a wife and was the father of two girls and two boys, including Dunnan, Jr.

Then tragedy struck. Dunnan's wife died suddenly, although typically, the records fail to say why. Dunnan was forced to act as both mother and father to his children, a predicament I'm sure he didn't appreciate. Dunnan rectified the situation in 1830, when he married a woman more than twenty years his junior. Some quick arithmetic indicates his second wife was not much older than his children. Dunnan's young bride must have rejuvenated the old boy, because he fathered three more sons within the next ten years. No word on how the missus felt about this turn of events.

In 1836, Dunnan, his wife, and the children who hadn't yet moved out on their own moved to Georgia, drawn by the belief—completely mistaken—that the government was giving away free land. Despite his bitter disappointment, Dunnan tried to make a go of it, but when the life he hoped to find didn't pan out, Dunnan uprooted his family again and headed to Polk County, Tennessee.

An 1850 census report paints a sad picture. Now nearly seventy, Dunnan was as poor as always. He owned no land, and his net personal property was worth all of two hundred fifty dollars. He died later that same year and was buried in a pauper's grave.

Dunnan Presley, Jr., had been born in Madison, Tennessee, in 1827. Like his father and grandfather before him, Dunnan, Jr., was illiterate and on the few occasions it was necessary, he signed his name as an X.

Dunnan, Jr., was a low point in Presley family history. There's not much good to be said about him. He was a bigamist and twice an army deserter. Old Andrew, had he known, would have had a seizure at how his grandson turned out. He no doubt would have blamed it on Dunnan's wayward ways.

Junior's first army desertion dates back to the Mexican American War when he was just twenty. Joining the army probably seemed like a good idea at the time, but Dunnan, Jr., decided in no time that he wasn't overly fond of being shot at. He was a private in Company C of the Fifth Tennessee Infantry when he took off for back home. He was quickly caught and spent a short time in military jail before being sent back to the front. All in all, the government was very forgiving—when he was mustered out in 1848, he received two dollars for clothing and a land grant of 160 acres.

In 1861, Dunnan, Jr., married Elvis's great-great-grandmother, Martha Jane Wesson, in Itawamba County, Mississippi. The only hitch is that the evidence clearly shows that he was already married with at least one child—Dunnan III. That family lived in Tennessee. It appears each knew of the other. Even Dunnan, Sr., would have raised his eyebrows over this.

On May 11, 1863, Junior joined Company E of the regiment of the Mississippi Cavalry as a corporal. Not only was the government generous, they had a short memory, since he left his last tenure as a private. He enlisted for a year and received three hundred dollars for supplying his own horse. True to form, Dunnan, Jr., deserted the next month. This time when he took off, he deserted his family as well, leaving Martha and their two small daughters to fend for themselves in Fulton, Mississippi.

All told, Dunnan, Jr., was married four times. Whether he was ever divorced is another matter. His last wife, Harriet, was twenty when they were wed in 1882. Dunnan was fifty-five and evidently spry. They settled in Brown County, Missouri, and Dunnan, Jr., died in 1900.

One of Junior's children from his marriage to Martha was Rosella Presley, born in 1862. In her own way, Rosella was a chip off the old block. Whether out of rebellion against her father's bigamist ways, stubbornness, or whatever the reason, dear Rosella bore ten children out of wedlock during a twenty-eight-year period. As if that wasn't shock and horror enough for her neighbors, she also gave the children *her* last name. It's an interesting thought—Elvis could have been Elvis Brown or Williams or who knows what, had Rosella bothered to marry or at least identify the children's father or fathers, as the case may be.

As you can well imagine, Rosella and the kids didn't have much of a life. They were poor as dirt with no hope of getting anything better. Being bastards, they suffered the sharp barbs of disapproval of the local townspeople. Oddly enough, despite her sin, Rosella was considered a caring mother who did the best she could for her children. Except for one or two problem children, she managed to raise her brood to be polite and to fear God, and she took them to church every Sunday until they moved away on their own. She died young for a Presley, at sixty-three, without ever revealing the identity of her children's father or fathers, even to them.

One of Rosella's children who never did learn the fear of God was Jesse Presley, a young hellion who would keep up a way of life that was making the Presleys infamous. Jesse, called J.D., was also born in Itawamba County, Mississippi, in 1896. From the start, he was a hard-working, hard-drinking, hard-living hell raiser who caused more than his share of shock and gossip for a lifetime.

If J.D. ever didn't come home at night, it was a safe bet he was either out carousing with some questionable lady or sleeping off a bender at the local jail. Jesse no doubt caused Rosella many a sleepless night.

J.D. was a restless lad, and to him, sitting in a classroom all day was a waste of time. Against Rosella's wishes, he left school at the age of eleven to find a job; he was a willing but unpicky worker, who was more interested in a quick buck than a steady future.

When he was just seventeen, Jesse married Minnie Mae Hood of nearby Fulton, Mississippi. Minnie Mae was twenty-five and on the plain side, but she also came from a family with money. Whether or not J.D. married for love has always been a matter of family debate, but he certainly succeeded in marrying well. Supposedly, Minnie Mae's hand in marriage included a dowry, but whatever financial gain there might have been come the wedding day, before long, the couple settled into the hand-to-mouth existence that seemed the Presley lot in life.

J.D. was a favorite with the ladies. A good-looking man with a love for nice clothes, he would parade around the dusty town like a peacock, with his chin thrust high in the air. More than one local wondered how J.D. managed to maintain his dapper wardrobe. He drifted from job to job and apparently never had two dimes to spare, but his clothes were always of the nicest quality. Some whispered that he made extra money as a moonshiner, but if he did, he was never caught.

J.D. and Minnie Mae lived for the most part in Fulton and raised five children—two sons, Vester and Vernon, and three daughters, Delta Nashville, Gladys, and Dixie.

Even as he aged, Jesse was still considered one of the most handsome men in the area, and he had long ago grown bored with Minnie. So after thirty years of marriage, Jesse filed for divorce, claiming that Minnie Mae had deserted *him*. Outraged, Minnie wrote a scathing letter to Jesse's attorney charging that it was her husband who had walked out on *her*. Typically, the judge ruled in favor of the man, and granted Jesse the divorce. One has to wonder just how upset Minnie was about this as time wore on. Certainly her pride was hurt, and what little financial security Jesse offered was gone, but Jesse could be a mean s.o.b., and her life was more peaceful with him out of it.

Shortly after the divorce, Jesse married Vera Pruitt and they moved to Louisville, Kentucky, where he became a night watchman. On a whim, Jesse added an extra *s* to his name, and through the forties and fifties he went by Pressley. But by the sixties, he dropped the extra *s,* so the spelling of his last name matched Elvis's.

If nothing else, Jesse was a prize scammer. After Elvis hit it big, Jesse saw a perfect opportunity to share a little of Elvis's limelight. He recorded two songs; one was called the ''Billie Goat Song'' and the flip side was ''Swinging in the Orchard.'' They were put out by Legacy Records, but mercifully, these songs never received any air play. When Vernon told Elvis what his granddaddy was up to, Elvis let out a howl of laughter.

''His moonshine must be more potent than usual. I swear, I don't know who's crazier—Granddad or the record company. Jus' as long as he don' ask me to sing no duet.''

But later, as he grew older, Elvis would recall the incident with a lot less levity and cite it as just another example of people trying to take advantage of his success. ''I might as well jus' support 'em all—that's all they want from me, anyway.''

It is through Vernon's sister Dixie that Elvis and I are related, although to this day, Dixie is one of the family's best-kept secrets, and her tragic fate has been a skeleton in the family closet for decades. Dixie, who was Elvis's paternal aunt, was also my grandmother. I never really knew my Grandma Dixie, because she spent the last years of her life languishing in a mental institution and in fact died there.

Mental illness was a shameful thing to many people. If someone in your family was known to be institutionalized, it cast a cloud over the rest of you— contamination by association. Making matters even worse was the fact that Dixie's mental instability had been caused by an untreated bout of syphilis. Put the two together, and you have a scandal of major proportions. In a small town where everybody knows their neighbors' business, it meant an indelible stain marked the relatives.

Dixie simply ceased to exist to her family. Period. J.D., Minnie, Vernon, and Vester never spoke about Dixie after she left, nor did they include her in any family remembrance. Vernon and Vester never acknowledged they had a sister named Dixie and, in fact, preferred to deny it rather than reopen the wound.

My family wasn't much better. Grandma Dixie was pretty much a forbidden topic, and the Greenwoods were only too happy that the Presleys were so determined to bury her shame and memory. That was another reason my family didn't broadcast being related to the Presleys, they were mortified at having a common ancestor who died in a loony bin. They didn't want to be socially tainted by the Presleys' bad bloodline. To this day, both branches of the family prefer to pretend Dixie simply didn't exist.

Before she was institutionalized, Dixie married my grandfather, Tom Greenwood, and they had seven children. One of my dad's brothers, Ben, grew to be very close to Jesse, Elvis's granddad, and the two could often be found together drinking until all hours of the night. Naturally, each family thought the other a bad influence. My father married Nora MacMullin, whose family was far removed from the antics of the Presleys and the Greenwoods. My mom brought our family a bit of respectability—and God knows we needed it.

What's never been made clear was how Dixie contracted syphilis in the first place, but since Tom was apparently healthy, it can only be assumed that adultery can be added to the scandal sheet. In any event, Dixie was spirited off in the middle of the night to the closest mental ward, which was in nearby Jackson, with the family offering curious neighbors the flimsy explanation that she was off visiting relatives. One day she was home, the next day she was gone—never to be seen again.

There was plenty of speculation by the locals, but

neither the Greenwoods nor the Presleys ever admitted to the real problem. More than her ravings and odd behavior, it was the specter of syphilis that horrified the families. Bad enough that Dixie disgraced the family by being what they called a loose woman, but did she have to add further shame by being diseased as well? Compassion can be a hard commodity to come by in families.

Like his dad before him, Vernon Elvis Presley was a handsome youth, but the similarities between father and son stopped there. Vernon was a dreamer who preferred to pass the time watching the clouds roll by while he was fishing, rather than break his back in the fields. He'd grown up poor and expected nothing different. Vernon's aversion to work and responsibility and his lack of personal pride had always been a source of irritation to Jesse, and as a result, their relationship was strained throughout Vernon's life. When his son was just fifteen, Jesse kicked him out of the house, and Vernon went to live with relatives until his father's temper cooled down enough for him to return home. But Vernon was so easygoing, he never once expressed any hard feelings against Jesse in all the years I knew him. Either he was terribly forgiving or, like Elvis, he swallowed his bad feelings and kept them buried inside.

One of Vernon's more surprising acts of defiance was marrying Gladys Love Smith, a vibrant girl who loved dancing and music. Gladys and her family had moved to Tupelo in the spring of 1933 from nearby West Point, shortly after her father, Robert Smith, died of pneumonia. She was twenty-one and working in a garment factory. Gladys and Vernon met at the First Assembly of God church one Sunday, and they eloped just a few months later, shortly after Vernon's seventeenth birthday. To just about her dying day, she knocked several years off her real age, not wanting to look like a cradle snatcher.

Vernon was smitten with her prettiness and her worldliness—being four years older, she seemed very sophisticated compared to other girls he'd known. Young Gladys had a laugh that sounded like the tinkling of crystal and a strength and belief in the future that drew Vernon to her. They fed off each other's dreams, and the headiness of first love made them believe they could overcome their surroundings and move up in the world.

Vernon knew Jesse felt him incapable of providing for a family, and knew his father would be angry at him for running off to marry a girl he barely knew. Just plain irresponsible is how Jesse would see it. Whatever else bad can be said about Jesse, no one can argue that he had a point about Vernon, which would become all too apparent to Gladys as the years went painfully by.

But in the first days of their courtship, Gladys couldn't see beyond Vernon's handsome face and his endearing gentleness—and on a more basic level, their physical passion for one another was apparent to anyone who saw them together. She also found herself caught up in his sweet daydreams and let herself believe he had the wherewithal to make them come true. Little did she know that once he was confronted by the effort of turning dreams to reality, Vernon would quickly be content to let his fantasies live on in his mind only.

Because she was new in town, Gladys and her family weren't familiar with the unflattering reputation the Presleys had earned and probably thought she had a fairly good catch in Vernon. He was personable, attractive, and already a skilled carpenter, although he'd make little use of this talent during his life. Like most people in Mississippi, the Presleys were sharecroppers who lived a humble existence, but Gladys believed Vernon shared her desperate desire to improve their social standing. Gladys never bargained for the severe poverty that would dog them until Elvis turned their lives around.

Like most suitors, Vernon had been on his best behavior—which ended shortly after he and Gladys eloped, when he reverted back to form. He was unable to work for long stretches because of his chronic bad back, and they were usually strapped for money. Vernon was the king of the odd job, preferring to flit here and there rather than seek out permanent employment, and part of Gladys's paycheck went to help support her family.

Lovely and vivacious when she married Vernon, within a short time her looks began to fade along with her hopes for the future. She tried to hide her bitter disappointment under a mask of stoicism, but it oozed out of every pore. The loving tones she once cooed at Vernon turned into clipped responses as the real character of her "good catch" became all too clear. Over the years, whatever affection they had for each other was buried beneath an avalanche of frustration.

I remember once walking home from school with Elvis. It was a dreary winter day, and he'd been quiet since the morning. By this time I had learned it usually meant things weren't going well at home, although he rarely admitted it unless pushed or very upset.

"Mama says we maybe have to move away," he said.

"Where to?"

"I don' know. I don' wanna, but she says we'll starve to death if we can't find work. Daddy says we ain't goin' nowhere. That got Mama all upset. . . . I hate it when they yell. I hate it when his yellin' makes her cry so bad."

"My folks were fightin' last week, but I don't know what about—they always stop talkin' when I walk in. If I want to hear, I got to go listen through the wall."

"I wish we had a wall so I *didn't* have to hear," Elvis said. "Mama cries all the time, no matter what I do." He looked at me, his eyes full of fear. "She's 'fraid we'll *starve* to death."

"You ain't gonna starve. You can always come to our house."

"Well, Mama ain't gonna."

After that, Elvis clammed up. Even though it was

cold and his threadbare jacket little use against the damp wind, I knew he was shivering more out of terror than the weather. He was all skin and bone as it was—the thought of having even less was enough to frighten anybody. I invited him to our house for some hot chocolate—he was tempted, but only for a moment. He said he needed to get home, his mama was expecting him.

"You know how she hates bein' by herself."

After Vernon and Gladys married, they needed a place to live. Neither of their parents' homes was big enough to accommodate them, so the newlyweds stayed with friends until Vernon built a two-room shack on Old Saltillo Road, near his family's home and on the property of landowner Orville Bean. Bean also happened to be Vernon's brother-in-law and my great-uncle through marriage, which is why he allowed Vernon to stay on his land, even though he rarely worked the fields. While she knew they were lucky for a roof over their heads, Gladys deeply resented Bean's limited generosity.

"Oh, he'll offer you jus' enough so you feel you owe him, but not enough to really help. Rich folks jus' like keepin' you on a string."

But she eyed Bean's nice house with envy and wished Vernon had the ambition to ask his brother-in-law for full-time work or at least a plot of their very own. But that wasn't Vernon's way, and as her hopes for a better life dimmed, Gladys felt the walls of her shack closing in on her.

To counteract the anxieties gnawing away at her, Gladys tried to make the best of it, refusing to believe things wouldn't get better soon. She worked hard to make their simple two-room house comfortable. She scrubbed it from top to bottom, stuffed rags in the cracks between the warped boards that Vernon had used to build their shack, and filled old milk bottles with wildflowers to brighten the otherwise drab and depressing interior. Typically, Vernon apparently didn't notice her efforts, complimenting her only after she burst into tears at his inattention.

"Ain't that jus' like him?" Gladys confided to my mom. "We could disappear int' the ground and he wouldn't notice 'til come dinnertime."

The first break in the clouds engulfing her came in the spring of 1934 when she realized she was pregnant; at least that part of her life with Vernon had stayed good. Gladys glowed in the knowledge that a baby was growing inside her and saw it as an omen—maybe starting a family would get Vernon moving and get their dreams back on track.

2

Despite their limited resources, both Vernon and Gladys were thrilled with impending parenthood. Pregnancy seemed to recharge Gladys, and after a few weeks of mild morning sickness, she basked in the glow that blesses certain expectant mothers. The mother-to-be kept her job in the dress factory well into the pregnancy, cheerfully saying the several miles she walked each way to work and back was good exercise for her. She also believed it would keep her strong and healthy for future pregnancies.

"Other than improving their lot, Gladys talked most about having kids," my mom recalls. "She wanted lots of 'em and looked forward to a household filled with the sounds of little voices callin' for mama."

For his part, Vernon looked forward to the extra hands that a big family could provide down the road to work in the fields, which would translate into more family income. And take some of the pressure off him and his aching back. So for different reasons, Gladys's pregnancy represented the young couple's hope for the future.

Elvis Aron Presley was born around noon on a cold, windswept winter's day, January 8, 1935. It was a long, hard labor and difficult birth for Gladys, who lost a great deal of blood. The family consensus is that Elvis arrived first, and his unfortunate twin was born dead within minutes. Both Gladys and the doctor expressed surprise at the double birth, but instead of joy and celebration, a pall fell over the tiny shack. While Vernon struggled in vain to comfort his wife, Gladys clung to her surviving child, blocking everything and everyone else out. The doctor finally had to pry baby Elvis out of her arms to clean him off and wrap a blanket around him.

Vernon and Gladys named their dead son Jesse Garon, and the following day he was laid out in a tiny coffin in their small shanty. The Presleys were so poor that the local church donated both the coffin and a plot of land in the closest cemetery, which was also owned by the church.

Medical care being what it was in the rural South, infant mortality was high and not an unusual occurrence, but Jesse's death shook Gladys's very soul—it was an ill omen of the worst kind. Her still born baby symbolized a bleak future. Gladys was numb and uncommunicative, except in her attention to little Elvis, and the family tried to comfort her by telling her to be grateful that she had one healthy baby boy.

"Gladys wouldn't have any of it," my mom says. "For as attentive as she was to Elvis, she dwelt even more on the baby she'd never hold."

After a sad funeral attended only by Vernon and Gladys, Jesse was buried the very next day in an unmarked grave. The Smiths, Presleys, and Greenwoods were all surprised at Gladys's vehemence they not come, but she said she wanted to grieve in private and expected everyone to respect her wishes. Gladys was weak and in pain as she shuffled to the cemetery, but she insisted on carrying Elvis the whole way there and back, even though Vernon repeatedly offered to help.

Gladys tried to overcome her heartbreak by pouring every ounce of love and devotion in her being on to Elvis. It was also a way to avoid dealing with Vernon, who stayed off to the side like some boarder.

"Gladys had a one-track mind," my mom says. "She would hold that baby so tight I thought he might suffocate. She wouldn't let nobody carry him around but her—not even Vernon.

"Vernon would just stand around, shuffling his feet, acting like some stranger who happened by. Gladys didn't even notice he was there half the time. He didn't understand she woulda come 'round with some patience. Instead, he spent more time with your Uncle Ben sneaking moonshine than he did at home with her. It's no wonder she turned to the baby for comfort—he sure didn't know how to give her any. But then again, she never gave him the chance."

One thing that everybody seems to agree on, things between Gladys and Vernon were never the same after they laid Jesse Garon to rest. A big chunk of life had gone out of them as individuals and as a couple. It didn't help that Gladys wouldn't be able to have any more children. She confided that tragedy to Ben's wife, Agnes, her tongue loosened by a glass of Ben's liquor. Over bitter tears, Gladys cursed her fate—but once she walked out Agnes's door, her eyes were dry, revealing nothing.

Jesse's tragic death turned him into a mystical figure spoken about in near-reverential tones. He became a golden child, remembered for the man he might have become and the deeds he might have accomplished. This was especially true of Gladys, and seeing as how he wasn't around to disappoint her, those fantasies stood no chance of being shot down. Alive in mind alone, Jesse was the perfect child.

As Elvis grew up, Jesse was an unseen but ever-present entity. For as long as could remember, he had "talked" to Jesse daily, a habit that sprang from Gladys's urgings to pray to Jesse and ask him for guidance—after God, of course.

Most children love hearing the story of their birth— all the excitement and funny stories, real or fanciful, that become part of your personal history. Not Elvis. Any mention of his arrival inevitably brought on a wave of melancholy—because his entry into the world had been accompanied by death. One part of him never learned to control the guilt he felt over being the one who had lived, while the better one had died. On a more spiritual level, Elvis saw Jesse as his other half. Each was part of a whole that could never be whole until they reunited in the hereafter. Throughout his life, the belief that half his soul died at birth prevented Elvis from ever fully enjoying the good things that would happen to him.

"If only Jesse could be here" was a constant refrain once Elvis's career had taken off.

Over the years, Vernon often expressed dismay at Gladys and Elvis's mutual obsession but felt helpless to do anything about it.

"I tried to tell her it ain't nat'ral, but she 'bout took my head off," he once lamented to Ben as they tried out some local moonshine. "I thought it was jus' a phase at first—who knew it'd go on permanent?"

Vernon's concern over the appropriateness of his family's ties with the other side had something to do with his professed ignorance as to the location of Jesse's gravesite when it came up many years later. Elvis had never thought to ask about it until after Gladys's death, and when he did, Vernon gave him a blank stare. Not knowing where his brother was buried became another obsession for Elvis, and he'd bug Vernon about it constantly.

"Elvis, how many times I gotta tell you, the grave wasn't marked 'cause we couldn't afford no headstone," Vernon would plead.

"But how could you forget where you buried someone, regardless?" Elvis asked Vernon.

"It was a long time ago, son. Nobody knows where half their relatives are."

Elvis sighed in frustration, and after his dad left the room, he paced in circles.

"How am I gonna find Jesse to bury him here if nobody'll tell me where he is? How could he forget?"

I shrugged. "Who can say, Elvis—maybe it hurts too much to remember."

"It hurts me too much not to know. If I could only

find him and bring him here . . . and bury him next to Mama, I'd feel better. Every time I think about it—of him out there, by himself—I get this uneasy feeling inside. He wants to be here, I feel it when I talk to him. Mama would rest easier.

"Isn't there anything we can do?" Elvis begged, eyes welling with tears.

There wasn't. Only Gladys and Vernon had attended the funeral and seen the location of the grave. And since the local community in those years didn't take the time to accurately record who was in what burial plot, especially if it was a pauper's grave, there were no records to turn to, either.

A big part of Elvis's obsession with Jesse Garon was his belief that they had been identical twins. Vernon occasionally pointed out that the doctor who delivered them said it was impossible to tell if Jesse and Elvis were identical or simply fraternal twins, but good luck trying to convince Elvis of that.

"Even if nobody else knows, I do. I can feel it. There's no mistaking it. And Jesse knows it, too."

Vernon would just shrug and disappear into the kitchen for some peace, not interested in debating the issue. Elvis watched him go, angry.

"He couldn' care less what I feel. He's never understood anything 'bout Jesse—no reason for him to start now."

Elvis sank into a chair with a pained expression. "I miss him. I miss having someone around who knows what I'd be thinkin' because they'd be thinkin' the same thing, too. No matter how close you and I are, Earl, it would be different with Jesse, because we'd be the same person. That's why it feels so . . . soothin' talkin' to him. Asking for advice."

"Does he answer?" I asked. Elvis ignored my tone.

"Yeah, sometimes. But even when he don't, I know I feel better after. Maybe that's answer enough."

Elvis was a cute, chubby baby who grew into a toddler of fair complexion with blonde hair and enormous blue eyes that could penetrate right through you. As adults we would sit and laugh at each other's baby pictures.

"Look at those ears," Elvis would tease me.

"I wouldn't talk—you had a flat nose and fat lips."

"Not anymore, which is more than I can say about your ears."

When I'd start to argue with him about it, he'd laugh his head off—he loved to lead people on. His laugh was so genuine and infectious when it got going, I'd end up laughing right along with him. It was hard to stay irritated at Elvis for very long when he let that boyish side show.

As a little girl, Gladys had dreamed of being a dancer—dance was her first love, but music was a close second. So it's not surprising that Gladys claimed Elvis had been born with a gift for music.

"I remember taking Elvis to church, and even when he was an infant, he'd squirm in my lap whenever the singin' would start. Your daddy, Elvis, thought it was the colic, but I knew you was jus' feelin' the music. He tried singin' before he could even talk."

"You still can't talk," I'd mutter under my breath to Elvis, and Gladys, with her bionic hearing, would chide me.

"That ain't no way to talk, Earl. Elvis got a knack for it—the voice of an angel."

Gladys grabbed hold of Elvis and hugged him as if he were going somewhere. He grimaced under my amused stare, but at the same time, Elvis couldn't hide his pleasure that mama was so proud of him.

In one of her favorite stories, Gladys would describe a three-year-old Elvis jumping off her lap to go running up and down the church aisle, singing and dancing to the hymns. Since he was only three and didn't know the words to the songs, he just kind of tootled along. Elvis's unsolicited performance must have pleased some of the stuffier members of the congregation no end—not that anybody in town was a paragon of sophistication.

Tupelo in the late 1930s was strictly a farming community of about six thousand people. Believe it or not, it was the county seat and, compared to the neighboring towns, a thriving metropolis. Downtown Tupelo consisted of a shopping area that covered a single square block, bordered by the two main roads. We had one movie theater, a Montgomery Ward, a general store, and a pharmacy. The rest of Tupelo was farmland and sharecroppers.

Most of our streets were just country roads, made of dirt or gravel, that kicked up choking dust in the summer and turned into rivers of mud during the spring rains. The church was located out away from downtown, as were the one or two factories, including the dress factory where Gladys worked. Despite Tupelo's relative size, it was an extremely poor area. Mississippi has always been poor. To this day, the state is poor. For most of the residents there was nowhere to go, and no way to get where you might have wanted to go.

When Elvis and I were young children, Mississippi was suffering through the Great Depression and a debilitating drought. It got so bad that the government had to step in, forming a work labor force called the WPA. When you're starving, you do whatever the government tells you to do. The work could be anything—from fixing local roads to cutting back dangerously combustible brush—and it paid twenty dollars a week. The Presleys did it, my family did it, everybody did it in addition to working the fields.

Except for the big landowners, everyone we knew was poor, but Vernon and Gladys were among the poorest. The incentive he'd shown after marrying Gladys had fizzled out and was all but gone after the tragedy of Jesse Garon. With Gladys reluctant to leave her baby, the sole burden of supporting the family fell onto Vernon's shoulders, and he sagged under the weight. If his back wasn't acting up, he'd go out with the intent of scrounging up some work—and would occasionally get some—but he was never overly upset if none appeared.

The people of Tupelo were polite but cool to the Presleys and didn't think too highly of them. Most people felt sorry for Gladys, because she was at the mercy of her husband's inability to keep a steady job. They whispered among themselves, my family included, when they saw Gladys, with baby Elvis bundled in her arms, walking barefoot down the road in the snow during the dead of winter, because she couldn't afford to buy a new pair of shoes. Gladys simply pretended not to see the stares or hear the hushed comments—and in fact would go out of her way to greet the people she passed. Gladys would never hide her head in shame—that would be admitting defeat. While she didn't ask for handouts, she would accept help if offered. My Uncle Ben would give them what little extra money he could spare, and my family offered food and clothes. She was grateful, but never subservient about it. She refused to believe this was to forever be her lot in life.

But that's another disadvantage of living in a small, country town—everybody knows too much about everybody else, and once a family gets a reputation, it's almost impossible to be rid of it. The Presleys would always be the white trash of Tupelo, regardless of what they did.

Neither Vernon nor Gladys had many friends outside of family. There was no place to socialize, anyway, except for church, and that wasn't what most people would consider a hooting good time. They kept pretty much to themselves after the baby came, each involved in their own worlds—Gladys with Elvis, Vernon visiting his drinking buddies.

Despite their youth, both had aged terribly during the three years since Elvis's birth. Gladys especially. She lost her girlish figure for good after giving birth and paid less and less attention to her overall appearance—the only thing that mattered was her darling baby boy, who shared his parents' bed, giving Gladys an excuse to put off Vernon's romantic advances. The passion that once engulfed them for all to see had dried up and scattered like the dust swirling on the Tupelo landscape.

But, as bad as things were for them then, it would get worse.

By the time Elvis was three, Vernon was at the point of desperation. He confided to my Uncle Ben that Gladys was still grieving, which is how he explained the tenseness and lack of physical love between them.

"Vern's a sensitive boy," Ben told Agnes, "but he can' see the forest for the trees, if he thinks that's all the matter 'tween 'em. Gladys might feel like lovin' him more if he put food on the table."

"Maybe he'd pay more 'tention if you didn't offer him liquor nearly so much," Agnes said to her husband with disgust. " 'Sides, he knows he can count on you."

"What am I supposed to do—let 'em go hungry if I can help it?"

"Jus' don' be so quick to offer, that's all."

Even though his track record says otherwise, in my heart I still believe Vernon's intentions were in the right place, he simply lacked the character to make good on them. Or, when he did try, he made a worse mess of things, which is exactly what happened after Vernon went to work for the Leake and Goodlett lumber company.

Vernon thought he had finally done something right when he landed a job loading wood at Leake and Goodlett. Who knows what prompted him to do it, but in a moment of sheer stupidity, Vernon forged a company check for a hundred dollars—a grand sum of money to a poor southern farmer. Needless to say, he was caught within hours and the money retrieved. The unforgiving lumber company pressed charges, and all of a sudden, Vernon found himself on his way to prison, and Gladys found herself homeless and the center of all the local gossip.

My family was horrified that a known relative had been convicted of a crime and sent to prison. Although they never treated Gladys with anything but kindness, she must have known the disapproval they felt in their hearts. It further isolated her and drew her even closer to her toddler.

Since Vernon wasn't going to be around to periodically go through the motions of helping work Bean's land, Gladys had to vacate their two-room home to another family. She went to stay with my Uncle Ben and his wife, Agnes, who lived next door to us. Being close in age, Elvis and I were thrown together as playmates and companions.

"Elvis thought you were his personal playtoy," Mom says. "He loved helping give you a bath and dressing you. One night he insisted on feeding you your supper. While I was mixing up a bowl of toddler food, Elvis was behind my back trying to stuff an apple down your gullet.

"I heard this funny gurgling sound and turned around to see your little eyes were bugged straight out of your head. Elvis couldn't understand what he'd done wrong and felt so bad, he wouldn't come out from beneath the table."

Forgiving child that I was, I held no grudge, and we formed an attachment during that time that was to last.

Six days a week, after helping Agnes clean house and cook, Gladys made the rounds to former clients. She picked up small sewing and tailoring jobs, which she did late at night, after Elvis was put to bed, her eyes straining to see in the poor light.

Out in public, Gladys held her head high. She braved her weekly walk to the welfare office for food with dignity, looking everyone who passed her in the eye, although she seemed to grow older with each trip. In private, she wasn't so sturdy, and turned more and more to Ben's moonshine for comfort. Sometimes, after several drinks, she'd sit with Ben and Agnes and let the tears flow.

"How could he be so stupid?" she asked. "How could he leave us to fend for ourselves? Maybe he did it on purpose to be free of us."

"Now, hon, Vern loves y'all—he jus' got impul-

sive,'' Ben said, putting his arm around her. ''He'll
make it up t'ya.''

''How? By leavin' us to starve to death? I can hardly
blame ever'body for sayin' what they do.''

''You're imaginin'—''

Gladys cut Ben off. ''Just cuz' I can' hear the words
don' mean I don' know what's bein' said. I'd move me
and Elvis if we had anyplace to go. I try so hard, but
Vernon seems to cross me at ev'ry turn. I can' do it
myself, but Vernon's no'count and Elvis is too little.
I don' know what to do.''

Her terror was so vivid that Ben and Agnes said
nothing about Gladys's increased drinking. They considered it ''medicinal'' and appreciated the calming
effect it had on her.

Naturally, Gladys's biggest concern was Elvis—
providing for him and protecting him from nasty comments and pointed stares. Her solution was to lock him
up in my aunt and uncle's house, and not let him outside even to play. After watching his sad little face
pushed up against the front window for a couple of
weeks, wondering what he'd done wrong, Agnes finally
put her foot down. She told Gladys she couldn't keep
Elvis a prisoner—one in the family was bad enough.

''A boy needs air, girl. He thinks he's bein' punished
and he ain't done nothin'.''

Besides alcohol, Gladys found some measure of comfort in church and spent most of her spare time there.
Elvis must have spent more time in church than any
child in Mississippi. It's no wonder he got hooked on
hymns—it's all he heard for a solid year from three to
four. Church was the one place Gladys felt she could
sit in peace, where no one would dare cast aspersions
her way in the house of the Lord. Unfortunately, whatever restraint the folks of Tupelo had been exercising
when it came to the Presleys disappeared almost overnight after Vernon's conviction. They were now considered the white trash of the community.

What do you expect, they would say to each other
while doing the laundry. You know what kind of stock

Vernon comes from, what with his grandmother having all those kids without once getting married.

And that father of his, they'd righteously note after church, a drinker and a womanizer. It's no surprise to me Vernon ended up the way he did. All those Presleys are white trash—they belong in East Tupelo.

As you might gather, East Tupelo was the "bad" end of town, on the far side of the tracks. Even the poor have their own class distinctions, and the Presleys had just sunk to the bottom of the heap.

Gladys absorbed the disapproval that came from the townsfolk with a steely resolve and adopted an "us" versus "them" attitude.

"We don't need nobody but us," she'd tell Elvis at bedtime.

If she saw a worried look on her young son's face, she'd comfort him by invoking their family protector.

"We'll be jus' fine 'cause we got Jesse lookin' after us. He's our guardian angel in heaven, and you're mine here on earth."

Gladys clutched Elvis to her side during church services and dared anyone to make a remark to her face. But the effort it took to stand tall in public was exacting a high price. Whether it was caused by the drinking or just a simultaneous affliction, Gladys's health weakened. She developed a cough that racked her body and robbed her of easy breath. Her ankles swelled and walking became painful—and again, Gladys found relief by sneaking a glass of liquor. More than once, Agnes and Ben would hear Gladys crying herself to sleep on the couch but were helpless to comfort her.

Although he was only three going on four, Elvis wasn't oblivious to the scandal around him. He was old enough to feel his mother's tension and be aware of his father's absence. Elvis had always been a cut-up kid, full of laughs and good humor, but during the time of Vernon's sentence, shyness overcame him. He walked around like a puppy waiting to be smacked with a newspaper. Gladys hadn't wanted to tell him the truth, but family sentiment prevailed—better he find out from his mama than on the street. So while his daddy was away being punished for doing a bad thing, Elvis experienced his own punishment by association.

Gladys tried to hide her fears and humiliation from Elvis, but occasionally cracks would show, especially after drinking. If Elvis saw his mama cry, he'd burst into terrified tears, too. Gladys would hold him gratefully.

"I don' know what I'd do without you, Elvis Aron. You keep me goin'."

Elvis intuitively adopted her "us" versus "them" posture, and it got so he didn't want to leave his mama's side at all. He also became very protective and once took a swipe at Ben when he went to hug Gladys goodnight. Rather than reprimand him, Gladys held him, kissed him, and called Elvis her "little man," a role he would take very seriously from then on.

As he got older, he became even more sharply aware of his family's standing in the eyes of his neighbors as their remarks became more directed at him personally. I'll give him this, though, whenever he heard an unkind remark about his family, he held his head high like his mama, until he was alone. Then there might be tears or, more often in later years, swallowed anger.

One time, after Elvis had just managed to avoid being beaten up by some local bullies, he came over to my house, and we went for a walk through my dad's dairy barn. We sat on a stack of hay and Elvis described his close call.

"They were waiting for me down at the end of the road, near where the big oak tree is," he said, still out of breath from the fear and the run.

"How many were there?" I asked.

"Don't know for sure, three or four—I was runnin' too hard to notice. They jumped out from the side of the road and tackled me, but I kicked one of them and was able to get away. They tried throwin' some rocks, but they missed me. I thought for sure they'd be waitin' for me by home, so I came here 'stead."

After he caught his breath and calmed down, we mulled over several plots for revenge.

"We could toss a skunk at them," I suggested.

"You wanna catch a skunk?" Elvis asked. "That'd be worse than gettin' beat up."

"I know—we could ambush one of 'em, tie 'em up by the pond, and let the mosquitoes get 'em."

Elvis liked this one. "Can you imagine? Soon as the sun went down, they'd be covered with great big ol' mosquitoes sucking the blood out of 'em. They'd be beggin' me."

"Wouldn' it be great—wanna do it?"

"Yeah . . . but we can't."

"Why not?"

" 'Cause, I don't want to hurt anybody."

"They wanted to hurt you."

Elvis shrugged. "Mama would blister my behind. Yours, too. She says revenge is the Lord's."

Again, he was right. Both of us had been raised to say please and yes, ma'am, and be polite to our elders, addressing them as Mr. and Mrs., and listen to the Bible and turn the other cheek—even if you were provoked. It was a curse to be raised to know better.

"Why'd they wanna get you, Elvis? You do somethin'?"

"I don' know why they don' like me. I never did nothin' to 'em." After a moment he added, "They called Daddy a jailbird and said that made me no good, neither."

"Aw, they don't know nothin'."

"I hate it when they call me names like that. I wish they'd just leave me alone."

While Vernon was serving his time in prison, Gladys's drinking became yet another topic of local conversation. While she didn't partake in public, her bloodshot eyes and the lingering aroma of day-old liquor was all too familiar. A lot of women were known to enjoy a snort or two, but a lady boozer was much more scandalous than a man. A fellow would be the topic of conversation, but there was an extra amount of disapproval if a woman turned to the bottle.

The neighbors shook their heads but weren't too surprised—Gladys was merely in keeping with the rest of the Smiths, all considered alcoholics. Between having to live down both the Presley side and the Smith side, it's a wonder Elvis came out of Tupelo with any sanity at all. As it is, he took being called white trash to heart and, as much as he tried not to, accepted it as fact.

Gladys didn't make a spectacle of herself with noticeable public displays of drunkenness, although as time went on she did start missing work. When he was little, she'd use the excuse Elvis was sick; later it would be migraines. Regardless of the reason, there was often a lingering smell of alcohol around her. Gladys's sister was a heavy drinker as well. They were both very nice ladies, so it kills me to say these things. But it's the truth, and it would have an effect on Elvis later in his life.

Like her sister, Gladys took to eating large chunks of onion, which disguised the booze and everything else, but certainly didn't improve her social standing. Gladys's drinking was never discussed, nor did Vernon ever acknowledge it.

"He'd rather have her soused than on his butt," Ben opined.

Because Elvis was young and because money was scarcer than ever, Gladys made few trips to visit Vernon in prison, but their separation was cut mercifully short. Vernon was released from prison after serving only eight months by declaring hardship for his family. Since his crime was minor, prison officials gave him a break and sent him back home with freshly laundered clothes and two dollars in his pocket. Vernon arrived back in Tupelo looking none the worse for wear. Despite having to work the prison fields—obviously, prison officials had no compassion for his bad back—he'd been amply fed and cared for in jail.

Except for his pale skin, he actually looked better than when he left.

The same couldn't be said for Gladys. Vernon was shocked at his wife's bloated, haggard appearance. Her once-shiny black hair was streaked with strands of gray, dark hollows beneath her eyes gave her a weatherbeaten look, and her skin was splotched with red.

Gladys was more relieved than happy to see Vernon, and Elvis greeted his daddy shyly, no doubt sensitive to the tension between his parents. The little boy also harbored his own anger both at being left and at Vernon's coming back. While his daddy was gone, Elvis didn't have to share Gladys. He was particularly upset at being replaced in his mama's bed. For weeks after, he'd cry until Gladys brought him back to bed with them.

Whether it was because Vernon had been separated from Elvis during such a vital time in his childhood, or because Elvis tended to reflect more his mother's feelings than his dad's, a shyness and restraint sprang up between them that never really went away. Even in an area so poor, fathers would still find the time on occasion to go fishing with their sons or throw a baseball or football around. Elvis and Vernon never shared that kind of companionship.

Vernon and Gladys had their own barriers standing in the way and usually communicated through Elvis, rather than to each other. He was their reason for being together. From here on out, what little they shared as a couple was embodied in their son.

But that might have been the case even without Vernon's arrest. From the day he was born, Elvis was his mama's son. She hated for him to be out of her sight and instilled it in him that a boy's place was with his mama—they only had each other. Even after Vernon's return, Elvis always had to know where his mama was—not that he'd run to her, but just to know.

Nor did Elvis have close ties to his granddad, Jesse. Up until Jesse left Minnie, they lived a stone's throw from each other, but seldom spent any time together.

Hardly too surprising since Jesse and Vernon had never been especially tender toward one another. Vernon's jail time had humiliated Jesse and confirmed his worst suspicions about his son. Perhaps J.D. assumed that Elvis would be a chip off Vernon's good-for-nothing block and not worth investing any time in. Whatever the reason, the kinfolk on the Presley side seemed happier when they didn't have to deal with one another. Maybe if they had, Elvis wouldn't have adopted my family as close to his heart as he did.

You might think that several months in prison would change a man's outlook on life, give him a resolve he might have previously lacked, and see his freedom as a second chance. Not Vernon. About all it seemed to teach him was not to mess with company checks anymore. He still couldn't hold a job for any consistent length of time, still suffered from his chronic bad back, and still did just enough to get by and little more.

As the country celebrated the new decade, the people in northeast Mississippi prayed for the next ten years to be better than the previous ten—or else we'd all be either moved or dead. That New Year's Eve going from 1940 to 1941, my family and Elvis's family were over at Ben and Agnes's place. The smell of baking warmed the house and gave us a very safe, secure feeling.

The men were playing cards at the dinner table and the women were in the kitchen talking, cooking and quietly toasting out the old year with a few slowly sipped drinks.

Since it was a special occasion, Elvis and I were allowed to stay up late. It was a happy night, one of those rare times where you didn't sense that the grown-ups were upset at matters you couldn't begin to understand.

It was already dark outside and cold, so we were housebound and searching for ways to entertain ourselves. Elvis and I stood around watching the men play cards, but that got boring after a while, as did our repeated requests to play, too. I'm sure the men were relieved to see us leave to wander into the kitchen. This was better, with lively chatter and the smell of food making our mouths water. We staked out a spot in the corner and sat down with some freshly baked bread.

"Now, you know what's going to happen later, right?" Elvis asked me.

Since my mouth was full of warm bread, all I could do was shake my head no.

"Real late tonight, midnight, it's going to turn into 1941, and when that happens, we're all going to sing a song."

"Like a Christmas carol?"

"No, a New Year's song. It's called 'Auld Lang Syne.' "

"Old who?"

Elvis laughed. "Not old, 'Auld.' But you're close. Mama says it's Scottish for old. We're Scottish. Our relatives way back came to America from there."

"Why?" Even then, I couldn't imagine anyone coming to Tupelo by choice.

"Stop interruptin'—I'm trying to tell you about the song. When the radio says it's midnight, we're all going to sing. At least, I will."

"I don't know the words."

"That's why I'm going to teach you. Listen:

" *'Should old acquaintance be forgot*
And never brought to mind . . .' "

I'll never forget Elvis's clear voice singing me that song, so gently. His singing voice was high, but incredibly clear. Out of the corner of my eye, I could see Gladys and Agnes turn to listen, and I saw tears in Gladys's eyes.

Elvis repeated the song to me several times, to the point where I could at least hum the tune close enough to his liking. We each ate another thick slice of bread, followed by a milk chaser. Over the protests of the moms, Ben gave us shot glasses. Elvis played bartender, carefully pouring the milk from a large glass to the two small ones. We prefaced each shot with a robust "Happy New Year."

We finished our milk in record time and waited impatiently for midnight, while our parents looked forward to a new decade and a fresh beginning.

Somebody must have forgot to pray for peace. The day the Japanese bombed Pearl Harbor a scary quiet silenced Tupelo. Children didn't understand the full implication, but saw the fear and worry on everyone's face. When the people you count on to tell you everything is going to be okay are frightened to death themselves, a child knows the news isn't good.

We gathered at Ben's house to listen to the radio. The men looked like a close relative had died, and in fact, the whole atmosphere in the house reminded me of a funeral. Elvis stayed close to Gladys, who grabbed his hand tightly—Vernon sat on the other side of the room with Ben and my dad.

The next day, nearly every guy of proper age was on his way to sign up. Back then, people were so poor they would join the army as a means of getting regular meals and a roof over their heads. Now that there was a reason, half the county was ready to go. I saw Elvis later on—he had finally got loose from home.

"Mama was afraid to let me go anywhere. . . . I think she was worried we might get bombed."

Now there was a thought that perked me up. "Really? I hope they blow up ol' Orville's field."

"Yeah, then he'd have to work for a livin'." I knew Elvis was echoing Gladys, who I had heard say the same thing countless times.

"What'd we do?"

"We'd have to all hide down in the storm cellars. It'd be just like having a tornado 'cept a lot worse," Elvis said. "And just think, no school if it got blowed up."

"They couldn't bomb Tupelo," I decided. "The army would shoot them down before they got here."

"Yeah, I s'pose you're right. I guess we only have to worry if spies come and take us prisoner."

"I hope they take my sister."

"Is your daddy joining up?" Elvis asked.

I shook my head. "He's too old. Is yours?"

"Nah, he's got to take care of me and Mama and his back's bad. I could take care of us for him if he really wanted to go. I wish he would join."

"You wanna to be a soldier when you grow up?" I asked him.

"Sure . . . but who'd stay with Mama?"

That was Elvis for you—always looking out for Gladys. He was only six and already felt responsible for her well-being. The sad state of affairs within their family had forced him to assume the role that should have been Vernon's.

Vernon got himself exempt by declaring his family was totally dependent on him, and he watched his cronies head off to battle. While the war caused its share of fear, it also boosted the area's struggling economy. It was still a poor county and would remain so, but the WPA once again stepped in, creating jobs to help the war effort. Vernon was one of those hired to help build a prisoner-of-war containment facility somewhere in the state, and it was one of the few times he finished a project he started.

After the first rush of excitement and confusion, the war became like a familiar background noise— something you were aware of, but that you only paid marginal attention to. You listened to the news bulletins on the radio or read them in the newspaper, but for Elvis and me, the war seldom touched our lives directly. Not even when the son or husband of an acquaintance was shipped home in a flag-covered coffin did the war become reality.

The truth is, the war years were some of the most fun and carefree of our entire lives.

3

As the battles raged in Europe and in the Pacific, the poor of Tupelo found themselves having to face the additional sacrifices of doing without sugar, nylons, and other goods reserved for military use. The townsfolk attended Sunday services in droves, to pray for peace and prosperity equally hard, and they spent a great deal of time after church talking about Japan and Hitler and Italy, and right versus might.

But during the rest of the week, life went on with barely a ripple of difference. The Presleys were still struggling against their poverty and each other to make ends meet and provide Elvis with the bare essentials. Gladys did the best with what she had. Regardless of how worn or how old or how few the hand-me-downs Elvis had to wear—more often than not a pair of ill-fitting dungarees and a two-toned shirt—Gladys made sure his clothes were always neat and clean.

"You don' need to be rich to look proper," she said, fussing over him.

But should Elvis ever complain about wearing the same clothes over and over, Gladys's smile would snap off and she'd grab him by the shoulders for a good talking to.

"I don' ever wanna hear none o' that. Yer daddy and I are doin' what we can—don' be an ingrate."

Elvis would hang his head, his eyes filled with tears. In fact, Gladys often did go without so that Elvis would have presentable clothes and shoes. She would go around town wearing two or three pairs of socks because she didn't have enough money for both of them to get shoes. (Fortunately for Vernon, his heavy boots had a long lifespan.) Elvis would beg Gladys to get shoes for herself, too, when they were at the second-hand store—partly because he hated her doing without, and partly because he cringed at the stares and whispers that followed his shoeless mama around town.

But Gladys was stoic, and her explanation carried a double-edged blade.

"It don' matter I go without, jus' so long as you have . . ." whatever it was.

Elvis never got anything he didn't in some way feel guilty about. If he was benefiting, it meant his mama was suffering a little extra in some way. And unfortunately, Gladys never let Elvis forget her sacrifices on his behalf. She truly loved her boy with all her heart, but she couldn't rid herself of that ever-present anger and frustration at being trapped in a life of impoverished hell. She just wasn't made to accept her lot in life like a lamb—she would always keep looking for a way out.

If it were just a matter of Vernon, she could still leave, try her luck elsewhere—but with a child, it was too late. Elvis was both her reason to live and her warden. So when he complained, even about the littlest thing, how could she help but feel riled— she had already given up so much for him. He might not understand its source, but even a child intuitively picks up on unspoken attitudes—and Elvis translated what he felt into a belief that he was the cause of his mama's troubles and unhappiness.

The depth of Elvis's guilt reached its lowest point when he learned the real reason he was an only child. Whenever he'd ask as a little kid, Gladys would sit him on her lap and give him a big hug.

" 'Cause, honey, you's ever'thin' we could ever want."

But one day, Vernon evidently decided his eight-year-old son was old enough to know the truth when Elvis enthusiastically announced for the umpteenth time he'd like a baby brother to play with.

"Now don' you go hasslin' your mama 'bout havin' you a brother," he ordered.

"Why not—ever'one else got brothers and sisters. How come I can't?"

Vernon sat Elvis down beside him on the outside step, buying a few moments to regroup before his first man-to-man chat with his child.

"You're a big boy now, so I wan' you t'listen. It upsets Mama when you talk 'bout wantin' a baby brother, 'cause she'd dearly love t'do jus' that."

"Why don' she?"

" 'Cause she can't. She got hurt inside real bad when you and Jesse was born. Somethin' broke, and the doctor ain't able to fix it."

"Mama's hurt?" Elvis's eyes swelled with tears of terror.

"No, no, boy, not no more," he patted Elvis's shoulder awkwardly. "Jus' when you was born. It breaks Mama's heart she can' give you a baby brother, but she knows it's God's will. Now, I'm countin' on you t'do right by Mama and stop all this brother talk, you hear?"

"Yessir," he said in a little voice, quickly wiping his eyes.

"This was jus' our secret, okay? Man to man."

Elvis nodded.

"Good. Now you go play and 'member—no more upsettin' your mama."

Elvis kept his promise and never told his mama this secret. He wouldn't mention it to me until he was already a star. But despite his silence, it had weighed heavily on his mind over the years and this guilt became so entrenched that he would always feel "It's my fault"—whether it was started by his inability to help out financially, or his mama not having shoes, or her sudden crying jags, or her heartbreak at not having more babies. Which is why no matter how much Elvis gave Gladys his whole life, he could never do enough to make up for all her sacrifices.

It also cemented his reliance on the one brother he did have—even though that brother was dead.

The seeds of future behavior might have been firmly planted in the fertile soil of Elvis's unsuspecting young mind, but their full effect wouldn't show up until later. Despite the pressures of poverty and a tense home life, Elvis was still a kid, still capable of putting worries aside long enough to have fun, especially during the summer—if he could get away from his mama.

Gladys was always finding a reason to keep Elvis by her side. He had to help her clean house and do other chores, and keep her from being lonely. It wasn't unusual for Elvis to go home because his mama needed company while preparing dinner. Vernon might have been her husband, but Elvis had become her emotional partner in life.

One warm summer night we were heading back to his place after Elvis had stayed over for dinner—it was one of Gladys's unbreakable rules that Elvis had to be walked home if it was dark out. It was a bright night, with the moon pretty full, and we pointed out the different constellations to each other. As we neared his home, I asked Elvis if he wanted to go fishing the next day.

"Yeah, but I can'. I gotta help stack wood for Orville Bean, then I gotta go shoppin' with Mama."

"Can't you come after?"

"Maybe. I wanna, but . . . I gotta think o' somethin' to tell Mama. I gotta lot o' chores to do."

"Your mama sure is strict."

"You're lucky you don't hafta do chores."

"I do."

"Yeah, but you got so many older brothers helpin'. If Jesse was here, it'd be easier, but I don' mind helpin'."

"Too bad he ain't. You'd have twice as much time to play."

"To be a loafer like you," he teased, nudging me with his shoulder.

On days Elvis did have time to play, we'd pass the time fishing, tossing a battered ball that looked like a cross between a football and a softball, or making up games to fit the day. Sometimes, I'd go play with Elvis at his place, but mostly he'd come to our house. Elvis liked nice things and the fact was, he preferred my home to his. The Presleys lived in what was known as a shotgun house, because it was straight through, like a tube. It had two rooms, and Elvis grew up sleeping on a beat-up sofa in the front, which was a combined living room/kitchen. Every piece of furniture and all the utensils were second-hand or throw-aways. No matter where they moved, and they moved plenty, they always wound up living in the same type of house.

If it was raining out, we'd go into my bedroom, which I shared with another brother, and play with some old, beat-up plastic toy cars. We built humongous highways out of old pipes and boards and anything else we could drag in the house without my mother seeing, and spent hours just rolling the toy cars up and down. We'd make up stories about where the cars were driving to. I'd usually pick a spot on the West Coast, while Elvis preferred to stay in the South.

Sometimes, we'd team up with other kids for a game of football, tag, or hide-and-go-seek. It was a funny thing about Elvis. He was really a cut-up kid, and when we were alone, he was just as outgoing and talkative as I was. But when we'd team up with other kids we knew, he would get very quiet and just kind of follow along, almost hanging back from the rest. Because he got so much taunting from the local kids, he automatically went into a shell, drawing back like a puppy waiting to be kicked, but always hoping to be accepted. Once he saw they weren't going to get on him, then he'd open up, join in, and let himself have fun.

Oddly, games were an equalizer, an unspoken truce time. But it would hurt and confuse Elvis that the same kids who'd root for him to score a touchdown would snicker at his family a month later in school. But with every succeeding year, it took longer for him to open up, because it was harder for him to forget the comments he'd heard. The older he got, the shyer and more introverted he got.

Nobody ever said anything nasty to Elvis in front of me, but I knew it happened. He suffered abuse about everything—his father's not working, his father's having a prison record, his family's checkered past, and even their being so poor. That's the strangest, because everybody was poor, but the Presleys were considered the bottom of the heap.

On days when the weather was comfortable, we'd go behind my Uncle Ben's house and drag out these two old car tires that he kept especially for us to fool with. They were as smooth as porcelain and were completely worn through in a couple of spots, but they were perfect for us.

We'd take them out to one of the dusty roads that hardly got any traffic and race with them. Back and forth we'd tear down the road, desperately trying to keep the tires under control. Half the time we'd end up going in opposite directions and take ten minutes to travel a hundred yards. We'd raise such a cloud of dust, you'd have thought someone was drag-racing cars down the road.

A couple of times we got really daring and found the steepest hill in the area, which was really more of a gentle slope.

"Okay, you go first," I'd tell Elvis.

"Why can't you go first?"

"You're older. Besides, you do it better."

Even then, Elvis was susceptible to flattery.

"Awright. Watch for cars."

So as I kept one eye peeled for any runaway flatbed pick-ups, I would hold on to Elvis's tire as he squeezed himself into it. Once he was curled in tight, I would give it a push and watch it wobble down the hill, while he would bellow out squeals of laughter. On reflection, it could have been screams of terror, too.

Half the time, the tire would tip over after just a few turns, but sometimes, if everything was perfect, you would roll all the way down the slope, across the road, and land at the edge of a cotton field. When that happened, you'd climb out and be unable to keep to your feet, never admitting your stomach was about to come out of your ears. No carnival ride ever was as much fun or made you feel as sick. Part of the thrill was the element of danger, that you could be flattened by a racing car if the timing was just right.

Sometimes my dog would come with us and chase after us, barking and trying to nip at our feet and hands as we rolled by. Elvis loved Spunk and talked a lot about wanting to have a dog of his own, but the Presleys could barely feed themselves, much less a dog. Actually, Spunk was an outdoor family dog, not a pampered pet. He often fended for himself when it came to getting dinner, being a fairly accomplished hunter of rabbits and squirrels. More than once my brothers would tear after Spunk when they saw him catch a rabbit, hoping to have it in our pot instead of poor Spunk's stomach. He was the cutest little thing, but feisty. Had to be—the Depression was tough for animals, too.

I don't know who cried more on the day Spunk got run over, me or Elvis. He was chasing a car and just got too close. I'll never forget hearing his yelp. I ran and found Elvis. Gladys's eyes welled, and she gave Elvis permission to come help me bury Spunk. He gently held Spunk in his arms, rocking him and crying into his fur.

We dug a grave and buried him on the edge of my dad's property. We made a cross of sticks, tied together with some of my mom's thread, and carved his name on it. After we said a prayer, Elvis put his arm around me.

"He'll be okay. Jesse'll watch after 'im."

Spunk was the closest thing to a pet Elvis ever had

growing up. But Elvis loved animals dearly, and years later, Elvis made up for not being able to afford a dog as a child by having a small kennel at Graceland. Dogs made him laugh and he could spend hours watching their antics. When he got upset, he'd reach out to his favorite dogs before people.

One time, one of his dogs got sick with some rare disease. The local veterinarian in Memphis told Elvis the best animal doctor for this particular ailment was in Boston, so Elvis had the dog flown to Boston on a chartered plane. The pet was there for four months, and it cost Elvis a small fortune, but he said it was worth every penny. The dog came back home and lived to a nice old age.

Vernon was appalled at the money spent, but Elvis wouldn't listen.

"They love you no matter how much you do or don't have. They don't want anything except to be with you, and they don't leave you like people do. You can count on them more than you can most people you know, that's for sure."

Out among the cotton and soybean fields were several creeks and ponds where you could fish and swim. Elvis and I would go out back and dig up some worms from the early morning soil, put them in an old tin can with some moist dirt, and set out for our favorite pond, with some hooks and thread to serve as test line When it was really hot, we'd daydream about owning a bicycle—a real luxury item—as we trudged in the sticky heat.

By the pond it was always a few degrees cooler, which was worth the effort of keeping the mosquitoes at bay. We'd set the worms in the shade, lest they cook, and scrounge around for sticks suitable for fishing poles. Long, flexible branches were the best, because we loved watching the pole bend when a fish bit the bait. Nothing was more aggravating than when a fish took off with your worm and the pole snapped in two.

Some days, you wouldn't get a single nibble, not

that it mattered one way or another. If the fish weren't hungry, you'd put the poles away for a while and go for a cool swim. Our favorite pond had a big tree nearby with a branch that hung out close enough to the water so you could use it as a makeshift diving board. That first dive in always felt so wonderful as the cold water chilled you to the bone. The water was clear, and if Elvis and I had bad luck fishing, we'd try to catch them by hand, but the closest we got was to feel them shimmy through our fingers as they scurried away from us.

When we had enough of swimming, which could be hours, we'd sit on the grass and let the sun dry us. Sometimes my mom would have sent us out with lunch, usually peanut butter and banana sandwiches, knowing it was one of Elvis's favorite meals. We'd lounge around until the sun began its downward arc and it was time for one or both of us to get home.

After one of our fishing outings, I went over to Elvis's for dinner. Eating at the Presleys was a fairly rare occasion for me. I assume my parents didn't encourage it because they knew that Gladys and Vernon found it hard enough to feed three mouths. But on this day, Elvis and I had caught our dinner with a prized catch of a half dozen or so humble-sized fish.

The two-room house they were living in was tiny but clean. Vernon was outside when we got there and he slapped our backs, although Elvis didn't return the affection. Gladys was inside preparing dinner. Although the fish were so small that together it was barely enough to feed the two of us, she let out a surprised holler and fussed all over us, especially Elvis. He flushed deep red with her hugs and kisses, as if he was embarrassed that I was there to see it. He was proud and looked forward to enjoying a special meal.

For most families in the area, meals didn't vary much. Corn bread, black-eyed peas, collard greens, boiled potatoes, grits—what's popularly referred to now as soul food—were the staples. If it wasn't boiled, it was fried, but however prepared, there wasn't very much of it.

There were very few chubby sharecroppers. Those that were, like Gladys, owed their extra weight to drinking or avoiding field work. Alcohol was cheap—food might be hard to come by, but you could always find a drink.

Elvis had been a little bit fat as a toddler, but he lost it by the time he was seven or eight. He was a thin adolescent and downright skinny as a teenager. He didn't really fill out until after he graduated from high school. Some of it had to do with heredity—Vernon and Jesse before him had been thin men—but most of it was due to his simply not having as much to eat as he should have. It's miraculous that his health and teeth were as good as they were, considering the conditions he grew up under. When he did come down with snif fles or a cold, he'd ignore it and never complain.

Elvis and I wolfed down our fish, which Gladys had prepared by frying in a hot skillet with butter. Dinner was very pleasant. Vernon and Gladys asked me a lot of questions, but they never addressed one another. Each of them spoke only to me or to Elvis. After dinner, Elvis and I helped Gladys with the dishes, and Vernon excused himself and left for parts unknown. Gladys watched him go, but kept her thoughts to herself. In some ways, they seemed to be a regular couple, like my parents, but they lived very separate lives. Gladys's world revolved around whatever shack they currently occupied, and Vernon found every reason to be out of their home, even if it meant just sitting for hours on the front stoop. About the only time they were together was for meals and church.

Their common denominator was Elvis. They would have loved nothing more than to spoil him. If Vernon or Gladys came into some extra money, rather than spend it on something sensible like food or clothes, Gladys would buy something special for Elvis, trying to make up for their poverty.

Vernon would want to tear his hair out at what he

thought was a frivolous expense, but Gladys always got her way. Take the time he got his first guitar. Gladys skipped meals and made do with raggedy clothes, scrimping and saving until she had enough money to buy Elvis a guitar—a gift that meant more to her at the time than to him.

While it's true Elvis had a thing for music, what he really wanted was a bicycle.

"But I saved all this time to git you a gu'tar," Gladys said, shocked. "For you t'use singin'. If you git good 'nough, maybe the minister'll let you play in church. You don' want no bicycle."

That was that. Gladys took him to the second-hand store and proudly counted out her accumulated change. The shop owner showed Elvis how to hold the guitar and how to strum it, while Gladys beamed with pride. From day one, Gladys dreamed of her son being a star, partly because as a young girl, she'd wanted to be a performer. If she couldn't live out the dream, maybe, just maybe, she could live it through Elvis. It was a fantasy that kept her going. She would tell Elvis time and time again how happy it made her to see him sing, so he knew one sure way to please her.

Once it was his, Elvis spent hours strumming and grew to love his instrument. What little he could play, he taught himself simply by experimenting. He'd sit alone and try to play along with the radio, singing and strumming and looking to be in seventh heaven. When he wasn't plucking out a tune, he carried the guitar around almost constantly. After having spent his whole life doing without, he suddenly had something that few others had. It made him feel special.

Every Saturday night we'd listen to the Grand Ol' Opry on the radio, and Elvis would try to come over and listen to it at my house. If the whole family was there, which wasn't that often, Elvis would sit off to the side and just listen, silently mouthing the words to the songs. When it was just us and my parents or one of my brothers, Elvis would start singing along. My parents seemed to enjoy it, as long as he didn't get so loud that he drowned out the radio. I swear he lived for Saturday nights, so he could sing old songs and learn some new ones.

I have to admit, I never liked country and western music—I still don't—which was too bad for me, because all we ever listened to was country music. But listening to the radio, especially on Saturday nights, *was* something to do, and I sat there along with everyone else, never letting on my terrible secret. A southern boy who didn't like country? I was sure I'd be ridiculed if I let it be known. Years later, when Elvis confided in me that he had felt pretty much the same way, we shared some good laughs over it. As the world would eventually come to know, the music that most stirred Elvis was gospel, and the sound that excited his creativity was blues music, which he would first learn about as a teenager in Memphis, when he heard black musicians playing and singing on Beale Street. But as a child he took what he could get, so when church wasn't in session, country and western would have to suffice.

For as much as Elvis revered music, I was obsessed with the movies. Elvis enjoyed going to the cinema, too, and the top priority of any week was to make sure we had the two-bits it cost to see the local double feature. My parents would take us most of the time, but I made sure I had back-up in case they came up short on any given week. After Elvis was done with his chores, we'd head on out to the main road and search through the grass for discarded pop bottles, or volunteer if there was an odd job to do for one of the neighbors.

Most of the films we saw were old by the time they reached Tupelo, but they were still a breath of fresh air. Usually, it seemed they played westerns, but one movie I remember in particular was the old version of *The Titanic*, with Barbara Stanwyck. About twenty years later, I reminded Elvis of that when he announced that Ms. Stanwyck had been signed to play his mother in one of his films.

"Hey, wasn't she old enough to be my mama back then, too?" Elvis laughed.

Most of the time, my parents would drive us into town to see a movie on Saturday. During the winter, we'd go to the matinee, but during the summer, it was usually after the Opry. My parents always invited Elvis and treated him to the show, because they knew I wanted him along, and they also knew he couldn't go otherwise and would have been left out.

That's what families were like back then, if you could help, you did. My parents never expected to get anything back from Vernon and Gladys—if you did someone a good turn, you just hoped that maybe later on they could do something for you. Vernon never really helped out my family through the years, but Elvis sure did. He'd always offer to help with chores when he was over and, when he became successful, always made sure none of us was in need. He felt obliged to repay the debt for his whole family. No matter how often we'd invite him to the movies, Elvis never took it for granted and was always genuinely appreciative—almost surprised that we really wanted him to come along.

My parents would load us up in the back of our old truck, a pick-up with a flatbed, and we'd bounce into town, hanging on for dear life. When we were younger and even sometimes when we were almost teenagers, they would wait for us outside until the movie was over. There was always a double feature, and of course, they played the worst one first, so you had to sit through both of them.

In that dark theater, we were all eyes, utterly fascinated with the magic of it all. I think we would have liked anything we saw—we didn't know any better. The technology back then might not have been what it is today, but I for one still think the movies were better; they were about people, not special effects, and they gave some of us hope that there was life beyond our dead-end towns.

When the films were over, I was a bundle of energy and full of dreams.

Elvis would roll his eyes to tease me.

"I still dunno how you're gonna get famous in Tupelo."

"You can'. When I grow up, I'm gonna move to Hollywood."

"I can jus' see you, drivin' a fancy car and wearin' big ol' sunglasses, like some big shot. Nobody'll know you. 'Course, nobody'll admit knowin' you anyway," he said.

"I'll be at my station pumpin' gas and you prob'ly won' even 'member my name."

I'm not saying this to pat myself on the back, but I think my desire to reach my goals had an effect on Elvis when we got older. The more he saw my determination, my fascination with the possibility of succeeding in an artistic field, the more he began to believe that maybe it *was* possible.

If he had been alone in his room and hadn't had someone to share his dreams with, someone who believed they could be more than just dreams, I don't think he would have pushed as hard. By yourself it's scary. Luckily, we had each other, and together we held each other up. In the end, Elvis had the talent and the special qualities it took to achieve his dreams.

Although Elvis became notorious for displays of sudden, violent temper as an adult, he seldom displayed anger as a child. Nor did he get into trouble, having been raised with manners—and an abhorrence of Gladys's displeasure. Gladys could wound Elvis more with the pain of disappointment than a whipping stick ever could. He hated feeling that he failed her.

There is one incident, though, when he was eight, that stands out as a double rarity with Elvis getting into mischief and displaying his usually well-guarded rage. We had met up after school to fool around for an hour, and on our way home, we passed by a roadside fruit stand with a load of apples for sale—big, beautiful, shiny red apples. Elvis stopped to admire them, and the idea forming in his head showed on his face.

"Earl, you got any money?"

"Uh-uh. Why?"

"Look at them apples. Mama loves 'em—I wanna get her one."

The farmer came over to us, eyeing us suspiciously. "Can I he'p you boys?"

"How much?" Elvis asked, pointing at the pile of apples.

"Nickel each. Quarter for ha'f dozen."

Elvis patted his pockets again, knowing full well they were empty. Still, he stubbornly just stood there, staring at the fruit.

"You boys run alon' now."

"Thank you, sir," I said, grabbing Elvis and pulling him away. We got about twenty yards away when Elvis stopped and yanked his arm out of my hand.

"Let's go find her one on a tree," I suggested.

"No, I wanna get one of *those*."

"Elvis, come on. We don't got money."

"We never got no money," he said absently. "Hold my books."

I was getting nervous, 'cause I knew what he was going to do.

"He got so many, he ain't gonna miss one. And he ain't gonna sell 'em all, either, so they'd just spoil."

The farmer was sitting by the front of his truck, so Elvis snuck up from the back, plucked a plump apple off the cart, then quietly retraced his steps. Halfway back to me, he broke into a run and flew past me, laughing and triumphant, his face flushed as red as the fruit he hugged. Once I caught up, I dumped his schoolbooks in his arms and made a hasty goodbye.

Elvis walked home and proudly plopped down the apple in front of a very surprised Gladys. Just as he'd hoped, his mama was delighted and wanted to know what tree had such beautiful fruit.

"I dunno, Mama," Elvis said.

"Why not?"

When he told her he got it from a roadside stand, she asked how he had paid for it. Elvis stood there, mute.

"Elvis Aron Presley, did you steal this?"

"No, Mama, I, uh, didn't mean to—" the words caught in a stutter.

"I jus' wanted you to have it," Elvis sobbed out. "Ain't you hungry for it?"

"You *never* take something without paying unless it's a gift," she shouted at him. "You wanna end up in jail like your daddy someday?"

Elvis was frightened by the intensity of her reaction. How did he know she was terrified of him getting a reputation in town as a thief, or turning out to be like Vernon. It was a child's silly mistake, but to Gladys, it was a portent of Elvis's following in the unfortunate footsteps of the Presley clan.

"But he had so many, and I just wanted one."

"Ain't it bad 'nough we're poor? The good Lord he'p me if we're gonna be thieves on top of it."

She grabbed him by the shirt collar and led him out the door. He begged her to stop, but no amount of crying and carrying on could sway Gladys. Curious neighbors peeked out their windows at the sounds of Elvis's pleas, and the humiliation made him so angry he cried out even more. He struggled, but Gladys had a grip of iron. She half-dragged Elvis back to the stand, her face blotched with fury. The farmer jumped up at the commotion, and Gladys planted Elvis directly in front of him.

Gladys held out the apple. "Take this, and tell the man how you got it."

Elvis stood there crying, head hung in shame.

"Tell him."

"I took it off the cart."

"Now apologize."

"Sorry."

"Sorry what?"

"Sorry, sir."

Gladys gave back the apple. "I'm so sorry."

"Aw, you know boys," the farmer said, a little taken aback by all the emotion.

Gladys and Elvis walked back home in silence, her head held high, Elvis's chin digging a hole in his chest.

When they got back home, Gladys ordered Elvis to stay inside as punishment for what he'd done. "You gotta learn, if you can't pay for it, you gotta go without."

Gladys left, partly to calm herself down, and partly to give Elvis a chance to think about what he'd done. But the thoughts he had weren't what Gladys intended. Shamed beyond words, frustrated that he had lacked a lousy nickel in the first place, and mortified that his mama was so disappointed in him, Elvis had a tantrum. He attacked the walls of their shack, peeling off the cheap wallpaper Gladys had put up in an attempt to make it less shabby. Elvis tore at the paper with a vengeance, wanting to rip everything about their life into pieces. He had ruined two walls and was midtear on the third when Gladys came back in and caught him.

For a split second, they stared at each other, Gladys with stunned surprise, Elvis with defiance. Then in a flash, Gladys scooped Elvis up and gave him the spanking of his life. In fact, it might have been the first and only spanking he ever got.

The only thing Elvis would say about the apple incident later in life is that none of it would have happened if they hadn't been so poor to begin with.

The biggest event of the year was the Mississippi-Alabama Fair, which came once a year. The people of Tupelo and the surrounding areas looked forward to this more than they did any holiday. Men put on clean shirts and trousers, and women pressed their nicest dresses to go on rides and see livestock. The biggest attractions of the fair were the farm animal shows—best hogs, best cows, which cows gave the most milk, hog-calling—and people took serious interest in these things.

For the kids, the rides were what made the fair special. The cornerstone, of course, was the Ferris wheel, which creaked and jerked as it groaned through its revolutions, but we'd wait in line an hour to get on it. At the top, you could see the flat farmland stretch out forever, and you'd strain to find your house in the distance. By today's standards, the fair was strictly small time, but it wasn't small time to us then. It was the most important thing that came through town.

In the weeks before the fair, we'd do double duty scouring the roadsides for bottles to redeem, because it wasn't enough to go to the fair just once. A lot of times, Elvis would meet me inside the fair after having snuck in by climbing over the fence. A couple of times I did it, too, as did most of the population of Tupelo between the ages of six and eighteen.

Once you got away from the livestock end, the fair took on a wonderful aroma. Chili cook-offs and baking contests were enough to make your mouth water. If you timed it right and looked hungry enough, it was pretty easy to get a nice sampling of pie for free. Besides the rides, eating was the best thing about the fair.

People from all the towns in the area—Aberdeen, Okolona, Shannon, Oaklawn, Willis Heights—converged on Tupelo for four days of the year. The highlight of the fair for many people was the talent contest. Anyone with even the slightest ability, from juggling to singing to playing the spoons, participated.

By the time Elvis was ten, his voice was developing into a thing of crystal beauty, and when the fair came to town that year, everybody in the family thought it would be a wonderful idea for Elvis to enter the talent contest. Everybody but Elvis. The thought of just standing in front of a crowd of strangers was too terrifying.

"Aw, Elvis, honey, come on," Gladys urged. "You sing so beautiful, ever'one'd love to hear you."

"I don' wanna."

"You sing in church, you don' mind that."

"That's diff'rent, Mama, it's jus' prayin'."

"Then do it for me. It'd make me real proud for ever'one to see how special you sing."

"Mama, if the boy don't wanna sing—"

Gladys cut Vernon off. "O' course he does, he's jus' a little shy."

That was an understatement. Elvis had grown into an increasingly insecure young boy to the world at large, with a tendency to disappear in crowds—mostly because he feared negative attention, whether it was about family, or his looks, or doing poorly in school, or whatever.

Finally, after a great deal of persuasion and manipulation on Gladys's part, Elvis agreed to compete. The promise of free entry into the fair and complimentary lunch made the decision easier, but mostly it was because singing was the one thing he did that often resulted in positive reactions—even from strangers. It set him apart in a good way, but most of all, it was a refuge from outside barbs and inner feelings of inadequacy and failure—that, and knowing how disappointed Gladys would be if he didn't.

The day of the contest, Elvis was very nervous, and distracted himself by obsessing over the clothes he'd wear. Not that he had much to choose from, but he tried every possible combination ten times. Gladys was in a state of barely controlled mania. She fluttered over him like a butterfly, constantly smoothing his already plastered-down hair and adjusting his clothes. Elvis had on a jacket that was at least one size too small and pants that would have fallen off him without a belt, but I could tell he was excited and thought he looked rather spiffy. He clutched his worn guitar for dear life, and I noticed that his hands were shaking as he strummed.

Attempts to make conversation were futile—he was thrilled and hyper one second, talking a mile a minute about his free lunch and everybody coming to see him; then he'd plummet into near-catatonic paralysis. At one point, he told Gladys he was going to be sick.

"No, you ain't, honey, that's just nerves foolin' with ya."

She made him sit with his head between his knees and he felt better. By the time we left for the fair, Elvis had settled into a calmly numb state, while the rest of the family chatted merrily, full of anticipation.

My family found seats next to Vernon, who saved one for Gladys, still back with Elvis, and we settled in to wait. We were almost dead-center in the audience, a spot great for seeing but murderously hot. The tent was packed, and it must have been a hundred degrees. People fanned themselves with pieces of paper and kept climbing over the packed rows of seats to go out and buy lemonade.

Backstage, Elvis silently mouthed the words to his song over and over, while Gladys re-wet his hair for the hundredth time.

"What if I forget the words, Mama, and ever'one laughs at me?"

"They won't, 'cause you won't." She looked at him right in the eye. "I'm jus' so proud o' you. Prouder than I ever been of anyone." She hugged him a last time, then was shooed to her seat by one of the contest's officials.

The official patted Elvis on the shoulder and gave him some advice.

"If you feel yourself gettin' scared, son, just close your eyes and pretend you're all alone. Or just pick out one person to sing to. Works every time."

Elvis nodded, then started mouthing the words to his song yet again.

Gladys returned to her seat just as the first act was introduced. She gave us a look of hope and crossed her fingers for good luck. After what seemed like hours of countless poorly sung country songs—you know how thrilling that was for me—I saw Elvis standing in the wings waiting to go on. He had a death grip on his guitar and a silly grin on his face, which was flushed a deep red. His shoulders rose and fell rapidly—his adrenaline was pumping so hard he was on the verge of hyperventilating.

Vernon noticed, too. "He'll pass out cold if he don' calm hisself. That'd be one hard act t'follow," he laughed.

Gladys poked him in the ribs, but was too focused on Elvis to be overly angry at her husband.

When they announced his name, Elvis strode uncertainly toward center stage—which was nothing more than bare earth at the front of the tent. A friendly chorus of chuckles greeted him when he got to the microphone, because he was too small to reach it. One of the judges brought out a chair and told Elvis to stand on it so everybody could see him, then retreated so Elvis could perform.

He stood there quietly for several moments, unmoving, almost frozen, as he scanned the audience. His eyes grew big, then abruptly closed. After a few more tense seconds, during which Gladys looked as if she would faint, Elvis opened his eyes, put his guitar in playing position, strummed twice, then warbled out Red Foley's "Old Shep"—all the while looking straight into the first row. The song is a tearjerker about a boy and his dog, and a number of sniffles could be heard among the people around us. Elvis looked so small and vulnerable up there, but he grew more secure as the song went on, and by the end he was singing in a clear, strong voice—a cappella, since he forgot to strum the guitar after the first two times.

When he finished, the place erupted into an avalanche of applause. The sudden noise scared him at first, but then Elvis broke into a big smile before leaving the stage. Luckily, he was one of the last acts, so we didn't have to wait long for the judging.

They brought all the contestants back on stage to announce the winners. Gladys grabbed Vernon's arm in between wiping away her flood of tears. To Elvis's surprise and to the screaming and cheering of his family, he won second place and walked off with five dollars in prize money.

After a final bow from the winners, the contest was over, and Elvis ran to meet us.

"I did it! D'you see it, I did it, and they all clapped and ever'thing," he said in one breath, literally hopping with excitement.

"Not only are you the best singer, you're rich," Vernon said. "Don't spend it all in one place."

"Here, Mama—you take it," Elvis said suddenly, bringing even more tears to Gladys's eyes.

No doubt it was the happiest day in Gladys's life, and it was a turning point for Elvis. It was his first taste of public approval, and he was almost drunk with the unaccustomed feeling of affection and acceptance. The smile never left his face, and Gladys couldn't stop hugging him. Elvis even returned Vernon's hug, all was so right with the world.

"Congratulations, boy, you did a good job," people would come up and say.

"They never even said hi t'me before," Elvis said.

"It's 'cause you're famous," I said.

"Yeah, that's it, huh."

For that day, at least, Elvis was the object of everyone's congratulations and good wishes, instead of their scorn and ridicule. By singing a song, he had been accepted, even if only for a day. The next morning, it was just a sweet memory, and nothing had changed, except perhaps inside Elvis. But it was enough to set the ball in motion. It was enough to instill in his mind that singing equals loves equals acceptance. Elvis would seek that sensation of approval and public love, like a junkie after a fix, for most of his life. No matter how famous he got, how successful his career, every time he set foot on a stage, he was still a little boy seeking love and acceptance, trying to shuck off a hundred years' worth of family shame.

Part II

GROWING PAINS

4

In 1948, the country prospered in the postwar economic boom. Even Tupelo enjoyed increased trade and commerce—although for the bottom-level poor like the Presleys, life went on with frustrating sameness. For Elvis, as the winter wind swirled the dirt in the barren fields, the coming year seemed indistinguishable from the ones preceding it, and resignation overwhelmed him and made him turn inward. Nothing could have prepared Elvis or his parents for what would be a year of abrupt change, renewed hope, and dashed expectations.

While still a young woman in her thirties, Gladys moved like someone twice her age. Her health had steadily declined as her drinking increased, and that, combined with poor nutrition and the Smiths' family history of weak constitutions, had taken a sharp physical toll. Most days found Gladys hung over and suffering from nausea and splitting headaches. The official family line, though, had her battling lingering flu or suffering from female troubles.

Vernon took Gladys's ailments calmly, seeing them for what they were, but Elvis fretted constantly about his mama's health, terrified she might die and leave him to fend for himself. Gladys was more than his anchor and the person who loved him more than anyone, she had become his reason to be—he was put here to care for her. If she were gone, he might as well be, too.

If it weren't for Gladys, Elvis would have ignored Vernon completely, but she insisted Elvis treat all elders with courtesy and his daddy with respect. But while Elvis was cordial to his father, he felt no warmth for Vernon and no strong emotional bonds—only resentment at his apparent lack of concern at their situation and anger that they were stuck with him.

But even at this point, it might have still been possible for Elvis and his dad to grow close if Vernon had been capable of reaching out to his son, because the thing Elvis craved most in life was love. Unfortunately, like most men of his era, Vernon had been raised to keep a lid on his feelings and take things as they come. So the gulf between father and child deepened, and Elvis interpreted Vernon's self-containment as a lack of true caring. And if Vernon wasn't going to love Elvis, Elvis sure wasn't going to love him. He had already been rejected too much in his life by schoolmates and neighbors to risk much more.

Elvis was a skinny, awkward thirteen-year-old—shy but eccentric. Being an outcast, he wasn't a slave to peer pressure, since his peers already considered him an outcast. Elvis's way of dealing with all rejection was to stop caring, or do a good job of pretending to, which is one reason why when everyone else wore crewcuts, Elvis boasted long, flowing blonde hair that fell almost to his shoulders.

For a kid who was already the target of schoolyard taunts to set himself apart even more just shows what a stubborn sense of individuality he could muster. Some of the boys in school called him a sissy or Miss Elvis, but he ignored it; he was used to being called names. Not caring what they said showed they couldn't hurt him, showed fitting in wasn't important to him— even though he was desperate for that acceptance. But since they didn't like him anyway, he figured he might as well do what *he* liked and he liked his hair long. So did Gladys—much to Vernon's bemusement.

"If it makes 'im happy, what's the harm?'' Gladys asked. "He got beautiful hair.''

Elvis *did* have nice hair, and it was the source of great vanity. Besides being tangible proof he didn't care what others thought, his long hair compensated for his too-thin face, punctuated with prominent lips and eyes. Plus, being teased about the length of his hair was the least of Elvis's troubles.

In addition to his personal standing, Elvis was ever more acutely aware of his family's social and financial status. He realized with infuriating bitterness that Vernon was never going to be a consistent breadwinner and was quite content to scrape by, no matter how it upset Gladys. They were constantly changing shacks but never improving their living conditions—he regularly experienced hunger and they made do on the barest necessities of life. All the while, Elvis felt partly to blame—for being too slight to work enough in the fields, for being the only one there to help, for just being helpless to help enough. He was angry at so much but swallowed his feelings, lest he rage at his father. Anger wasn't proper, and he couldn't bear the thought of giving Gladys another reason to be disappointed in him.

What confused and frustrated Elvis was that it was still his responsibility to be the man of the house, a notion Gladys had instilled in him since Vernon had gone to prison. He wasn't allowed to be mad at Vernon, but it was okay to do his work for him, as it were. Elvis resented bailing Vernon out, but would do anything to make life easier for Gladys. He took any legitimate opportunity he had to make some extra money to help out, even if it meant getting up at four in the morning to deliver milk before school. Between working, helping Gladys at home, and going to school, about the only free time Elvis had was Sundays after church.

Unless the weather prevented him, Elvis would wander the countryside on those Sabbath afternoons, preferring not to sit in whatever shack they were currently occupying and be reminded of their destitution. While he felt increasingly responsible for Gladys, at the same time Elvis was less apt to stay home and keep her company, even when she made it clear that's what she wanted. The inner conflict between wanting to take care of his mama, wishing it wasn't all up to him, and needing to take care of his own needs had already started—a juggling act that would permanently retard his emotional development and undermine his independence.

Among most sharecroppers, alcohol was a popular item, but good liquor was expensive. But even though most people couldn't afford store-bought spirits, they could afford the homemade variety. Even though moonshining was illegal, moonshine could be found in most homes. Uncle Ben was long suspected of having his own personal distillery hidden away somewhere, and of being the one who kept Gladys in good supply as well.

The majority of moonshiners were in it for strictly personal consumption, and the local authorities usually turned a blind eye in that case. But their sight suddenly improved if you attempted to turn it into a business, like Vernon.

One chokingly hot summer day, the local sheriff came knocking on our door, wanting to search the house.

"Sorry, ma'am, but Vernon Presley's been apprehended runnin' an illegal still. He says he's your cousin, and we hafta check all his relations' homes, too."

"You think we got a still, too, 'cause we're kin?" my mother asked, irritated all over that her husband was related to these people.

"It's jus' procedure. Won' take but a minute."

My mother, and my sister who was visiting, were indignant, but of course let him in to see if Vernon had left a stash in our house.

I came out of my room at the sound of a strange

voice and watched the sheriff search our house, although my mother refused to explain why.

Ben and Agnes came over right after the sheriff left, and the atmosphere was as gloomy as a funeral. Later that day, Gladys and Elvis came calling, and they both looked ashen and grim. But while Gladys's eyes were swollen and red from crying, Elvis's eyes were dry, although he looked frightened.

Elvis and I were sent to my room, but we could still hear what was being said. Vernon had been caught red-handed distilling moonshine and trying to sell it for profit, a crime that could have sent him back to jail. Elvis was very quiet and mostly just stared at the floor, while Gladys tearfully told my parents, Ben, and Agnes how the sheriff had taken Vernon away to the local jail in broad daylight for everyone to see.

"I had no idea he was runnin' moonshine. He said he was doin' a little work for Orville. Why would I think otherwise?"

" 'Course you wouldn't," my mother said.

"Ever'one was starin' and whisperin' t'each other," Elvis said quietly, but his jaw was clenched so tight you could almost hear his teeth grinding against each other.

"They took 'im away in handcuffs like a common criminal for the world to see. How could they be so cruel to Elvis? How could *he* be so stupid? Why'd he do this to us again? Wasn't the first time enough?"

Tupelo had a mayor and a prosecutor, but the sheriff ran things and was free to make certain decisions. He decided to give Vernon a choice—either go back to jail for several months or leave Tupelo for good.

"At the jail, he said the most awful things to us, acted like we were dirt," Gladys said in a pained voice.

"He told Vernon he was a disgrace to the town, jus' like the rest o' his relations. He tol' us to get the hell out and never come back. If he does come back, the sheriff promised to put Vernon in jail without a second thought, so what choice we got? And even if he let us stay, I couldn't go through it a second time. It'd happen all over again—the talkin' behind our backs, neighbors shakin' their heads when we pass and avoidin' us. I jus' could not live through it."

Nobody said much for a while, then my dad broke the silence and suggested they go to Memphis. My parents had already decided to sell the land and dairy in Tupelo, move to the city by the beginning of the school year, and buy a couple of gas stations. He even told her he'd hire Vernon to work at one of the stations.

"Memphis is as good a city as any," my dad said. "At least there you'll have family."

Gladys broke down again at the kindness and sobbed, while I was hopping with excitement.

"Elvis, you hear that? You're gonna come to Memphis with us."

He didn't answer. He didn't even look at me. It took me a second to realize he was flushed a deep red and his breathing was labored—then he stumbled as if dizzy.

"What's the matter—you okay?"

"I jus' hate it that the whole town saw us that way, with Mama cryin' and all. Daddy didn' even say he was sorry. I wish they'd jus' leave 'im. We'd be better off without 'im."

I was stunned to hear Elvis talk like that.

"But what d'you think about comin' to Memphis with us? Don't you wanna?"

He shrugged.

"Just think, no more cow barns, and there'll be things to do all the time."

"I won't know nobody there."

"You'll know me."

At that moment in time, Elvis couldn't have cared less. His mind was on other things.

"They came in and messed ever'thing up for no reason, lookin' for moonshine, and got Mama all upset."

"Did you have to ride in the police car?"

Elvis shook his head. "We walked, and the whole way down the road people were lookin' at us mean. I

even heard two women whisperin' and laughin'. Like
we're a big joke.''

"Oh, they don't know nothing. Ignore 'em.''

"Mama heard 'em, too.''

"Who cares what they say? You ain't gonna be
around them anymore, anyway. We'll be in Memphis,
people'll be nice there.''

"I don't care where we end up, I jus' never wanna
come back here,'' he said with a sudden violence in
his voice. "I wanna go somewhere they'll leave us
be.''

They released Vernon the next morning, and the
sheriff gave him a couple of weeks to get his affairs in
order. During that time, Elvis suffered through conflicting feelings about the move. While he was anxious
to get away from the stares and disapproval of their
neighbors, the thought of moving to a strange place
scared him. Life in Tupelo might be horrible, but it
was familiar.

"It's different for you, Earl. You make friends easy.
I can't.''

"You could if you wanted.''

Elvis just shook his head.

"Don't you wanna go to Memphis?''

"I jus' wish people liked us better here. I wish
Daddy hadn' of done what he did, this time and the
other time. I wish we were leavin' 'cause we wanted
to, not 'cause the sheriff's makin' us.''

"Everything's gonna be better in Memphis, you wait
and see.''

"What if nobody likes us there either, 'cause of
ever'thin'? We'll of moved all that way for nothin'.''

"Nobody's gonna know unless you tell 'em. If anyone asks, just say your daddy moved to Memphis because there were more jobs. That's not a lie.''

Only thirteen, Elvis struggled to cope with the
weight of responsibility and humiliation he carried on
his slight shoulders. One of his favorite escapes was
walking. It relaxed Elvis and cheered him, too. He
loved the sights and smells of the country and felt

recharged after spending the day in its embrace. Most
of the time, I'd walk with him until it was time for
supper. Sometimes he came home with me for Sunday
dinner; when he didn't, he'd walk me home than go
on his way, a solitary roamer, his blonde hair blowing
in the warm breeze.

There wasn't much to see on these treks except for
soybean and cotton fields, until the day Elvis stumbled
upon a new world that moved his imagination and
stirred his soul.

Like the rest of the South, Tupelo was segregated;
the black section was so far out of town as to not be
part of it at all. In fact, the only time blacks mingled
with whites was at the Alabama-Mississippi Fair when
it came to town. Even then, each group stayed to itself,
as was the custom.

One day, Elvis and I found ourselves in the black
section, which, if it were possible, was even poorer
and more rundown than the poorest white section in
Tupelo. A couple of bent old men were tending a
wilted-looking garden, and a few women and children
gave us curious looks as we walked by.

"You think it's okay for us to be here?" I asked.

"Sure it is," Elvis said, with a rare display of authority. "We're jus' walkin'."

Elvis was intrigued by the unfamiliar surroundings
and a new perspective—here were people even more
outcast and poor than his family.

"D'you hear that?" he asked me.

"Hear what?"

"Jus' listen—it's singin'."

Sure enough, there was someone singing. It sounded
low and mournful.

"Maybe it's a funeral," I suggested.

"It's comin' from that way."

Elvis pointed toward the far end of a nearby field,
and we headed in that direction. The singer turned out
to be a man on a porch step, who appeared to be using
the music to keep time while he whittled on a stick.

"What song is that? I don't recognize it."

Elvis shrugged. "Don't know the name, but it's gotta be gospel."

"It don't sound like any gospel hymn I ever sung."

"Maybe they jus' sing 'em *better,*" Elvis said.

Fortunately, Elvis didn't run up and down the church aisles any more when the congregation sang, but he still loved hymns more than any type of song. This new way of singing a hymn clicked with something inside him, and we walked through the area until we found the black church.

"There's no service now, and even if there was, we're not dressed proper," I complained, thinking he wanted to go inside.

"I just wanna see when they get together on Sundays."

"You want to go to church here next Sunday?"

"No, I jus' wanna come listen."

"Why?"

"I wanna hear 'em sing. I betcha it's different from the way we do in church."

We noted the time, which was a little later than our regular service, and headed back home, with Elvis trying to mimic the old man's song and low, deep voice.

"You sound like a bullfrog," I said.

"Earl, you never knew good singin' when you heard it," he shot back.

We raced each other back to my house, and I promptly forgot about it until the following Sunday after church. Elvis walked over to me, away from Gladys and Vernon who were chatting with Ben and Agnes.

"I'm goin' over to that other church—you wanna come?"

"Sure, I'll meet you at my house."

Elvis came over about an hour later, and we ran full speed until we got to the church. After catching our breath, we walked quietly to the side of the beat-up building, straining to hear.

"Let's go by the window," I said.

We bent over and tiptoed to the window. We could hear the preacher talking, and a smattering of "amens" being said in reply. After about ten minutes I was getting antsy, but Elvis was determined to stay until he heard what he'd come for. When he wanted something bad enough, he had a will of iron.

Finally, the congregation rose to sing a hymn. Elvis sat on the ground, his back against the outside wall, eyes closed, knees keeping time to the music.

"Don' it sound like how heaven's gotta be? Relaxin' and peaceful, with no more hurt."

Elvis made the trip to that little church on the outskirts of town regularly after that and, except for me, kept it his secret. Not that he was doing anything wrong, but Elvis somehow sensed it might not be approved of if anyone knew, and the last thing he needed was more abuse.

As moving day approached, Elvis's spirits rose, mostly because Gladys had come to see Vernon's arrest as a blessing in disguise. Vernon had begged her forgiveness and promised to get a steady job and take better care of his family. It gave Gladys hope and convinced her Memphis would be a fresh start. Things *had* to be better for them there, and that gave Gladys a sense of anticipation. And anything that made his mama happy, made Elvis happy.

If we hadn't been on our way to Memphis, who knows where Vernon would have taken his family, and who knows if Elvis would have ever gotten the chance to sing. The mysterious way life works out fascinated Elvis as he got older, and he could only come to one conclusion.

"Jesse's hand was guidin' us."

Spiritual assistance notwithstanding, it was Ben who staked Vernon a hundred and fifty dollars so he could buy a beat-up 1939 Plymouth for the trip and have some cash to help him get settled once in Memphis. My mother suspected Ben gave Vernon the money, because she believed Vernon had been working Ben's still when he'd been caught, but if that was the case, neither ever admitted it.

Moving day for the Presleys came in mid-August. What little packing there was to be done only took a few minutes. Gladys simply took a large cardboard box and filled it with all their belongings. There was room to spare.

Gladys stood in her empty shack, nervous and fretting, worried she was forgetting something and suddenly emotional at leaving. Vernon was outside, saying goodbye to Ben and Agnes. Elvis and I walked a ways out in the fields. It was ungodly hot and the air was thick, but I felt a pang. So did Elvis.

"It's funny thinkin' this'll be the last time we'll be here together," Elvis said, watching the sharecroppers bent over in the fields. "Ain't you gonna miss it at all?"

"No."

"Not even the pond? I bet they ain't got that in Memphis. And how 'bout the colored church?"

"But they don't got cotton fields there, either."

"Yeah, no more choppin' wood, either." He smiled. "When you comin' up?"

"In time for school, but I wish I was going with you right now."

"Me, too."

We headed back to the shack just as Vernon finished loading the trunk. The men shook hands, the women hugged, and then it was time for them to go. I ran after the car a way, waving and yelling that we'd see them soon. Elvis looked back through the window and waved, clutching his guitar in his free hand.

It was a long, bumpy four-hour drive to Memphis. While Vernon and Gladys sat in their respective silences, Elvis strummed his guitar and watched the landscape change from rural to urban the closer they got to their destination. Cotton fields gave way to industrial smokestacks spewing bad-smelling fumes, and the road became crowded with cars. Elvis felt his heart sink as the crowded city came into view—the life he had known was over forever. He felt an incredible sadness and anger every time he looked at his daddy.

Having no specific destination, Vernon drove to downtown Memphis. In the heart of the city, prosperity and enthusiasm surrounded them. Every other car they passed was shiny and new. Clean, shop-lined streets were filled with men in suits and women in fashionable dresses and matching hats. Unlike sharecroppers who trudge their way through life, these city folk walked with a spring in their step. Even breathing was easier, the air free of choking dust. As he watched the purposeful movement and felt the energy, the pain in Elvis's chest temporarily eased. Maybe his mama was right. Maybe Memphis *was* a promised land of opportunity.

After splurging on a lunch of cheeseburgers, fries, and milkshakes, Vernon set out to find his family a place to live. At first they were awestruck at the stylish houses nestled on neatly manicured streets; the thought of living in such splendor made them dizzy. But their high hopes were rudely snatched away by harsh financial realities. The neighborhoods that most appealed to them were way beyond their means and out of reach. By nightfall, they were fighting crushing discouragement, and a shroud of despair settled on Elvis.

In Tupelo, only a privileged few didn't have to work in the fields, and even those who owned small plots of their own weren't *that* much better off. Someone really well off, like Orville Bean, was easily despised and dismissed. But mostly, whatever their bank accounts, they were all simple farmers with dirt under their nails. Memphis was different. Being so close to the good life made being poor even more unbearable, and Elvis felt more an outcast and more hopeless than ever.

Elvis wanted to go to a drive-in for supper, but Vernon didn't want to spend any more of their precious stash of money on fancy meals or even a hotel, so they ate peanut butter and banana sandwiches Gladys had brought along for dinner, then parked on a deserted street to sleep. Elvis lay awake most of the night, unable to sleep in the unfamiliar surroundings with the strange city sounds. In the dark, Elvis was suddenly aware how close they were to being homeless, especially now in a new city with no relations. Frightened by their uncertain future, he cried himself to sleep before dawn, and he never lost the fear of being on the street with nowhere to go.

The next morning, they resumed their search, and with each passing hour, the weary family moved on to increasingly dingier neighborhoods until they finally found an apartment they could afford at 572 Poplar Avenue. It was a boxlike, single-room, furnished apartment in an industrial part of town. They unpacked what few belongings they had and tried to adjust to their new home.

The little apartment was dark and depressing, with small, dirty windows that barely opened wide enough to let air in. There was a communal bathroom on their floor that they would share with five other families. Elvis fought back tears while pleading to Gladys.

"I don' wanna live here, Mama, please, let's go home. I don' like it here."

"We ain't even settled."

"I don' wanna get settled here, I wanna go home, please, Mama," he begged, tears spilling down his cheeks.

Gladys hugged him briefly, then spoke in a firm voice. "Now you stop—big boys like you're too old to be carryin' on so. You're gonna make your daddy feel bad. We can' go home. This is our home now."

Elvis spent the next days in a daze, hoping the empty feeling would stop hurting. Nothing put him at ease. While it was true their new apartment was nicer than the shacks they'd lived in before, it didn't feel like a home. In Tupelo, Elvis had always been able to escape outdoors and feel free in the open flatland, or clear his head with the sweet, heavy smell of a summer night. Now, instead of a front yard, there was a concrete sidewalk and a busy street clouded by exhaust fumes

and the acrid discharge of nearby factories. No more
lying on the grass watching the sun set over lazy farmland, they were surrounded by the ugliness of city industry.

Scenery aside, Elvis missed the sense of community
he had previously taken for granted. The Presleys had
hardly been the favorites of East Tupelo, but at least
there Elvis had known who his neighbors were. City
people seemed happier to stay to themselves.

This suited Vernon and Gladys just fine—no nosy
neighbors asking embarrassing questions. But it also
meant they were more isolated than ever, especially
Elvis.

"That boy's too shy for his own good," Vernon
complained to Gladys. "He oughta be out havin' fun
with youngsters his own age, instead of just staring
out the window all day long, miserable."

"Nothin' wrong with him keepin' his mama company for a while. He'll be in school soon 'nough."

"I swear—"

"You ought t'be glad he ain't out runnin' loose
straight off. He'll be fine."

I had given Elvis our Memphis address before he
had left, and we'd only been in town a few days when
he showed up at our door. I came running when my
mom called that Elvis was there—then stopped dead
in my tracks when I saw him. His blonde hair was
gone, replaced by jet black, lacquered locks. He could
have hit a truck head-on and survived.

"Elvis . . ."

"Oh, yeah," he said, his hand reaching for his head.

"I hardly recognize you," I said.

On this note, my mother beat a hasty retreat.

"When did you do that?"

"Couple weeks ago," he said, again smoothing his
hair, as if a strand was capable of moving. "Wha'
d'you think?"

"It's different."

"You don' like it."

Clockwise, from left: Elvis's school picture at Humes High School in Memphis, Tennessee. Elvis, age 18, was the prom date for his first love, Dixie Locke. Elvis at age 14 in Humes High School.

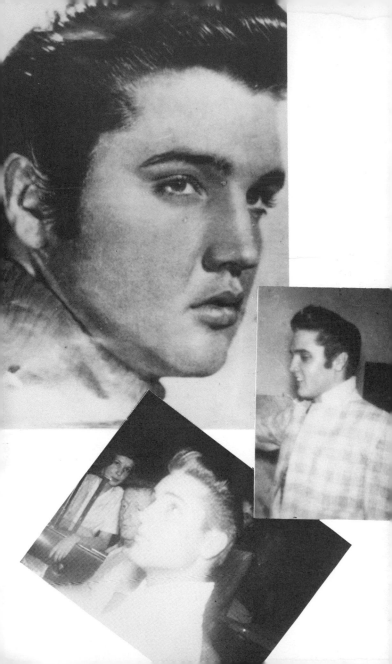

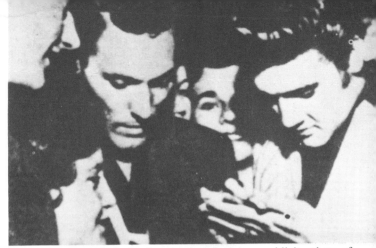

Opposite page, clockwise from upper left: A rare publicity photo of Elvis in the 1950s. Elvis at a private party at Graceland in 1957. Elvis and Red West driving out of Graceland in 1957. *Above right:* A young Carl Perkins and Elvis at a concert at the Overton Shell in Memphis on July 30, 1954. *Right:* Elvis with early session musicians Scotty Moore (left) and Bill Black. *Below:* Elvis with deejay Dewey Phillips, the first deejay to place Elvis on the air.

Upper left and center: Elvis performing at the Mississippi-Alabama Fair benefit for the Elvis Presley Youth Recreation Center on September 27, 1957. *Remaining photos:* Elvis performing in Memphis in 1958.

Above: Elvis accepting a check from a cashier at a movie studio. *Right:* Elvis studio-dubbing for one of his early films.

Opposite: Elvis in front of Graceland in 1957. *Inset:* The late actor Nick Adams motorcycling with Elvis in the 1950s.

This page and preceding page: Elvis at a press conference on a train en route to Los Angeles in 1957.

Clockwise, from upper left: Elvis's friends did a comedic artist's conception of Elvis in uniform. Elvis with a fan in front of Graceland in March 1958. Elvis in Hawaii for a benefit show in November 1957. Earl Greenwood photo of Elvis behind Graceland. *Opposite:* Elvis in Ft. Chaffee on March 27, 1958, during his army physical.

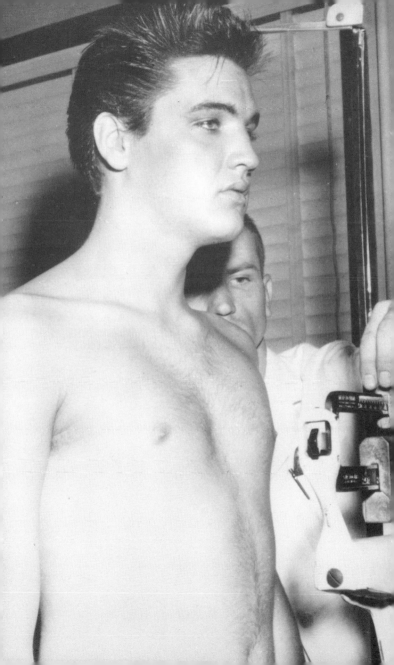

Above: Elvis standing in front of Grace-
land in his army uniform in 1958. *Right:*
Elvis in a Gruenwald Hotel suite in
Frankfurt, Germany, in late 1958.

Right: Elvis in the army mess hall in Frankfurt, Germany, in 1960. *Below:* Elvis and Earl Greenwood in Elvis's rented house in Killeen, Texas, the day Elvis left for Germany, September 19, 1958. *Bottom:* Elvis in army barracks in Germany in 1959.

Top: Elvis in army barracks in Germany in 1960. *Above:* Elvis in his Gruenwald Hotel suite. *Right:* Elvis returning home from Germany in March 1960.

Clockwise from left: Vernon Presley with two visitors at Graceland in 1960. Vernon Presley at Graceland in 1960 shortly after Elvis's return in 1960. Vernon Presley with a visitor at Elvis's rented home in Killeen, Texas, in 1958.

Clockwise, from upper left: Elvis with close friend Laurie Lutz in front of Graceland in 1957. Earl Greenwood snapped this photo of Elvis at Graceland. Elvis and friends at a party at Memphis's Rainbow Skating Rink. Elvis and Earl at the skating rink.

"It's not that—I'm not used to it. You sure stand out, though."

Elvis gave a small laugh. "This place's so big, you could have green skin and nobody'd notice. You'll fit right in."

We exchanged a few playful punches and dropped the issue of his hair, because that's when I noticed he was wearing mascara.

"You got on makeup!"

"Not much. Jus' 'nough so they match my hair. Mama says white lashes'd look silly with dark hair."

As if anyone would notice his eyes once they saw the black lacquered helmet on his head. I started to voice that thought, but something in Elvis's eyes stopped me. It was both a challenge and a plea for acceptance.

Elvis broke the awkward silence. "Gonna show me 'round?"

The neighborhood was a nice, residential community with tree-lined streets, and like the other houses on the block, ours was older but spacious. I gave Elvis a tour of our two-story home, which ended with me throwing open the door to my room with a flourish.

"You got your own room? I don' believe it."

"I told you everything would be better here."

Elvis kind of shrugged and sat on my bed. "Same as always."

"Are you living nearby?"

"Uh-uh. We're over on Poplar. It ain't nearly nice as all this. There's no yard or trees or anythin'. You're livin' in a mansion."

"We are not," I said, suddenly feeling bad about my good fortune. "It's old and creaky. It's just bigger than what we're used to."

"Our place's like a prison it's so dark," Elvis said. "I hate it, but Mama says it's only for now."

Elvis took a longing look around my room, then stood up. "I gotta go. Mama's 'spectin' me to help her with supper. She ain't been feelin' too good."

"Wait, I'll walk you."

Elvis hesitated, then shrugged. "If you wanna."

It was a long walk, and it gave us a chance to catch up with each other's lives. But Elvis was more comfortable listening than talking, and when he did speak, I was struck by the weariness in his voice. His first months in Memphis had been one hurdle after another, and he was emotionally wrung out. School had been particularly painful.

It was Elvis's freshman year of high school, and Vernon went with him on the first day. Gladys stayed home, feeling particularly "under the weather" that day.

Their determination to see Elvis educated was Vernon and Gladys's one shared passion, and it had set them apart from most of the other sharecroppers who thought kids only needed to know the basics of readin', writin', and 'rithmetic before going to work in the fields full time. The Presleys were among the minority who believed a high school diploma guaranteed you a better life, so it was serious business.

Vernon sat with Elvis through the whole registration process, then left when classes were about to start. No sooner had he returned home than Elvis returned home, too.

"I shut the door behind me only to hear it open right back up. In walks Elvis, sayin' it'd be better if he went job hunting instead of staying in school," Vernon enjoyed telling.

Gladys sprang out of bed, her head suddenly cleared.

"You get yourse'f right back to class, young man."

"It's too big, Mama. And there's too many people— I couldn' find where I was s'posed to go."

The mere size of Humes High, with fifteen hundred students, had terrified him. To someone used to sparsely populated country schools, it seemed bigger than all of Tupelo.

Gladys was unmoved and over wails of protest marched him back to school. This time he stayed, probably out of fear that if he didn't, Gladys would sit right there in the class with him to make sure he did.

He was having trouble with his math and history classes and felt completely alone, a total outsider.

"Ever'body already has their friends picked out," he complained.

"That's no reason not to introduce yourself."

"Jus' 'cause you can talk to a turnip. I ain't like that, Earl. I wanted to try out for football, but Mama wouldn't hear of it. She's afraid I might get hurt," he said, sounding disappointed.

"I bet you can change her mind if you try hard enough."

"It's too late, now, anyhow. Next time, I'm jus' gonna do it. I shoulda known better to even mention it."

"What's your daddy doin'?"

Elvis gave me an exasperated look. "Same as usual, workin' on 'n off, dependin' on his back."

"My daddy says he needs help at the gas station," I said.

"I wish he'd let me take it."

As we passed through a busy shopping area, the sidewalk got more crowded.

"There's jus' so many people here," Elvis said. "Sometime I feel like I'm gonna get swallowed up."

"I think it's fun."

"You *would* like gettin' trampled to death by all these people."

"Better than getting trampled to death by cows in Tupelo."

Some of those who passed us, especially if they were older, gave Elvis strange glances. He shyly avoided direct eye contact, but he wasn't put off by the attention.

"Let 'em look—I like it."

All of his life, except for that one day when he won the talent contest at the fair, Elvis had gone virtually unnoticed. He could disappear in a crowd and not be missed. Adopting a fashion style as drastic as he did was an attempt to stand out in the crowd, create his own unique identity and force people to notice him—

to leave some mark, any impression. Proof that he existed in the eyes of others. For good or bad, Elvis was suddenly impossible to miss.

Elvis's neighborhood had a rough, city feel to it and wasn't a safe place to walk around alone at night. Gladys hugged me and made me tell her all about my new school, how my parents were, about the gas station, and anything else that came to mind. Elvis looked uncomfortable. While Gladys was always wonderful to me, she only got this talkative when she'd been drinking. The only thing that shushed her was Vernon's gentle chiding.

"Mama, leave the boy alone—his tongue'll wear out if you don't leave him be."

"Earl don' mind, ain't that right?" she said, hugging me close.

"You ready? I'll walk you down." Elvis looked at me.

"Why don't you stay for dinner?" Gladys asked in a loud voice.

Elvis was waiting by the door, jaw tight.

"No, ma'am, I already ate."

"That's okay, I'm just being an old chatterbox. You won't be too long sayin' goodnight, will you? Dinner's waitin'."

"No, ma'am," Elvis said, opening the door.

"What's this ma'am business? You ain't too old for a mama now, are you? Come gimme a kiss."

Elvis went and gave his mom a kiss on the cheek. She gripped him tight, before he gently pulled away. Elvis walked me to the sidewalk, his shoulder arched and tense. He watched me go, and as I turned the corner toward home, he slowly shuffled up the stairs.

The combined Presley income in the autumn of 1948 was about thirty-five dollars a week. Gladys occasionally found work in a factory, although it seldom lasted more than a couple of days, and Vernon sometimes drove a truck for a wholesale food company. Elvis also contributed to the family earnings by spending weekends and afternoons after school offering his services to mow lawns, clean out gutters, or anything else someone might want done in the neighborhoods that could afford such help.

Although they were making more money than they had in Tupelo, it cost more to live. So despite their combined efforts, the Presleys were still swimming upstream and slowly sinking in over their heads. Despite having been in Memphis for just a few months, their dreams of a new way of life were all but dead. Memphis was supposed to have been a new beginning, but nothing had changed except their address. Gladys, in particular, looked like she was about to be done in. Her frustration at their inability to improve their standard of living drove her to drink even more. Bloated and aging rapidly, Gladys's outbursts of despair and rage toward Vernon accelerated, unlocked by the key of liquor.

She covered the same ground time after time—no food, bills and rent due or past due, no steady job, Vernon not trying hard enough . . . on and on. Vernon seldom argued back, and his acceptance of their lot heightened Gladys's rage to greater heights. Elvis's nerves took a beating with each sharp word; his resentment of Vernon soared, and his determination to somehow rescue his mama from her torment stiffened.

After one of their arguments, Elvis would try to do something to help out. He would even go and sell a pint of blood, if that's all there was to do. He daydreamed about getting her all the things she had gone without—a washing machine, decent clothes, new shoes. But for now, he had to settle with merely helping to keep them from being evicted.

Even as Elvis desperately sought out a way to rescue Gladys and fantasized about his dad's being out of the picture altogether, he was simultaneously aware it *should* have been Vernon's responsibility, and he resented Vernon for his failings as a husband and father. His frustration grew as he saw classmates after school playing touch football or leisurely walking home, homework their biggest concern—he *might* get to do homework, if he wasn't too exhausted after working at whatever job he currently had. In Tupelo, where more children his age worked in the fields than attended school, there wasn't so much a reminder of what he was missing as there was in Memphis. Elvis's anger was always indirect—he'd slam doors and punch walls, bust out windows of deserted tenement buildings with rocks, or just run as fast as he could down the streets until he wore himself out. Or he'd turn inward and sit with his guitar for hours, shutting the world out.

At no time did he ever say a word to Vernon about it directly. Not then, not later. Remember, the way you're raised in the South is to respect your family, especially your elders. You had no right to talk back. It was a confusing but unwavering double standard. Regardless of how bitter her words to Vernon were, Gladys would have smacked Elvis if he dared be disrespectful to his daddy. You did what you were told and kept your mouth shut. Which is exactly what Elvis did throughout his life, at least in front of those in authority. Out of earshot, his control occasionally cracked.

"He don't give a damn 'bout Mama, or me. Jus' as long as she gets his supper and I bring in money, that's all we're good for. Why does she still love 'im after all he's done t'us?"

In the spring of 1949, the Presleys were in desperate straits. Their car had broken down, they couldn't afford to get it fixed, and they were behind in rent and afraid of losing their apartment and being kicked out on the street. Vernon and Gladys were forced by their bleak situation to swallow their pride and apply for welfare. Elvis was so shamed by this setback that when he told me he couldn't look in my eyes. He also made me promise not to tell anyone in my family.

"Mama's kind of embarrassed so I'm not s'posed to say anythin'."

"Nothin' to be ashamed of—we all used to get assistance in Tupelo," I said.

"That was diff'rent. I tol' Mama that I'd quit school. If I got a full-time job, we wouldn' need no handouts anymore."

"You're quittin' school?"

Elvis exhaled with a snort. "No—Mama says over her dead body—and it'd break her heart if I ever mention it again."

"What's gonna happen then?"

"Mrs. Richardson came t' see us. She's from the Housing Authority," he said carefully. "They gotta know for sure we're poor enough for welfare."

"Are you?"

Elvis gave me a sarcastic look. "What d'you think?"

"Sorry."

"It don't matter. She looked 'round a lot and took notes on a big pad o' paper."

"Shc said the plumbin' was bad. She musta never seen an outhouse." Elvis laughed suddenly.

"I don't think this lady ever seen a cotton field, either. All dressed up wearin' a ton o' perfume. But Mama felt better after, 'cause Mrs. Richardson said the city was gonna help us."

"Are they gonna help your daddy find a job that pays better?"

Elvis shrugged. "I still think Mama and I'll be better off if they find me one."

As it was, he told me he was always getting yelled at by his teachers because he kept falling asleep in class. He had a job delivering papers or something at the crack of dawn, and by early afternoon he couldn't keep his eyes open. Of course, they didn't know that—they probably just thought he was lazy.

Years later, I was going through some boxes at Graceland, and came across the report that Mrs. Richardson had made to the Memphis Housing Authority. It was ironic to read it while sitting in the splendor of Graceland. One of the more interesting revelations was

that they had checked out Vernon's salary and noted
that he was sending ten dollars a month to Miss Minnie,
Elvis's grandmother, in West Point, Mississippi. While
his wife and son were doing without, he was secretly
helping support his own mama. He and Elvis might
have been more alike than either guessed.

That Elvis went to a fair amount of trouble to obtain
a copy of that report showed how deep an impression
going on welfare had made on him. Like people who
show off their first dollar to show how far they've come
in life, Elvis kept that report as a haunting reminder of
where he'd been, and where he feared he might someday return.

In May of 1949, right before Elvis finished his freshman year at Humes High, the Presleys moved to 185
Winchester Street in the Lauderdale Courts, a government housing project.

Even though it was a project and in need of repairs
itself, their new apartment was like a dream come true
for Vernon, Gladys, and Elvis. There were two bed-
rooms, a separate kitchenette, and a private bathroom.
It was the most luxurious place they had ever lived in,
and for now, they were as proud as if they had just
bought a house.

"We don't hafta go sit in the hall t' study," Elvis
said as he showed me into his room.

"Or to go to the bathroom," I added.

"This is like a real home. Mama spent the first two
days scrubbin' it top t' bottom. She says it's the best
way t' make a place your own."

Elvis's delight was shattered as the reality of the South
rose to the surface. During the last week of school,
Elvis overheard a cutting remark and the accompanying
laughter from some girls in his history class—about Elvis living with the "coloreds in the projects." He didn't
know how they knew, but their knowledge was bound
to make Elvis even more of an outcast.

The apartment where the city relocated them was in-
tegrated and mostly black. The Presleys had been so
relieved and so happy with the comparative luxury, they

hadn't paid much attention to who their neighbors were. But in the South in the forties and fifties, racial discrimination was alive and well and considered correct. It *was* a stigma to live "with coloreds," and even my family was taken aback.

"I don't see why the city couldn't put them with their own kind," my mother said. "It's not proper. I jus' hope our neighbors don't find out."

If your own family reacts that way, you can imagine the response of most strangers—especially if you're already considered weird because you have a helmet for hair. A few days after Elvis overheard the two girls, a swaggering bully walked by and called him "so weird only the niggers will let you live near 'em. Don' get too close—who know's what we'll catch."

Elvis squeezed his eyes shut so tight he saw yellow flashes. Here they were, living in the nicest home they'd ever had but looked down upon as something worse than white trash—as scum. All the frustration and rage, bottled up since he first heard taunts while still a toddler, exploded to the surface and let loose. Elvis turned and landed a direct punch on the side of the boy's head. It ended up being more a scuffle than a real fight. The other boy's friends broke it up, and when the dust cleared, it was Elvis who emerged with hardly a scratch, while the boy's nose and lip dripped blood.

There was a surprised silence among the students. Because Elvis was so shy, people had made the mistake of thinking he was a pushover. And maybe up to that moment he had been, but now he was old enough and tired enough to try and put an end to the verbal abuse and silence his tormentors. It was a turning point and also a painful lesson. Even if punches could keep words from being spoken, they couldn't force people to like and accept you.

5

Elvis began his sophomore year at Humes with a new sense of determination and desire. He yearned to enjoy school and participate in activities more than he had the previous year. Elvis argued with Gladys for a solid week about trying out for the football team, an often heated discussion that left her teary-eyed with fear for her baby's safety. Exasperated, Vernon settled their tug-of-war by putting his foot down on Elvis's side.

"Mama, he's safer bangin' heads in one of them uniforms than he is crossin' the streets 'round here or walkin' home at night. Give 'im room to breathe—do 'im good."

Elvis was surprised that Vernon spoke up at all, but accepted the support with a detached, mumbled thanks.

Gladys was still unsettled over that turn of events when Elvis dropped another bombshell that was even more traumatic for her. Elvis had reached an age where he wanted a little less smothering and a little more autonomy, but Gladys coddled Elvis constantly, worried about him, and generally treated him as if he were about two years old. Ever since Elvis had been old enough to go to school, Gladys had walked him there at least a couple of times a week, high school being no exception. On top of everything else, he didn't want the other kids at school thinking he was a baby who needed his mama looking after him like that.

On the first day of school, Elvis stopped her at the door and took a deep breath.

"Mama, there's no need for you t'go."

"I always walk you."

"I'm jus' sayin' you don't hafta anymore. I'm okay."

Gladys looked at him a moment, then burst into tears.

"You're 'shamed of your mama—who can blame you—"

"Mama . . ."

"Your daddy and I cause you nothin' but grief.'

"Mama!"

Gladys turned away from him. "I worry 'bout you so. If anythin' ever happened and I lost you, too—"

She wailed, and Elvis's resolve melted in her flood of tears—but not completely.

"Mama, please stop cryin'. Why can' I jus' go t'school like ever'one else? That's all I want. Got nothin' to do with you."

It took awhile, but Gladys eventually calmed down and apologized for getting so emotional.

"You'll always be my baby. Mamas never stop worryin'."

She agreed to a compromise, and for the rest of his sophomore year, whenever Gladys wanted to walk him to school, she did—but from at least a block behind.

Unfortunately, Elvis's efforts to join the football team were not as successful. When he went to sign up during the first week of school, the coach was standing nearby and called Elvis over. After saying hello and finding out Elvis's name, the coach gave him a long look.

"If you want to even try out for the team, son, that hair's gotta go."

"How come?" His voice was unsteady.

"It's a school rule. Athletes have to keep their hair short. Promotes cleanliness."

"But my hair *is* clean."

"Rules are rules. If you don't get it cut, you won't be able to try out. I'm sorry."

Several other boys heard this exchange, and when Elvis turned around, he could see the smirks on their faces.

"One of 'em offered to cut my hair for me if I wanna play so bad," Elvis told me later that afternoon. "Coach told 'em to mind their own business, but I still felt like punchin' the smiles off 'em. 'Cept it still wouldna got me on the team.

"Mama was right—who needs it."

With football out of the question, Elvis switched his attention to other activities. He liked shop class and joined the ROTC, and got off on the precision drills and military talk. He was teased a little in ROTC about his hair, but not as much as you'd expect. After he became famous, Elvis went back to Humes and donated enough money so that the ROTC drill team could buy brand-new uniforms, partially out of appreciation for their letting him participate.

Elvis's best subject in school was English, his worst were math and history. Part of his problem was that both subjects required a lot of homework time, which he simply didn't have.

That fall, Elvis got a job as an usher at Loew's State Theater in downtown Memphis. Elvis worked from five to ten each night and earned $12.75 a week. He gave most of it to Gladys, but always saved a little for himself, a secret stash fund to buy clothes or a cheeseburger and fries after school. Elvis liked the money, but the hours were taking their toll. His grades began falling, and his teachers complained that he was sleeping through class, so he reluctantly quit.

School officials stepped in again a year later when it was learned that Elvis was working a full-shift job from three to eleven, during a period that both his parents were unemployed. Elvis's counselor sent Vernon and Gladys a letter requesting a meeting, where they were told Elvis was carrying too heavy a load and they had to make a decision.

"He simply can't do both. He's too tired to concentrate in class and is on the verge of failing—and I don't think that's what you want to see happen."

"I had no idea," Gladys said, ashamed.

"We've had a little bad luck," Vernon said. "He was jus' helpin' out a bit."

"Well, you have to make a decision," the counselor said, with little sympathy toward Vernon. "Unless he devotes more time to his schoolwork . . ." He shrugged to finish the thought.

Elvis argued with Gladys that night when she told him he was to quit—but his heart wasn't completely in it. He looked forward to having more free time. Now sixteen and a junior, his interest in girls was reaching a fever pitch. Elvis was still thin, but he was filling out and growing into his looks. Even if his speech and grammar were still rough, his voice was changing and gaining a silky resonance that he was learning to use to its full advantage.

Elvis began doing his own clothes shopping and loved browsing through racks of old and out-of-date shirts, jackets, and pants at thrift shops and second-hand stores. It didn't matter if there were a few holes or tears, because Gladys was still a whiz with a needle and thread. His wardrobe reflected a style that was as startling as his hair—pink shirts matched with green pants and a striped jacket; plaids and polka dots freely mixed.

Elvis was aware not everyone shared his taste. "At least it'll be easy to spot me if I ever get run over."

But he felt good about his choices and loved it when he noticed people do a double take as he walked by. Elvis's desire to belong hadn't diminished—he just wanted to belong on *his* terms, with his own style.

Elvis's sudden rush of independence rattled Gladys but not as much as his interest in girls would. Elvis's hormones kicked into high gear the summer before junior year when he was rehired by the Loew's State Movie Theater and became smitten with a candy-counter girl named Sue.

There had been crushes before, but they'd been confined to stolen glances and wishful thinking. Sue's blonde hair and sparkling green eyes consumed Elvis's thoughts and ignited his fantasies—not to mention paralyzed him with fear. Most of us are shy and awkward at that age, but Elvis took it to new heights. He was poor, living in the projects, and embarrassed about it. Plus, he considered his awkward body and face ugly and assumed any girl thought him homely.

But Sue stirred his dormant sexuality to such a degree that he went out of his way to introduce himself and talk to her. Unfortunately, their potential romance met an untimely demise after Elvis was fired for fighting with another usher who was also a classmate of Elvis's.

"What you hit him for?" I asked.

"I heard 'em tellin' Sue that nobody liked me 'cause I was weird and lived with coloreds. He only said that 'cause *he* wanted to take her out and was jealous 'cause she was talkin' to me so much.

"I didn' mean to hit 'em, but he made me mad. I did it 'fore I knew what I was doin'."

"Did you tell your mama you got fired?"

"No, and I ain't gonna. I'll get somethin' else. She don't care *where* I work, jus' as long as I help. She got a bad cold and had to quit her fact'ry job."

"Maybe she should see a doctor."

"She jus' needs rest, you know," he said vaguely, dropping the subject. "I bet that girl over there is real sweet." He nodded toward the corner.

Elvis had a tendency to like well-dressed, blonde, pretty girls, but claimed only their "goodness" attracted his interest. By coincidence the sweetest girls he saw also happened to be the prettiest.

"What about Sue?"

"Aw, I'll never see her 'gain." He watched the young lady in the corner while sipping his Pepsi. "Got a pretty smile, don' she?"

"Rather than just sit here and tell me about it, why don't you go over and say hi. Introduce yourself."

"There's too many people with her."

"She's just with two friends."

"Don't matter. I doubt she'd talk to me anyway."

"She sure won't if you don't at least try."

"Those girls are too high class—prob'ly the snooty kind. I wouldn't feel comfortable. But I wish there was *someone* I could take to the movies this weekend—'sides you."

"Elvis, to get a date you have to ask. They surely won't come asking after you."

Elvis finally got the courage to ask his first girl out, and was surprised it was so easy.

"Louanne's goin' to the movies with me," he said, a shy smile on his face. "She must really like me."

To his dismay, fireworks didn't blind either of them, so he set out to find his next companion. Elvis became single-minded in his pursuit of a Saturday night date and through sheer doggedness, more often than not, found one. The faces changed on a regular basis, but not much else did. Elvis would take the girl to a movie, stop in at the local diner for a cheeseburger, then take her home. He seldom saw the same girl more than once or twice. But with each date, he built up a little more confidence, and he kept on asking, hoping to find the girl he'd want to call his own.

Elvis's eyes lustily took in the rich, cultured girls with their perfumed skin and comfortable lifestyles. Some would look back, snared by Elvis's brooding looks. Startled by their attention, Elvis melted into the background, knowing he was out of their league and resenting *them* for it. He explained his professed disinterest by claiming he was looking for a girl who was pure, innocent, simple.

His view of women even at that young age was based on a double standard. A woman who was good, simple, and pure did not exhibit sexual desire and passion, and she certainly didn't have any prior "experience"—a viewpoint with little basis in reality. Sexually, Elvis would develop into a young man alternately repressed and obsessed, with a fair share of kinks. Sex became more a weapon than a tool of love, and from the beginning of his life, it represented conflicting meanings and emotions.

As an infant and toddler, Elvis shared his parents' bed. Later when he moved to the couch of the one-room shack, he was still privy to their sexual relationship. Despite Gladys's emotional distance and estrangement from Vernon, she still enjoyed sex with him and until liquor doused her passion, pursued it with gusto.

According to my mom and Aunt Agnes, one of Gladys's favorite stories was the time Elvis attacked Vernon after he'd been released from jail.

"I guess we was gettin' carried away makin' noise, and Elvis comes runnin' over, hittin' Vernon's backside, tellin' him to stop hurtin' his mama. Oh, my two men fightin' over me."

After that, Vernon and Gladys tried to be quiet, but their creaky bed didn't always cooperate, and Gladys would come calling with another risque tale.

"Last night we were, you know, romancin', and sure 'nough, Elvis wakes up like a bolt, wantin' to know if I'm okay—he thought I'd cried in pain. Well, Vernon didn't want his rump bruised again, so he jus' froze 'til we could hear Elvis was back asleep. But we stayed that way so long, Vernon got a cramp in a most painful spot," Gladys said, giggling like a schoolgirl. "I tol' Vernon he's gonna have to explain to Elvis 'bout the birds and bees before he suffers a serious injury."

Thousands of youngsters before and after Elvis have been exposed to their parents' sexual relationship, but his confusion arose because instead of turning to Vernon after their act of physical intimacy, she'd turn to her young son for emotional intimacy, and it set son against father on the most primitive of levels. When he was a toddler sharing her bed while Vernon was locked up, Gladys told him he was her little man. Not only was Elvis Gladys's son, she also made it clear he was her mate. When Vernon returned, he took back what Elvis thought was his rightful place, and the little boy felt an intense rivalry and jealousy. So the sounds of pleasure were interpreted as pain. Recalling it later stirred budding desires, forbidden fruit buried beneath a mountain of repressed guilt.

While this classic confrontation played itself deep in Elvis's subconscious, Gladys complicated matters further by adding her own suffocating possessiveness and jealousy. Like many moms, she felt no girl would ever be good enough for her son, but it went beyond that.

Elvis was aware that his mama was cool toward the idea of his dating. She didn't have a life of her own and resented anybody or anything that took Elvis's time and attention away from her. She let him know he was all she had, all she would ever have. Gladys would get terribly agitated that he preferred another female's company over hers and found reasons for him not to go out. Elvis stubbornly kept his plans—but only after Gladys managed to make him feel terrible.

One night Gladys begged Elvis to keep her company because Vernon was out and she was feeling low, knowing full well Elvis had a date.

"I can't, Mama. Remember, I'm goin' to the movies with someone tonight."

"Oh, well . . . That's alright, Elvis. You go along, then. Can't say as I blame you." Gladys looked at me. "Mamas aren't much fun for young folks, are they, Earl? And look at me—I'm a sight—who wouldn't want better comp'ny?"

"It's not that, Mama," Elvis tried to explain.

"You don't gotta make no excuses, boy. Of course you'd rather be with people your own age. You go on, I'll be alright."

Elvis stood there, torn and once again feeling like he was failing her. "I'll come home right after the movie, okay?"

"You jus' go and have yourse'f a good time. If you wanna come home right after, don't do it on my account. It's up to you."

Elvis learned quickly, and to keep the peace he either lied, using me as an excuse half the time, or let her know at the last possible minute as he was walking out the door.

Dating helped bring Elvis out of his shell, but in groups he often reverted back to wallflower status. Sometimes I found Elvis's shyness maddening, and it caused tension between us now and again.

Since I lived in a different neighborhood, I attended Tech High, and so did most of my friends, except of course for Elvis. For my Christmas party in 1951, Elvis came dressed for the occasion as only he would— red pants, green shirt, and black jacket to match his lacquered hair. Surprisingly, he hadn't brought his guitar.

"It's rainin', and I don't wanna get it wet."

"That guitar is so old no amount of water could warp it any worse than it already is."

"Don't make fun of my guitar."

"I'm making fun of you," I teased.

"That's okay, then." He smiled. He stood by the door, peering around at the other people.

"There's food and pop in the kitchen. Help yourself, then come back and find me."

Elvis said hello to my mother, who waited until he passed before turning to me and shaking her head. My parents hadn't been thrilled to be related to the Presleys in Tupelo, and as we got older, my mother honestly wished I would spend less time with him. She fully anticipated he'd follow in traditional Presley footsteps and didn't want him to be a negative influence on me. Despite her concerns, she uneasily accepted our friendship—and kept a wary eye out for the first sign he was leading me down a troubled path.

It's a little embarrassing to admit that, partly out of habit and partly to appease my mother, none of my friends knew that Elvis was my cousin. Nor did anyone guess. Even though there was a definite family resemblance, Elvis still sounded as if he'd just walked out of the cotton fields, while speech and theater classes had erased most of my drawl. You'd never know to hear us that we'd grown up a few miles apart. If Elvis ever suspected, he never let on.

Everyone was in a festive, holiday mood, and the living room was decorated with lights and a tree. Between the eating and the chatter, we were playing records when a girl asked me if Elvis was my friend who was the singer.

"Yeah, that's him." I talked about Elvis a lot, mostly bragging how talented he was, what a beautiful voice—good enough to be a professional someday.

"Come on, Elvis, sing something for us. I love to hear people singing," the girl said.

Several other people chimed in.

Elvis froze. "I, uh, can't," he finally said.

"Sure you can," I said. "They wanna hear you."

"I don't have my guitar."

"You still have a voice. You can sing to the records. You do that all the time."

"I can't sing without my guitar. It don't feel right. Maybe next time."

The girl looked disappointed; an uncomfortable quiet blanketed the room. Elvis shrank into the corner, and I was irked that he'd chickened out and put a damper on the festivities.

"I don't know how you're ever gonna be a singer if you're afraid to sing," I said to him later.

"Earl, I'll be lucky stayin' off welfare."

"With that attitude it's no wonder."

Dixie Locke was the first girl who stole Elvis's heart away. They sat across the aisle from one another in English class during the final semester of his junior year and became friendly straight away. Interestingly, in that same class was another person who'd play a prominent role in his life, Red West, but at the time they were barely casual acquaintances. Elvis asked Dixie out for a Pepsi after school, and that began their mutual attraction. One date later, he fell hard and fast.

Dixie was the girl of his dreams—pretty, petite, and blonde. A direct contrast to Gladys. To Elvis, she was the sweetest girl he'd ever talked to, with a soft voice and sparkling eyes. Dixie was quiet but more watchful than shy. Elvis sensed a familiar vulnerability in her and that drew them together.

My steady girlfriend, Karen, and I spent a lot of time with Elvis and Dixie. Double dating in Memphis was a challenge—there was nothing to do. They rolled up the sidewalks at nine. Your options were to go to a movie or to a restaurant. We weren't old enough to get into the nightclubs, so we'd drive around in a beat-up old Plymouth Elvis had bought for thirty-five dollars as junk and fixed up. He'd saved almost two years to buy that heap and was as proud of it as he would have been of a new Cadillac. Even then, big cars made him feel special.

Elvis was more himself around Dixie than with any girl before or since, and happier. He walked on air in her presence. Gone was the stooped shoulder and shuffling posture—replaced by a step that was positively buoyant. He began to smile and see the world in brighter colors at her side.

Dixie's girlfriends teased her about Elvis's choice of clothes and his dyed hair, but she ignored them or laughed about it.

"I'm glad he's not like all the other boys. He's got a mind of his own. I hate it when guys are like a pack of dogs chasing after the head mongrel, don't you? Besides, I think his hair is cute."

I'd heard it described a lot of ways, but never cute. It had to be love—no wonder Elvis felt so strongly about her.

During the time they were together, Dixie helped Elvis come out of his shell in a number of ways. First, just having a steady, pretty girlfriend who cared for him, accepted him, and found him attractive did wonders for Elvis's confidence. Dixie was also an upbeat girl with a sly sense of humor who craftily maneuvered Elvis into being more open in groups.

"He's becoming a regular chatterbox," Dixie teased

one day. "You should have seen him, Earl, he actually raised his hand in class—and made a joke."

"Everyone thought it was funny, too," he told me.

"Yeah, and suddenly all the girls in class started flirting with him, wanting to steal him away."

"They didn'," he said shyly.

"Uh-huh. I'm keeping my eye on you." She put her hand lightly on his knee for a brief moment, and the car abruptly accelerated in response.

Elvis was still very much the gentleman, but Dixie brought out a sensuality and sexuality in Elvis that had more to do with an increased sense of self-confidence than any physical activity between them.

He was still a virgin, and part of him desperately wanted to sleep with Dixie, but he felt too guilty to ever suggest it until they were married or at least engaged. He wouldn't want her to be the kind of girl who'd say yes—that would tarnish her image of being good, simple, and pure. All that aside, Gladys still exerted a strong influence on Elvis and warned him repeatedly that if he ever got a girl in trouble it would out and out kill her.

So their physical relationship was limited to kissing and light petting, but it was more than enough to do Elvis a world of good—it was the most pleasure he'd ever experienced. He had no idea what else he was missing; that demon was yet to be uncaged. The problem of privacy was solved by the Plymouth. They'd park on a lonely road on the outskirts of town, where the stars weren't dimmed by city lights. They'd climb into the back and press close together, denying their urgent longings, or sit on the hood, while Elvis sang love songs to her for hours at a time. It was in this pure, rather rustic setting that Elvis first told Dixie he loved her.

Elvis was very emotional and impulsive and confused love for crushes or sexual attraction throughout his life. But with Dixie, it was the real thing. Elvis knew she was *the* one after he tearfully told her his family was still living in the projects on assistance, and her response was to hold him and gently rock him. If she accepted that, she surely loved him. He was mad for her, too, and began to talk in terms of their future together.

His feelings for Dixie were not lost on Gladys, who tensed whenever her name was mentioned. The depth of Elvis's love was made clear when he told his mama he'd like to have Dixie over for dinner. Elvis had never invited anyone, other than me, to their apartment.

"Oh, honey, I wouldn' know what t'wear," Gladys managed.

"Dixie don' care 'bout that. I jus' want you both t'meet. You'll love her."

"But we ain't got no food, and I been feelin' so tired, I don' know if I'm up to the strain of makin' a nice supper. But if your heart's set on it, I s'pose I can."

The shade went down on Elvis's enthusiasm—he knew when he was beat.

"Never mind, Mama. No big thing."

"Honey, I tol' you it's jus' fine."

"No, please. I'll jus' bring her over before the movies one night, and we can get together that way."

Elvis brought Dixie home the following weekend and was confused by his parents' reactions. Gladys, who he expected to be embracing, was aloof and haughty. Vernon turned on the charm and made Dixie feel completely welcome. But instead of appreciating his daddy's efforts, Elvis was furious.

"He ain't nothin' but a dirty ol' man, givin' Dixie the eye like that. If he ever does that 'gain, I'm gonna beat the crap outta him, I swear I will."

"Maybe he was just trying to make her feel comfortable," I said.

"You don' know 'im like me. I see him out, flirtin' like crazy with any woman he passes. I never tol' Mama 'cause it'd break her heart. But he better keep his hands to hisself."

"Was Dixie upset?"

Elvis snorted and kicked the ground, but was suddenly calmer. "Can you believe she *liked* 'im. She thought he was funny—said that must be where I get it from. Doesn't that beat all. Me like him. Women."

"Dixie and your mama get along?"

Elvis shrugged. "Yeah, okay, you know—Mama's shy and all, but it'll get easier the more they're 'round each other."

"You really seen your dad with other women?"

"Yeah, talkin'. I seen him comin' out of the local bar, too. Better than moonshinin', huh?" he laughed a bit. "God, I hope he don' go tellin' Dixie 'bout that."

Every year, Humes High sponsored a senior class variety show that advertised all acts were welcome. It was a big event, one of the most anticipated of the whole term. The students who participated were stars for the week, and the winners' pictures were posted for the remainder of the semester.

Elvis, Dixie, and I were on our way to pick up Karen when Dixie brought it up.

"I think Elvis should sign up."

"Why don't you?" I asked him.

Elvis sighed and Dixie answered for him. "He says he's not interested, but it's really because he doesn't think he's good enough."

"It's not that," Elvis said in defense. "I'm just not ready to perform in front of so many people."

"If you're too afraid, it means you don't think you're good enough, and that just ain't so."

"You sang in front of thousands of people at the fair. Dixie, I've told you about the time—"

Elvis cut me off with a laugh. "Yes, you have, Earl, too many times. And it wasn't any thousands of people, neither. It jus' seemed like it 'cause the tent was so small."

"How would you remember? You were too busy singing to notice. And too short to see much beyond the first row. Dixie's right, now's as good a time as

any to start singing in front of a crowd again. You have
to sometime, if it's what you really want to do.''

''It's silly to be thinkin' like that.''

''Why?'' Dixie asked.

''It jus' is. I don't know the first thing how to go
'bout it.''

''You know how to sing, don't you?''

''Anybody can do that.''

''No they can't, Elvis, not like you,'' she said, giving him a long look.

''What would I sing?'' he asked her quietly.

''Anything but 'Old Shep,' '' I teased.

''How'd you and Karen like walkin' tonight?''

''Just pick something off the radio,'' Dixie suggested.

''And music? There'd be no band behind me.''

''All you need is that beautiful voice of yours,''
Dixie told him. ''That's all you'll ever need.''

''Just strum your guitar,'' I said.

''You're the most talented singer in that school—it'd
be a shame not to share it with everybody,'' Dixie
added. ''Just save the serenades for me.''

''Always. You really think I should?''

''Yes,'' I answered.

''I wasn't talkin' t' you.'' Elvis gave me a sly smile.

''Sorry.''

''Yes, I do, too,'' Dixie told him.

He reached over and squeezed her hand. ''Okay
then, baby, I'll do it. But you best be out there cheerin'
me on. I'm gonna be scared t'death.''

There were approximately thirty acts participating,
and before the show started, everyone was told that
whoever got the most applause would be the winner
and get to do an encore. That night when Elvis took
the stage, everyone there saw the potential of his power
and charisma. At first he was a little boy back at the
fair, self-conscious and gripping his guitar. But once
he got into the song, he was transformed, and it was
hard to take your eyes off him. Glancing around, I
could see I wasn't the only one affected by the sight

of him. Loud clothes and coiffed hair aside, Elvis displayed a brooding animal magnetism in front of the student body that night that had most of the girls squirming. He fed off the crowd, and his sexuality percolated with the mutual heat. At that moment he could have had almost any girl—and a few of the guys—who stood spellbound.

Sure enough, Elvis got the most applause. He was so proud of himself and so surprised by the power he had felt—I hadn't seen that exact look on his face since the fair so many years earlier.

"They like me," he said, breathless but focused. "They *want* me. I get to go up and sing again."

"Don't just stand here, go do it." Dixie gave him an impassioned kiss and pushed him toward the stage.

For the second time in his life, Elvis felt loved and accepted by the world at large through the simple use of his God-given voice.

A few weeks after his variety show success, Elvis and I were driving home after spending the afternoon cruising along Beale Street, famous for its blues clubs and the heart of the Memphis "sound." During the day, when the clubs were dark, aspiring black musicians gathered on the sidewalks to play and sing. Elvis would pull his car to the curb and listen in rapt appreciation, quietly singing along but too respectful to let himself be heard. Beale Street was a beacon for aspiring singers, and Elvis was similarly drawn.

A song came on the radio, "Tweedly-Dee" by Laverne Baker, and it got Elvis going. We drove to the beat of the music—me holding on for dear life while the car swayed and jerked in perfect harmony.

As the song mercifully ended we pulled up to a stop sign, in the middle of a quiet residential neighborhood. Quite a few people were either in their front yards or out enjoying a stroll.

"Earl."

"What?"

"I'm going to be famous one day, you know that?"

"Yeah, as the world's worst driver."

"No, I'm gonna be a big star. 'Member how they all clapped—I know I can do it. I wasn' so sure before, but now I jus' know. You're gonna hear me on the radio. I'm gonna make Dixie n' Mama n' ever'body so proud, and make ever'body who talked bad 'bout me sorry."

Before I could answer, he had opened his door and jumped out into the street, yelling at the top of his lungs.

"I'M GONNA BE THE BIGGEST STAR IN THE WORLD—JUS' YOU WAIT AND SEE."

I was so surprised I forgot to duck in my seat, lest anyone recognize me. We were blocking the street, and cars behind us started honking.

"Elvis, what are you doing? Get back in this car."

He stood there, pointing at the startled passersby. "They don' know me now, but they will."

"They're sure to if you don't stop screaming like a wild boar in the middle of the street."

Elvis laughed, his face flushed. "Earl, loosen up."

The fantasy of following in the footsteps of a Carl Perkins or Hank Williams had helped Elvis survive years of barely livable conditions. But what started as an escape, took on a life of its own. After thinking and dreaming about it so much, he felt the dream became more and more of a real possibility in his mind as time wore on, but he had hesitated to talk about it to many people. Now there was no need to be ashamed or feel silly—the variety show triumph brought Elvis's dreams of being a singer out of the closet for good.

On the other hand, Elvis also wanted to get married, settle down, and have a family. Realistically, you couldn't hit the road singing and be settled at the same time, but Elvis seldom let reality get in the way of his plans. With Dixie, he swam in new-found feelings and a self-confidence that was so out of character as to be awe-inspiring. Elvis felt invincible and capable of doing it all. He *was* going to be a singer, and he *was* going to have Dixie for his very own. Forever.

"You want to get married?" I was stunned.

"Why not? I love Dixie and she loves me. We'd be happy together. And I wanna have kids right away."

This was the most impulsive thing I ever knew him to contemplate.

"Where would you live? How would you support her and a baby?"

"Until my singin' gets goin', I'll work nights somewhere. Factories pay good. Don't matter. You don't hafta be rich to get married and have kids. People do it all the time, Earl."

Not people with a mama like Gladys.

"What about your parents? Told them yet?"

"Not yet, but I got it all figured out. Dixie'll move into my room, and we'll all live together. That way I can take care of both Mama and Dixie."

I gave him the hardest look I could muster.

"Don't you think you ought to ask Dixie how she feels about it, first?"

"She won't mind and neither will Mama. The only one I'm worried 'bout is Daddy. I don' trust 'im 'round Dixie—but he wouldn't dare do nothin' in front of Mama."

From Dixie's telling, her few meetings with Gladys had been tense and uncomfortable on each occasion.

"Oh, she was nice enough—just not especially warm, you know?" Dixie said. We were sitting together at the local diner, waiting for Elvis.

"I don't mean to be disrespectful about your relation," she added quickly.

"You're not. Gladys can be that way."

"I thought I smelled liquor on her breath, too," she whispered. One thing about Dixie, she pulled no punches. "I asked Elvis about it, too."

"You did? What'd he say?"

"That I was mistaken—but I know I wasn't. I felt bad after 'cause I think I got him upset, but I know it's why she was acting so funny. You know, fussing all over Elvis like he was still a little kid, hugging him

and asking him to give her kisses goodbye. It was kind
of embarrassing.''

Dixie saw through the loving-mama act at once.
Gladys meant to make sure she knew who was Elvis's
number-one girl. Putting these two under the same roof
was suicide, but there was no way to tell Elvis his
mama was jealous of Dixie.

"I don't know, Elvis. I think you're too young.''

He laughed as if I'd sprung a leak. "Too young?
Half the people in school'll get married before the end
of summer. Hell, in Tupelo they'd already be considered old maids.''

"Maybe so, but that doesn't mean they should. I
want to marry Karen, but I'm going to wait until I get
out of college.''

"Well, I ain't goin' to college, so there's no reason
to wait.''

"If you don't want to wait, at least think about it
some more.''

"What for? Ain't gonna change nothin'. Dixie and
me're gonna get married.''

I could feel the anger and tension between us. It was
as upsetting as it was unfamiliar.

"You already ask her?''

"Pretty soon. I hafta save up for a ring, then I'll
plan a real special night for us.''

As Elvis got older and especially since he started
going out with Dixie, he kept back more and more of
his earnings from Gladys, which gradually put increased pressure on his parents to shoulder a greater
share of the financial burden. Vernon in particular felt
the added weight. Gladys had once again taken to her
bed with an extended series of mysterious ailments,
leaving Vernon to take up the slack by himself. Both
Vernon and Gladys were so used to depending on Elvis
to help bail them out, it never occurred to them he had
been holding back.

Elvis was torn: He felt guilty about not helping out
as much as he had in the past, but he wanted the freedom to take Dixie to a movie, or fix his car, or even

to save up for an engagement ring. He was desperate to simply luxuriate in his passion and resented any intrusion—even from his mama. He was so wrapped up in his own world, he pretended not to see his family slipping back into a familiar hole.

In the winter of 1952, when Vernon's claim of a bad back forced him to quit his job, the Presleys fell behind in the rent and were past due on their utilities. The Housing Authority wasted no time in sending a notice announcing they were delinquent over thirty dollars and in danger of losing the apartment.

Gladys pulled it together and returned to St. Joseph's as a nurse's aide, but her take-home income pushed them over the city's poverty level, jeopardizing their welfare status. This had happened once before, and their options were simple: Lose the extra income and your "improved" financial status if you want to keep your subsidized apartment, or keep the job and look for a new place to live. Previously, they had elected to keep the apartment, but this time Vernon and Gladys decided to move to a smaller, non-funded apartment.

"I been cooped up here too long—I'm tired o' lookin' at the same four walls, and there ain't nothin' outside t' see, either," Gladys said. "We need a change."

Elvis wasn't as thrilled. "I jus' wish we coulda found a place as big."

Their new home was closer into the city—less industrial, more urban. Developers had divided a house into cramped apartments that were even more depressing than their place in the projects. Elvis went back to sleeping on the lumpy couch, where he would lie awake in the dark, trying to plan a course of action that would satisfy Dixie, Gladys, and his dreams. He was angry they had moved to this tiny, mildew-smelling apartment, but he held his feelings inside.

He also resented Gladys's resistance to warming up to Dixie and her refusal to accept the girl as family. Typically, he felt conflicting guilt at harboring animosity toward his mama, so instead of expressing his displeasure, he kept quiet and played the loving son doubly hard. While deep inside, his anger simmered like bubbling stew.

The senior prom was the event of the school year for the graduating class, and Elvis wanted to be a part of it. He'd been saving his money—sacrificing cheeseburgers and even a thrift-shop bargain or two—to have enough for the tickets, tuxedo, and fancy dinner. Between his excitement and his nerves, he was bouncing off the walls as prom day neared.

A week before the dance, Elvis went to pick out his tux from a store on Beale Street. When he tried it on, he was transformed from a slender, gangly youth into a surprisingly dashing young man. Part of the transformation was simply seeing him in clothes that fit perfectly.

"What're you starin' at?" he asked.

"I hardly know who you are."

"I look stupid, don' I?"

"Not at all. You look like you're supposed to look. Formal."

"Sure? I feel like a waiter or somethin'."

Elvis was being fitted in a white tux with white shirt and white cummerbund, which made his shock of black hair stand out even more, and made Elvis self-conscious.

"How 'bout the color—maybe the blue one'd be better, or the pink."

"The white is fine. Stop worrying so much. You're going to give yourself heartburn."

"I already got that. Can you believe there're people who go 'round like this all the time? Must be nice t'be rich like that."

Preening like a parrot, he studied every angle of his reflection in the mirror. He felt so good about himself that his cheeks glowed with exhilaration.

"No wonder people like dressin' up so much, makes you feel . . . clean. Dixie ain't gonna believe it."

Driving home, I asked Elvis if he had ordered Dixie a corsage yet.

"You mean a flower? I didn' know I was s'pposed to."

"Of course you are. And you get to pin it to her dress, too."

"What kind should I get?"

"It doesn't matter, just as long as it matches the color of her dress."

Elvis looked frustrated. He wanted everything perfect, and now he felt like he was messing up.

"I don' *know* what color it is."

"Then ask her."

"I don' wanna do that. It's s'posed to be a surprise. I don' wanna spoil that."

"Elvis Aron, I swear . . ."

"Don' get that way, I never done this b'fore. I thought I'd done ever'thin' there was to do, now you tell me this. Wonder what else I'm gonna forget."

"It's no big deal. If you don't know and don't want to ask, then just tell the florist to give you something neutral, like a white carnation or white rose."

"Okay, but what if her dress is white?"

I was about to scream, when I saw his sly smile. "I'm just foolin' with you, Earl. I ain't *that* dumb. A white rose—now that's nice. I never bought a girl flowers b'fore."

He suddenly laughed. "Havin' a girlfrien's sure expensive, ain't it? Mama'd have my hide if she knew what I was spendin', and Daddy would make me take ever'thin' back. But hell, you can only go t'prom once."

Elvis was determined to do everything just right, and one of the things giving him jitters was the prospect of dancing in public. He mentioned it later on when we were eating lunch at my house.

"Dixie's gonna be after me, and I'm gonna look the fool."

"You love bouncing around to music."

"I don' mean that kind, I mean romantic dancin',"

Elvis sighed, then half laughed. "With my luck, I'll step on her feet and break her toes and hafta carry her 'round the dance floor all night."

"I could show you how."

"You been takin' too many of those sissy classes after school," he teased.

"Come on, there's nobody around. Slow dancing is easy."

"Earl, we'd look like a pair o' fools if anyone saw us. I think I'm gonna wait and let Dixie show me when we get there. It'll be dark, so maybe nobody'll notice if I step on her a few times."

Gladys's eyes filled with tears when Elvis stepped out of the bathroom dressed in formal white down to his new buckskin shoes.

Elvis saw his mama holding a wadded-up hankerchief to her face, swallowing back rhythmic sobs. Elvis's intense focus on this night out with Dixie had made Gladys feel neglected. And sips from the bottle hidden in her robe added fuel to her emotional fire.

"Mama, it don' look *that* bad."

She waved her hand at his attempted joke. "Don' go makin' fun of me. You look so grown up, not my little boy no more. It's upsettin'."

"Mama, this is s'posed to be a happy time. It's jus' a dance. You act like I'm leavin' or somethin'."

"You will be soon, you'll be leavin' your mama all alone t' live your own life somewhere."

Gladys had worked herself into a full head of steam now. Elvis walked over and hugged her, although an edge of irritation hardened his smooth-shaven jawline.

"Why d'you have to be so upset, Mama? Nobody's goin' nowhere. I'm not gonna leave you."

"You will."

"No, I won', Mama. I promise. Jus' stop cryin', okay?"

She moved away from him and shook her head. "You look *so* handsome. You'll be the best-lookin' boy there."

Satisfied that Gladys had calmed down sufficiently, Elvis got ready to go, then stopped at the door.

"Why don't I bring Dixie back by so you can see how we look together?"

"Oh, no, honey, I'm all a mess—lookit my hair—and I ain't even dressed. No, you go on. I'll be fine. Your daddy'll be home soon, and I got to get busy fixin' dinner."

Elvis got even more irritated, but was determined that nothing was going to spoil this evening. He said goodnight and put his mama out of his mind—tonight was going to be the most important in his life.

6

By the beginning of the following week, I began to get worried. I hadn't heard from Elvis since the morning of the dance, and I hadn't seen him at his favorite diner after school. It wasn't like Elvis to stay out of touch, and I was worried that something was very wrong. The Presleys didn't have a phone, so I stopped by unannounced on my way home.

"Earl, what a nice surprise." Gladys seemed happy to see me.

"I was wondering if Elvis was home," I said, following her in to the kitchen.

"No, he's off who knows where," she said, piqued. "He's been gone in the mornings when I get up for work and stayin' out 'til all hours. Gettin' as bad as his daddy. They jus' go and don' bother tellin' me where."

"I haven't seen him since last week and thought maybe he was sick or something."

"He's prob'ly jus' been with that girl of his. He ain't got room in his head for much else."

I declined her invitation to hang around for dinner and walked home, deciding Gladys was right. Elvis and Dixie were probably parked in some lovers' lane, still swept away by the emotions from the prom. Everyone knew that was the one night of the year that many couples went all the way, as we called it then. Maybe Elvis just hadn't come up for air yet.

Comfortable with that assumption, I didn't give Elvis much more thought until he turned up at my house a couple of days later. I was in my room and looked up to see him standing in the doorway.

"Where've you been? I was beginning to think you'd gone back to Tupelo."

Elvis just shrugged. He stared at the toe of his shoe, which was grinding into the floor, not saying anything.

"Are you okay?"

Elvis looked terrible. His eyes were ringed with dark circles, he had lost weight, and his whole body seemed shaky—even his hair hung in limp strands over his ears and across his forehead.

"Have you been sick?"

He plopped on the bed. "Dixie broke up with me, Earl. We ain't gonna see each other again." His eyes were dangerously close to spilling over with tears.

I moved over next to him. "What happened—did you get into a fight?"

"I asked her t'marry me and she don' wanna." His voice cracked, and the tears splashed down his cheeks. "I wanna die, Earl. I jus' can't—I don' know what t'do."

"Did she say why not?"

"She says she cares for me a lot, but she didn' think gettin' married would work. She's wrong, Earl, I jus' know it. We been so happy together. You *ever* known us to fight?"

"Not that I've seen."

"That's 'cause we haven't."

He propelled himself off the bed, then collapsed back down. He was so upset, his eyes were wild.

"You know, when I picked her up for the prom, she was more beautiful than I ever seen her. When I was puttin' on her flower, I got shivers, Earl. She did, too."

He picked some lint off his pants for several moments then spoke quietly. "She kep' smellin' it, and said she was gonna put it in some old book and keep it forever. How could she say that, then not wanna marry me?"

We sat in an awkward silence, broken only by Elvis's sniffling.

"Did you mean to ask her or did it just kind of happen?"

"I wan'ed it to be the most special night we'd ever had, and ever'thin' started out so perfect. She was so pretty, I couldn' stop starin' at her. We danced, too. After dinner we drove out a ways and, you know— then I ruined it all by openin' my mouth. I shoulda waited."

"And she doesn't want to see you anymore?"

"What for, if she don' love me?"

"Just because she doesn't want to get married doesn't mean she doesn't love you. Maybe she wants to wait."

"No, that ain't it. I said I'd wait, but it made no diff'rence. She said she loved spendin' time with me but—"

I watched more tears fall.

"The worse part was drivin' home after. Things were so diff'rent between us, uncomfortable. Like we'd jus' met. When I walked her to the porch, she wanted to go right in. I know she was sayin' goodbye to me forever."

He threw himself back on the bed, covering his face with his hands. "What am I gonna do? I don' know how to go back bein' without her. I'm never gonna feel the same way 'bout another girl, ever. I can't go anywhere without thinkin' of the times I was there with her."

"Have you talked to her at all?"

He sat up and shook his head. "I saw her in a couple classes and we said hi, but that's all. Ever'body was starin' at us funny, and I jus' wanted t'crawl in a hole and die and not hafta look at anyone."

Elvis slid to the floor and leaned his head toward my knee, looking away from me.

"I don' get it, Earl. How could someone say all those sweet things and not mean it?"

"Elvis, you got no reason to think Dixie didn't mean what she said."

"If she'd meant it, she'd be marryin' me. You know, Mama was right—she always tol' me not t' believe anythin' a silly girl tells you. They lie all the time."

"No reason to think Dixie was lying," I repeated, knowing full well Gladys's motive in offering that bit of advice was not innocent.

"Mama tol' me not to get all wrapped up. She said Dixie would end up hurtin' me 'cause she was only a silly girl. I got so mad when she said that, too. I shoulda listened."

"Elvis, people break up all the time, then they go and find someone else."

"If I see her with someone else, I'll kill 'em, I swear t' God I will," he said with abrupt violence in his voice.

Elvis sat there looking like his life was over, disillusion washed over him like a waterfall.

"Don' tell anyone, okay?" he asked suddenly. "I don' want anyone to know. I don' want people laughin' at me. It's too embarrassin'. I haven' even tol' Mama, yet. I didn' want to hear her talkin' Dixie down."

It turned dark outside as Elvis sat and talked, covering the same ground countless times. His moods swung wildly, first agonized, then indignant, then hopeful that Dixie would change her mind and say yes.

He left late that night, still unable to cry himself out. He walked to his car looking like an old man, shoulders hunched under the weight of the greatest pain he'd ever known.

I went to see him the next day, a little surprised to actually find him home. His mood was the same shade of dark gray—and by Gladys's chirpiness, I knew he'd finally told her.

"Come on in, Earl, I'm glad you're here. Maybe you can he'p cheer 'im up," Gladys said.

Elvis was sprawled on the couch, looking pathetic. Gladys sat next to him, stroking his head, smoothing back the strands of hair, looking satisfied, almost smug.

"My poor baby," she said, caressing his cheek.

"Don't, Mama," he said as he pushed her hand to the side.

"Can't a mama hug her baby?"

"Not right now, okay?" Elvis stood up and looked at me.

"You ready? We're goin' out for a burger, Mama. I'll be back later."

As we were ready to walk out the door, Gladys grabbed Elvis and held him close. "Jus' you 'member, *nobody* loves you like I do. You always got me."

Translated to mean: You best not put any girl before your mama again. Dixie's turndown was vindication and proof. Gladys wanted to be everything to Elvis and wanted more from him than what was right or healthy to expect.

That night I sat with Elvis a long time, going over the same territory the way you do when you feel your world is falling apart, asking the questions that had no answers. Except in this case I did know the answers, because I had called Dixie and asked her.

"How's he doing, Earl?"

"I'd be lying if I said good."

"I feel so awful about what happened. I had no idea he . . . I mean, it never occurred to me he'd want to propose to me."

"Elvis really loves you, you had to know that."

"I care for him, too. I never wanted to hurt him, Earl, you know that, don't you? I know I handled the whole thing badly, he just caught me completely off guard."

"He thought you felt the same about him as he does for you."

"We never made plans for the future, we never even discussed it. I mean, he's gonna try to be a singer and all. I guess I assumed that when school ended we'd go our own way, that it would, you know, fade."

"If you didn't love him, why'd you keep seeing him?"

"He's fun to be around, we had a great time together, and I'll always be his friend, but . . ."

Elvis wasn't what she was looking for in a husband. Simple as that.

"I *do* love Elvis, I really do. I think he's one of the most special people I'll ever meet. I'm just not *in* love with him. I can jus' tell the difference."

Dixie was the first girl who showed Elvis heartfelt affection, and he was desperate to hang on to that. He honestly didn't believe he would find anyone else who'd feel the same way about him. He was sick with the fear of that loss. Plus, she had opened the door to his sexuality. He was still very attracted, felt possessive of her, and the thought of someone else having her was maddening—and demeaning. Suddenly all those old feelings of inadequacy flooded back, leaving him emotionally raw.

I've thought about Dixie a lot over the years. If she had said yes and married Elvis, imagine how the course of music and culture would have been affected. Elvis would have settled down right away with a steady job and had children. I think he might have been happier in the long run.

Instead, Elvis approached his adult life with an aching void inside him. He had counted on Dixie to be his savior—from a painful past and unsure future. Her love had given him validity; without it, he slid back down the mountain into the valley of worthlessness. His reactions were extreme, because he'd been such an extreme outcast throughout his life. His loss was greater. The hurt was so strong in him that he resembled a mental patient who'd had one too many electroshock treatments. His senses were deadened, and his body sagged inward. I'm sure he was clinically depressed, but psychiatric help wasn't well accepted then.

Elvis eventually managed his anguish through anger and by developing an armor that no woman would ever penetrate to the depths Dixie had. He wasn't about to let any woman hurt him like that again. Unfortunately, it also ensured he'd never love that way again, either. Other than Gladys, Dixie was the last woman Elvis would treat with pure love and respect. His unreleased anger would flare up as mistreatment and callousness for the rest of his life.

The break-up with Dixie put a damper on Elvis's excitement and enthusiasm for graduation. He was visibly proud of his achievement, but it wasn't the special day he'd looked forward to—the start of his grown-up life with Dixie.

Even though he was depressed, he wasn't about to ignore graduation or disappoint his parents. They were so proud, they both cried on the last day of school. Neither of Elvis's parents had attended high school, so his accomplishment was incredibly important. A high school diploma for Elvis had been their one shared dream, and now it was fact. He did what they hadn't. In fact, he was one of the first on the Presley side to finish high school. He was anxious to show up for commencement to hear his name called and have that diploma placed in his hand.

In honor of the occasion, my parents invited the Presleys over after commencement for dinner. Gladys insisted on cooking, so she borrowed our kitchen to make Elvis a special meal—pork chops, corn bread, black-eyed peas, and apple pie.

We didn't go out to any of the parties his classmates were throwing; even if he'd been invited, the last thing Elvis wanted was to run into Dixie somewhere. Instead, we hung around outside. It was a warm, still night. Elvis stayed to himself and spent half the evening sitting in the corner of the back porch, strumming his guitar, occasionally humming.

While our parents chatted politely, I thumbed through Elvis's yearbook. Humes High, 1953. I looked up his senior picture. Next to the photo it said Major: Shop, History, English. Activities: ROTC, News Club, History Club, Speech—the last three joined at Dixie's suggestion.

I opened the front cover and noticed with a pang that only one person had signed it.

I shut the yearbook and watched Elvis, absorbed in his music and his thoughts. He certainly wasn't voted the most popular, most talented, most charming, or most anything else of his class. On a whole, the students and teachers of Humes High had chosen to just ignore him.

Diploma in hand, Elvis wasn't sure what to do with himself as far as establishing a direction in life. The week after graduation, Elvis went job hunting with a vengeance. He signed up at the local unemployment office, scoured the want ads, and went on a number of interviews.

He was willing to do almost anything, but he needed to make a decent wage, because once again, he was the family's main breadwinner. Gladys had lost her job after staying home a full week, suffering from "exhaustion" that she claimed was caused by the strain of working full time in poor health during Elvis's senior year.

Seeing Gladys take to her bed and hearing her weak voice stabbed Elvis with guilt, and he took the first good-paying job offered—as a factory worker for Precision Tool Company. He hated it.

"It's too damn cramped and loud in there—I can barely hear myself think," he complained. "The boss is always yellin' 'bout somethin', watchin' ever'thin' you do, and he made me put a scarf on like some ol' lady."

"So quit," I suggested.

"I can't. Mama'd think I was bein' aimless. We need the money. I wanna move us to a nicer place soon as possible, too. I'm jus' stuck with it."

Elvis gave Gladys half of his check for bills and living expenses and kept the rest for himself. This arrangement saved him from going through the exercise of having to ask his mother for money—money that was his to begin with. Despite the cash in his pocket, his mood was definitely subdued as he dreaded facing a job he hated, but needed to support his family.

A few weeks later, the unemployment office called—Elvis had left the phone number of a neighbor since the Presleys still didn't have a phone—with the news that Crown Electric was looking for a driver who could fix his own truck if anything went wrong with it. Elvis jumped at the chance. The starting salary was forty-five dollars a week to be one of the company's two drivers, he wouldn't be cooped up inside a steaming factory all day, *and* he wouldn't have to wear a scarf. He was thrilled and called me to go out and celebrate.

While I was waiting for Elvis to finish messing with his hair so we could go cruising around, Vernon joined me on the stoop out in front. Vernon and I always got along, but in those days, I didn't see him too often—he was seldom home. That night, he stopped to chat before leaving on his evening walk. He asked about school, and I asked after Gladys.

"Elvis's new job perked her up quite a ways. It'll be good for the boy," Vernon offered.

"He'll be making good money, that's for sure," I said.

"Decent. But more important, he won' have some-one hangin' over his shoulder watchin' his every move. Yep, the worse thing 'bout workin' is the higher-ups tellin' you what to do. Bosses treat ya like dirt, and Elvis surely hates being ordered—but you know that."

"You never tell him what to do unless you're lookin' for trouble," I laughed.

"Only one he'll listen to when he listens 'tall is his mama, always been that way. At least drivin' he'll be somewhat his own boss. Elvis needs that. He's a lot like me in that regard."

Whether or not they were alike in any regard, over the years it became obvious that Vernon didn't mind living hand to mouth. His sense of freedom was more important to him than the security of a weekly pay-check or his family's peace of mind. Now that Elvis was out of school and officially a man, Vernon was content to let him assume complete responsibility.

That fact really burned Elvis, but he refused to confront Vernon on it, keeping his feelings inside when his father was around. As we drove away, I made the mistake of saying his daddy was proud of his new job, and Elvis's resentment burst out.

"Sure. He's jus' happy to let someone else do the workin'. If he weren't married to Mama, I'd have nothin' to do with him," he blurted out. "We'd be better off if he left one day and never came back.

"If I ever make it as a singer, I'm gonna give her everythin' he didn't and show her she don' need him for nothin'."

Elvis worked a forty-hour week, but had more free time on his hands than he'd ever known. After his shift was over, the rest of the day was his own. No more classes to study for, and Gladys had given up trying to get Elvis to stay home with her—his days with Dixie had broken those particular chains for good. Besides, he had somewhere he'd really rather be.

Elvis talked nonstop about singing but didn't have a clue how to go about breaking in to show business. One day he'd be wildly confident, the next depressed and sure he was wasting his time on an unattainable dream—but it was never out of his mind. Beale Street drew him like a moth to a lantern, and during that summer of '53, Elvis became a regular at the assortment of clubs that dotted the area.

At first, he'd wander around and stand out on the sidewalk, listening to the blues musicians playing inside. Just like at that church back in Tupelo. After a while, he built up the courage to walk inside—and found heaven. Sultry music filtered through the smoky haze of the club, and settled on Elvis like a flannel blanket. He slid onto a stool and let the atmosphere enfold him. People sat by themselves nursing drinks or enjoyed the company of friends in lively groups. He stuck out like a sore thumb but nobody bothered him, probably because it was so obvious how much he enjoyed and appreciated the music.

He quickly adopted Beale Street as his own, even though he was one of the few white people to hang out there regularly. Being some kind of outcast was old news to Elvis, but here the music gave him a sense of belonging even if his skin color said otherwise.

Beale became his favorite shopping center as well. There was a famous clothing store on Beale called Lansky Brothers, where many of the local black artists shopped. The store carried a dizzying array of styles and colors and patterns—just the clothes Elvis dreamed about. The prices were way out of his range, but Elvis loved walking through the racks, browsing and daydreaming. He went in so often he got to know the owners and became friendly with them. His hounddog eyes looking longingly at the rows of clothes must have gotten to them, because they told Elvis about second-hand stores where he could get similar styles that he could afford.

Elvis always remembered how nice the owners were to him, making time when they didn't have to. After he was famous, Elvis bought half of his wardrobe from Lansky's and would remember them every Christmas.

"The real reason you come down here to shop," I accused him once, "is just an excuse to wander over and listen to music later on."

" 'Cept for gospel, there's no other sound like it, is there? It's sung from the soul, deep down, the way you're s'pposed to. The best music is the kind y'feel, and you can feel this out on the street."

Elvis could listen to the blues all night, and frequently did. Gladys worried about Elvis spending the day driving after staying out late the night before, but he laughed off her concerns, not about to give up the one bright spot in his life. Spending time on Beale Street fueled Elvis's fantasies and gave him hope.

Memphis was home to a variety of nightlife, and Elvis didn't restrict his evenings out to just blues clubs. Blue grass and country bars had their own strongholds, and Elvis cruised through them all, taking in the different styles and sounds. He watched the performers and imagined himself up on stage, playing to the noisy crowds, and geared himself up for that eventuality. Equally as important, the clubs satisfied more than his thirst for music—they unleashed Elvis's sexuality.

The country western bars especially attracted a lot of women, who hung around looking for companionship or just a drink and loved anybody who could carry a tune. Elvis quickly noticed that singers were never at a loss for female company after a set, but as he spent more time at predominantly white bars, Elvis found himself the center of unfamiliar attention. Experienced women saw through the loud clothes and dyed hair to his sexual potential. Bar groupies weren't good, simple, and pure, and Elvis wasted no time immersing himself in their open arms.

Elvis wasn't comfortable talking about sex, but he couldn't contain himself after finally losing his virginity. He came and found me at our diner hangout and dragged me outside to talk in private.

"This better be good—I wasn't done eating yet."

"Guess what," he said, smiling a shit-kicking grin. I waited.

"I got me a *real* date last night."

"As opposed to a pretend date?"

"You know . . . I met a woman last night at Hernando's, and we got to talkin' and had a few drinks, then she, you know, invited me over."

"What she look like?"

"Pretty enough, although she was wearin' too much makeup, but that's 'cause she was older."

"How much older?"

"I don' know, twenty-five maybe. Don't matter. She got her own place, real nice, too, and when we got there, we had us a drink and then she wanted to, you know, *we did it.*"

He jumped in the air and punched my arm.

"You went all the way with her?"

"*All* the way. Three times. I coulda done it to her all night, but she got tired and tol' me she had to get some sleep for work. Can you believe it? Earl, it was great, you gotta get Karen to let you do it."

"Elvis!"

"I mean it, there ain't nothin' better. You'll see what I mean. It makes you feel so . . . *strong*. I hardly slept t'all but felt like I could go on forever. Now I know what women are best for," he laughed.

"What's her name?"

"Laura."

"Laura what?"

"I don' know—she didn' say."

"You gonna see her again?"

He shrugged. "Maybe. She ain't someone to take to a movie and dinner. She said she'll see me 'round at the club. I don' know—there's lots of girls to pick from, and I'm gonna do some plucking."

Laura was the first in a steady stream of one- or two-night stands. If the girl didn't have her own apartment, they drove to a secluded spot and climbed in the back seat of Elvis's car to satisfy their fevered urges. As he got more experience, Elvis developed a sexiness that bubbled to the surface, attracting even more ladies to fulfill his desires. Elvis used women with relish but considered them cheap. His attitude toward them was harsh, even hostile, once the sex was over. More than once after finishing with one girl, he'd go back to the bar and pick up another for more. The last thing Elvis wanted was to get emotionally involved, so the women he slept with were truly objects for sex, not human beings with feelings.

The control and power that casual sex gave him over women was quite a contrast to his home life, where Gladys still ruled the roost through guilt and obligation. Unwilling to let her hold over him loosen any more than it already had, she waited up for Elvis every night no matter how he begged her not to. Left alone more often now with both Vernon and Elvis out on their own, Gladys consoled herself with liquor but frightened herself with alcohol-hazed visions of desertion. Her biggest fear was that Elvis would find someone and want to move out on his own, and she brought it up regularly. If Elvis responded impatiently or without enough concern, a stricken look would cloud her face.

"I don' know what I'll do by m'self," she said in a shaky voice. "I don' mean t'be such a bother t'you. I jus' get scared."

"Mama, I've tol' you before, I'm not gonna leave you alone. *I promise.* Please stop worryin'."

"I can't. When you don' come home at a decent hour, I imagine all sorts of things. If anythin' happened to you, I'd jus' die."

"I gotta go out at night, Mama. If I wanna ever start singin', I gotta learn what t'do. And I'm learnin' by watchin' other people sing. Don'cha want that?"

" 'Course I do, baby. I'm jus' a silly ol' woman."

Elvis hugged her; the juggling act was as difficult as ever.

Elvis's first public performance after high school was a disaster of such proportions he was convinced his career was over minutes after it began.

Hernando's Hideaway, one of the seedier clip joints Elvis frequented, would hire anyone who was brave—or stupid—enough to perform. Elvis offered to entertain three nights for free—music to the owner's ears.

"I been thinkin' 'bout it a while now," he said, moving his french fries around his plate in a circle. His voice sounded calm enough, but his lack of appetite gave him away.

"I asked 'round a lot and talked to the guys I met who sing at the clubs, and they all told me you jus' got to *do* it. Record producers and deejays show up at amateur nights, so you got to be up to be seen. But I gotta get more comfortable in front of people before singin' where a producer might be. I gotta start somewhere. Hernando's as good as any place, I guess."

He was apprehensive but determined to go through

with it, and I admired his courage. He had picked a
rough audience. Hernando's was filled with what we
called red-necks—drunken red-necks with crew cuts
that weren't dyed boot black. Not the most receptive
crowd to launch a career in front of. As it turned out,
they nearly lynched Elvis.

It was a miserable night all the way around. Rain
was pouring outside. Hernando's was cold, drafty,
muddy, and reeked of mildew. Everything was damp
to the touch. The clientele seemed particularly edgy.
The tables were carelessly scattered around a tiny plat-
form that doubled as a stage, and there were as many
bouncers as there were customers. Hernando's wasn't
allowed to sell alcohol, but if you brought your own
bottle, they'd serve it to you in paper cups, so the
liquor flowed freely and often.

The manager introduced Elvis, and he stepped up
on the tiny stage accompanied by only his guitar. When
a few burly guys at the next table guffawed at his outfit—green pants, checkered jacket, pink shirt—I suspected a long night loomed ahead.

Elvis sang a selection of current hits on the country
charts, and his performance was a complete bust. None
of the charisma I saw at the variety show was there—
he looked awkward and unattractive, pale and damp
with nervous sweat. Instead of singing in his own distinctive style, he tried to copy a voice he'd heard on
the radio—so he wound up sounding like a bad recording. His voice, normally so rich and resonant,
sounded squeaky and unnatural. To top it off, he
strummed his guitar with no sense of rhythm and gave
the overall impression of someone who didn't know
what the hell he was doing.

Midway through the first song, a few people
laughed. During the second song, some hecklers
joined in. Beer-soaked men asked Elvis what he did
with the money his parents had given him for singing
lessons and what beauty parlor did his hair. By the
third song, Elvis's voice tightened up, choked by his
humiliation. He stopped altogether after an empty bot-

tle was thrown in his general direction, followed by a littering of wadded-up paper cups. He got off the stage and walked straight out the back door, shutting out the laughter behind him.

I found him sitting in his car, propped against the door, tears wetting his face. He looked away as I climbed in the car.

"Jesus, Earl . . . I can't believe what jus' happened. They didn' even give me a chance."

"You were just nervous. It happens to everybody."

"Not like that it doesn't, Earl. I thought I felt okay goin' up, but then I jus' felt ever'thin' fallin' away from me. I couldn't even remember the words. No wonder they threw things. I was terrible. I wanna be swallowed up. How can I ever go back in there and face those people again? They *hated* me."

"They didn't like your performance, it's got nothing to do with you as a person. Most of them don't even know you."

"Early, they tried to shut me up by throwin' a bottle at me. I coulda been *killed*. I don' know why I keep kiddin' myself that I can be a singer. I ain't foolin' anyone but me."

"You're giving up because of one bad night?"

"I heard everythin' they said. They called me a freak. It's bad 'nough you saw it—what if I'd brought Mama? It've killed her."

"But Elvis, you weren't yourself up there tonight. You were trying too hard to sound like the radio instead of just being you. If you'd relax—"

"*Don't* tell me how t'sing. You don' know the first thing about it," he shot back angrily. "It wasn't just the singin' they didn't like, it was me."

He tossed his guitar in the back seat.

"Don' matter. I'm the ignorant one. This was a stupid idea from the start. Instead of wastin' my time here I should be doin' somethin' worthwhile."

I felt bad for him but his wallowing made me angry. He was always so unsure of himself, it sometimes got irritating.

"If you're willing to give up so easy, then singing must not have been that important to you to begin with."

He slammed his fist on the dash and spit the words out. "How would you know how important anythin' is to me? *Everythin'* comes easy to you. You don't have to fight for nothin'."

"Go ahead and feel sorry for yourself, if that's what you want. Take the easy way out."

"You don' know what it's like to be run off a stage. You got your future all planned out, I don't. It's easy for you—you ain't got nobody countin' on you to take care of 'em. *I do*. It's all up t'me. It's *always* been up t'me, and now I don' know what I'm gonna do," he shouted at me.

The violence in his voice frightened me, but I didn't let him see that and I refused to yell back.

"If you want to quit, then quit, but don't go blaming it on anybody other than yourself."

Without a word, Elvis started the car and screeched away from Hernando's, the car fishtailing on the slick streets, the ride home ominously silent. When I got out of the car, Elvis didn't look at me or say a word, his face an unreadable stone wall.

I didn't expect to hear from Elvis for a long time, so I was stunned when he showed up at my house the following night and asked me to go with him to Hernando's.

"I have a date with Karen."

"Can't you be a little late for it? Or maybe you can both come."

"I don' know I want to take her to that place, it's a little rough."

He gave a small laugh. "Yeah, especially if you're singin'. Gotta watch out for those beer bottles."

"I thought you were quittin'."

"I told 'em I'd do it three nights, they're expectin' me."

"Why'd you change your mind?"

He shifted his weight, uncomfortable at the obvious tension between us. He looked at me and shrugged.

"I got home las' night, and Mama was waitin' up like always, and I was too ashamed to tell her what happened, so I lied and said it went fine. She looked so proud and was so happy—it'd mean so much to her if I made somethin' of myself.

"Then this morning I woke up thinkin' about the fair and the variety show I won, rememberin' the way those people *did* like me. They must've, or else they wouldn't have clapped like they did and been so nice to me after, right?"

"Right."

"I wanna see if I can get that to happen again. Jus' once more. If I can, maybe it'll mean I should keep tryin'. Can you come?"

"Let me call Karen, and I'll meet you there."

"Thanks, Earl."

Even then, Elvis wasn't one to apologize, regardless of the circumstance.

Elvis was tense like never before, expecting to see more beer bottles flying through the air at him. He stood off to the side of the stage, taking deep breaths to calm himself. After his introduction, he got up on stage, fixed his eyes at the rear of the room and started singing. The songs were the same, but this time he sang them in the style that came naturally to him, in a strong, melodious voice. Nobody paid much attention one way or another—no bottles, no hecklers, but no applause, either. Tonight, Elvis was just background noise.

When his set was done, he bounded off the stage, his face flushed with a sense of accomplishment. It wasn't a performance of the ages, but it was okay. And it gave Elvis enough to keep his dream alive. From that night on, he pursued singing with new-found vigor. Coming so close to losing it had done the trick.

Elvis searched out every amateur night or honkytonk looking for free talent in the greater Memphis area. He never had a regular set, just whatever was popular on the radio at the moment. He might hear something on the radio while driving to a club, be totally unprepared but try to sing it anyway, even if he only knew half the words, just because it was a hit song.

Some nights were good, many were bad. He took audience apathy or jeering personally. What he did was synonymous with who he was, so he construed any criticism of his singing as a personal rejection and it made him angry. And more determined.

"I'll show 'em. One day they'll see," he'd say whenever an audience gave him a cool reception.

Elvis became a planner. As the year came to a close, he wanted to plot things out as a way of knowing where his future was headed. He actually wrote it out on a piece of paper—his day, his week, his life. Topping his list was marriage and children, followed by caring for Gladys. Singing came in a surprising third. Sometimes, after a rough weekend of "clubbing," his confidence would sag and his enthusiasm wane, and singing was in danger of being erased off the list altogether.

"I'm just wastin' my time."

He kept going, though. "Ain't got nothin' better to do until I find me a girl to marry, anyway."

It was during a low period that Elvis decided he needed something to fall back on and announced he was studying to be an electrician.

"You're going to go back to school?"

" 'Course not. I can't afford no college. I'm gonna teach myself. I bought a bunch of books, and I can get others from the library. The guys at work tol' me which ones t'get. If I get good at it, Crown'll give me a better job. I don't wanna drive a truck all my life."

"Teaching yourself sounds hard."

"How hard can it be, learnin' to attach a few wires?"

I browsed through one of the books. "It's mostly math. You hated math."

"I was hopin' you'd help me, like you used to in school."

"This looks way beyond me."

Undaunted, Elvis doggedly studied his books at night during the week, but for all his efforts, he wasn't learning anything. Still, he refused to give up—his fledgling music career was stalled in Memphis's lesser honky-tonks, and he felt pressure to secure a solid future of some kind.

"I have to provide for Mama somehow," Elvis sighed. "God, I wish Jesse was here. We could take turns lookin' after Mama."

His parents were proud of his attempt to become an electrician, but Vernon especially was realistic about his abilities.

"I tol' him not to go practicin' on anythin' in here," Vernon told me. "The place'd go up in smoke. He got mad and didn't talk to me for a week, but it's the truth."

Other than myself and Gladys, Elvis got very little encouragement for anything he did. At Christmas dinner that year, my parents and brothers would ask politely about Elvis's singing, then pointedly inquire about his "electrical training." My family thought his ideas of being a singer were a crock and a pipe dream.

Gladys stubbornly supported his efforts, and Vernon backed her up.

"As long as it ain't interferin' with his job, no reason the boy can't spend his time where he pleases," Vernon said. "All kids wanna be famous—he'll grow out of it once he settles down."

"I don't want him to stop singing. He's got a beautiful voice, no reason he couldn't get somewhere with it," Gladys said. "You shoulda heard the record he made me for my birthday—as good as anyone on the radio."

"Elvis made a record?" My mom looked at Gladys with raised eyebrows.

Gladys called for Elvis, and he stuck his head in from the radio room. "Tell her 'bout the record."

"There's a place on the other side of town where you can make a recordin' of yourself and get a real record, just like in the stores—for jus' four dollars."

"You spent four dollars to hear yourself sing?"

"He spends it as fast as he gets it," Vernon sighed.

"It was for Mama's birthday," he said with an edge, then went back to the radio program he was listening to.

Gladys didn't fret how Elvis spent his money. Her biggest worry was that Elvis would fall into a bad crowd at the clubs and be led down an all-too-familiar Presley path.

"Elvis is easily swayed," Gladys said. "He can't seem to say no. You know how boys can be. And I can't always be there to watch over him."

Gladys had echoed my mother's own beliefs.

"It's the Presley in him," my mother said after they left. "Chasing after some fool notion instead of putting his nose to the grindstone. That boy has no direction in life."

"Yes he does. He wants to be a singer—or an electrician."

"Elvis has no chance of being either. It's nothing against him, Earl. Not his fault—that's how the Presleys are. I just don't want it rubbing off on you."

My dad cut in. "A man's s'posed to be responsible."

"He's got a good paying job."

"Earl, frequentin' bars and honky-tonks's a sign of shiftlessness. I know you've gone and heard him sing, but you better not be sneakin' out with him too often or I'll put a stop to it. You hear?"

"It's nothin' against Elvis," my mom repeated, seeing I was upset. "The Presleys have always been like that. They might be relations, but that don't mean we don't see 'em for who they are."

To be truthful, my parents had never been overly enthusiastic about my friendship with Elvis and would have preferred it if I didn't spend so much time with him socially. But to their credit, though, my parents never once interfered with our friendship. They trusted me enough to let me choose my friends. Even if one of them was a Presley.

Everybody had concerns about Elvis. Vernon generally kept his private, except for always being after me to fix Elvis up. Late one afternoon he cornered me while I was waiting for Elvis to get home from work. Vernon sat down next to me on the stoop, sipping a beer and smelling like he'd had several others.

"You boys goin' out tonight?"

"We're gonna grab a burger."

"And go find some girls, right? Maybe you can help Elvis find another steady girl. Do 'im good to settle down. Just don' tell his mama I tol' you so. She'll take to her bed for a week at the thought. She smothers him—always has."

I was too embarrassed to answer. This was the drunkest I'd ever seen Vernon.

"He's her life, but we know how women are, don' we? I s'pose all mamas hate seein' their kids grow up, but I tell you, boy, her attachment to that boy ain't natural. Most times she hardly knows I'm alive. Him, too. They'd just as soon I packed up and went back to Tupelo."

It might have been the drink talking, but Gladys *had* called Elvis her "man" since he was potty-trained. Mother and son formed a team that usually excluded the father; Vernon had suffered his hurts in silence for a long time.

I hadn't seen Elvis for over a week, since he'd spent the weekend in Louisiana at an amateur night, so we set out to Leonard's Drive-in to eat and catch up with each other. I ran into some friends there, and we joined their table. Elvis liked my friends and felt comfortable around them. They in turn thought of Elvis as a sort of celebrity and he fed off of it. Girls especially thought stories about his sporadic honky-tonk career were glamorous and exciting.

"Isn't it scary getting up in front of a whole room

of people?'' a girl named Julie asked. "I don't think I could face that many people staring at me.''

"Nah, it ain't so bad. You jus' pick out someone in the audience and sing right to 'em, then you forget 'bout all them people watchin'. Until they start throwin' beer bottles—then I just duck.''

"They weren't throwing any bottles at you last weekend. Elvis won an amateur night at the Louisiana Hayride and won fifty dollars,'' I told Julie.

"Fifty dollars just for singing a song?'' My friend Bob shook his head. "It must be great getting paid to just sing.''

"That was a special contest. Most times, with what they give, it'd only take me 'bout a week to starve to death,'' he laughed. "And you only get money if you win.''

"I hear there's lots of women at Hernando's that you can have for the price of a beer,'' whispered George, shielding his mouth from the girls.

"It wouldn't be proper to say in mixed company. You'll have to come see me and find out for yourself.'' Elvis winked. "Just don't bring no girlfrien'.''

"Can't I come see you?'' Julie asked.

"It ain't proper for a lady to go into no honky-tonks—unless you got an escort,'' he said.

"Couldn't *you* be my escort?'' She flirted with him.

"I'd like that.'' He flirted back, blushing.

For someone who slept with a couple girls a week, Elvis was still shy around proper girls who couldn't be dismissed as mattresses. Sex became a great equalizer for Elvis. He felt inferior around most girls, especially those with any kind of breeding, unless he'd conquered them in the bedroom, proving their cheapness and his superiority. As he got older, knocking good girls off their pedestals became a favorite pastime, and every time he succeeded in doing it, his disillusion with women grew. All of them failed the Gladys comparison test.

* * *

In January of 1954, Elvis went back to the Memphis Recording Studio to make a second record—the gift had been such a hit with his mama he thought he'd try the same tactic out on a girl he was desperate to impress—and get into bed.

That he ever made that first record for Gladys was a fluke. Elvis was on his way back to Crown after his last delivery of the day when he suddenly remembered it was his mama's birthday—he'd completely forgotten. He knew she'd be waiting at home, anticipating his present. If he walked in empty-handed, she'd be so disappointed.

As Elvis wracked his brains trying to think of a gift that would make his mama happy, he drove by the Memphis Recording Studios, and the answer jumped out at him: Make Your Own Record—Only $4.00. He had seen the sign countless times before without giving it much thought, but on this day—call it fate, happenstance, or destiny, whatever—Elvis pulled into the MRS parking lot and went in to make his mama a recording.

The secretary in charge of the public recordings had been so impressed with his unique sound she took a copy of his first record to MRS owner Sam Phillips, who was also the founder of Sun Records. Phillips listened politely than promptly forgot about it.

When Elvis returned, she remembered him immediately and greeted him warmly. After several minutes of blatant flirting, Elvis recorded "Casual Love" and "I'll Never Stand in Your Way," aware both of his rapt audience and the power he could exert with his voice. When he left, he had the secretary's phone number tucked safely away in his pocket.

That night at Leonard's Drive-in, Elvis presented the record to a petite blonde, sitting in a corner booth with three of her girlfriends. The girl blushed under Elvis's steady gaze but didn't avert her eyes when she agreed to a date the following Saturday.

"Maybe I ought to have you autograph this now for

when you get famous,'' she said, holding the record to her chest.

''You don' need my name on a piece of paper—you got me,'' he said, lightly squeezing her shoulder.

In less than a year, the whole country would have Elvis.

Part III

THE BOY BECOMES KING

7

Desperate to find new talent for his small-time label, Sam Phillips finally gave in and listened to the second recording by the kid with the sideburns his persistent secretary kept nagging about. Buried under the harsh static of a cheap recording, Phillips heard the sound of money.

When the wind-up alarm clock rattled him awake, Elvis had no inkling this was the day that would forever divide his life into before and after. He staggered into the bathroom for his clothes and got ready for work in the darkened apartment, careful not to wake his parents. He dressed quickly but spent considerable time greasing and combing his hair. He left, shutting the door gently behind him, to face another day of driving—and daydreaming.

The Presleys still had no phone, but their neighbor Jim gave Elvis free rein to use his. Elvis got home from work that afternoon and found a note on his apartment door to call Sun Records as soon as possible. Elvis assumed it must be the cute little secretary being forward and went to return the call with bedroom thoughts dancing in his head. When a man claiming to be Mr. Phillips answered, Elvis immediately thought it was a practical joke, but disbelief turned to excitement, then terror, then back to elation in quick turns as Phillips warmly complimented his voice on the four songs he had recorded, then ex-

plained he needed a demo singer for a ballad called
"Without You" and asked if Elvis would be interested.

Gladys came running out of the apartment at the
sound of Elvis's screaming, but she could tell by his
flushed, smiling face that he was excited, not being
murdered. While other startled neighbors peeked out
from behind their doors, Elvis grabbed his mama in
the dreary hallway and spun her around in a would-be
waltz before lifting her off the ground in a bear hug.

She squealed girlishly. "Elvis Aron, you put me down—
what's got into you? What'll the neighbors think?"

"Let 'em think what they want, Mama. I did it, I
finally did it."

Elvis stuttered out what had happened and Gladys
cried tears of happiness, even though she had no idea
what a demo was until he explained it to her. Elvis
was beside himself, wondering what it all meant—if
anything at all. He was unable to sit or stand in any
one place. His emotions needed more space than their
tiny apartment could give, so he spent the evening
driving the streets of Memphis, too preoccupied to
stop at any of his usual haunts. As the night wore on,
nervousness and self-doubt gradually elbowed aside
the heady thrill he had first experienced, and his mind
raced into dark and frightening corners. By the time
he got home, Elvis felt sick with anxiety. Drained and
tired but unable to sleep, Elvis lay on the couch wide
awake, staring at the darkness as he tried to see the
future.

The rest of the week passed in tantalizing slow motion. Elvis practiced singing until he was nearly hoarse
and stopped by my house several times looking for
company and distraction.

My parents took the news of Elvis's good fortune
politely but with typical skepticism.

"Is he getting paid for this?" my mom asked after
he left.

"I don't think so."

"I didn't, either."

* * *

Elvis showed up at Leonard's a few days after his big day in the studio. Instead of being full of stories, he was subdued and reluctant to talk about what happened until pressed.

"I don't know why but it was jus' awful. *I* was jus' awful. It was a pretty 'nough song but I couldn' get 'hold of it. Mr. Phillips made me sing it over and over, with a band, without a band. . . . He tried bein' nice but he hated the way I sang it, ever'one could tell. Nobody would look me in the eye. It was so humiliatin'. I wanted to run outa there and not look back."

Elvis let out a trembling sigh and looked up with puppy-soft eyes, his vulnerability apparent enough to break your heart.

"I couldn' believe it when he tol' me to come back the next afternoon 'cause he wanted me to try somethin' else. I'da *never* let me back in the door."

When Elvis returned the following day, Phillips introduced him to two musicians, Scotty Moore and Bill Black. Sam realized Elvis's biggest problem was a lack of training and experience, so he arranged for Elvis to practice his singing using Scotty and Bill as a back-up combo—who for their part thought it was a big waste of time.

Elvis spent hours at Scotty's house, rehearsing a number of ballads Sam had given him. With his musicians backing him up, Elvis tried out his new material at a couple of clubs with typically mixed and muted reactions. Not surprisingly, when they went back to the studio to try another demo, the results were disappointingly familiar.

Elvis knew he was on the brink of disaster and was paralyzed at the thought of blowing this opportunity. He kept telling himself to just relax, but his constricted throat betrayed him. With each take, the tension in the studio thickened, straining everyone's nerves. A tight-jawed Phillips called for five, and Elvis was left ominously alone. During the break, Elvis tried to calm his escalating panic by singing—except this time instead of a schmaltzy ballad, Elvis stood up and shook to the beat of an upbeat blues tune, "That's All Right, Mama." The sounds of his lilting high octaves brought them all running.

"They had me sittin' and singin' songs I jus' wasn' comfortable with, that's all. When I stood up and sang a song I liked, that made all the diff'rence. I need somethin' I can move to."

Sam knew a winner when he heard one, and was smart enough to go with it. He recorded "That's All Right, Mama" and Elvis cut a snappy "Blue Moon of Kentucky" for the flip side.

Elvis showed up at Leonard's soon after in a state resembling shock and disbelief.

"Did something go wrong?" I asked, fearing the worst.

"No . . . Mr. Phillips says he's real happy."

"You sure don't act like it."

"None of it seems real. The day started out so bad then ever'thin happened at once. I wouldn't be surprised if Mr. Phillips said he'd get my song on the radio jus' so I wouldn't feel bad 'bout screwing up on the other songs."

"You're gonna be on *the radio?*"

"That's what he said."

"You're kidding?"

Elvis flashed me a tentative smile and shrugged. "I can't believe it either."

"Elvis, what's wrong with you? Stop acting like your best friend just died. You did it—you're gonna be a real singer."

I was stunned and stuttering and found this turn of events mind-boggling. I had always thought Elvis was talented enough, but when a dream turns into reality, it seems more a dream than ever. I wanted to go celebrate and tell everyone the news, the occasion too important to keep a secret. Elvis shook his head and stayed glued to his seat.

"I can't believe it'll really happen, y'know? I don'

wanna get all excited over nothin'—ever'time I do, it gets ruined. I don' wanna jinx it.''

Still, he couldn't completely submerge his anticipation or keep from jumping ahead of himself. He replayed the day for me step by step, reliving the ups and downs with fresh emotion.

''Havin' music behind you makes singin' so much easier. They played it back and it sounded like a *real* record. I hardly recognized myself. They were all pattin' me on the back, tellin' me how great I was. . . . God, I didn' want to leave.

''Can you imagin' if he *did* get it on the radio? Mama'd be cryin' from now 'til New Year's. It'd sure be nice. . . . Mama'd be out on the streets tellin' strangers.

''I wish I knew what it all meant—it jus' don' seem real to me. I ain't never been lucky like this. Good things never happen to us. If it really happened, d'you think I'd make any money?''

A disc jockey named Dewey Phillips, no relation to Sam, agreed to play Elvis's version of ''That's All Right, Mama'' on his station, WHBQ, as a favor to the label owner. Elvis knew exactly when his record was going to be played, but he refused to listen. He was too scared he'd see disappointment in his mama's eyes or be ridiculed by others if it sounded awful. So he turned the station on for his parents then left to go on a long car ride by himself, feeling sick to his stomach from nerves. Vernon and Gladys were waiting for him when he got home and were genuinely thrilled, but he took their review as biased. What finally convinced him he hadn't been a disaster was when acquaintances came up to congratulate him, and girls found excuses to talk to him. Once again, he basked in the acceptance and read it as love.

The effect on Elvis was visible. His chest puffed out with pride, he laughed and smiled more with strangers, flirted more openly with girls, and even stuttered less. He was trying on popularity and liked the way it fit.

Within a week, Sun received over five thousand orders from people who wanted a copy of the record, and Elvis was a local hit—and destined to stay one. Despite an aggressive mailing by Phillips to deejays in all the major markets, Elvis's record never heard the light of day. It was a "country song" from a "country label," and Top 40 stations weren't interested.

"Listen, Elvis, that's you again!" I turned up the volume on his car radio.

Elvis sang along, moving his hips in time to the music as he drove. A look of wonder lit his eyes while the song was on, but when it ended, he shook his head.

"Ever'time it comes on, all I hear are the mistakes I made. If it wasn't for the guys in back of me playing, they'd be throwing bottles at the radio," he laughed. His desire for perfection couldn't diminish the pride he felt. Nor hide his disbelief.

"I jus' can't get over it, Earl. It was too easy. I thought you were s'pposed to have to work hard for a singin' career."

As word spread among his acquaintances, Elvis became a minor celebrity at the diners and bars where he spent his time. People who had barely given him the time of day before were suddenly going out of their way to say hello or buy him a drink. Elvis especially loved the increased female attention.

"I can't believe that's really you—it sounds so professional," said one girl. "To think I know someone on the radio."

"That's me alright, mama," he said, laughing at his own joke as the girl leaned against him, giggling.

"When you gonna be moving to Nashville?"

"Why would I go there?"

"That's where all the country singers go."

"I ain't no country singer, don't wanna be one, either. They jus' call me that 'cause they don't know what else to call it. Guess I'm one of a kind."

That initial rush of overt self-importance went over better in the bars than it did at home with his mama. Gladys was floating with joy over Elvis's leap from obscurity, but she was upset at how infrequently he was home. The first time Elvis dismissed Gladys in a sassy tone, she reminded him in no uncertain terms she was still his mama and was to be treated accordingly. He was leaving to go bar hopping when Gladys asked what time he'd be home—as she did every night.

"When I feel like it, that's when," he answered, not hiding his irritation.

Gladys was up and on him in a flash, grabbing his arm in a painful grip.

"I don' care how many records you got playin', you better learn respect. I ain't one of your bar whores and don' like bein' treated like one. You talk to me in that tone again, I'll slap that attitude outta you and don' think I won't.

"I was 'fraid you'd pick up bad habits hangin' out in bars filled with loose women and loafers. Don't make me sorry you're my boy. Jesse wouldn' treat his mama in a bad way, and I 'spect you to be the same."

Her words stung worse than any slap could and Elvis apologized, chastened and deflated.

Having the night off from performing, Elvis cruised the bars that had become his home away from home, intent on finding a women to dominate and control, needing to regain the potency his mother had sucked out of him. It didn't take him long to find a willing partner, and just like other similar encounters, he left feeling superior, but empty.

Sam Phillips's strategy to establish Elvis was to book him into any decent club and bar in the greater Memphis area, which were many. Phillips believed in Elvis's talent but worried at his lack of professionalism—he was often late and usually unprepared to sing, having failed to familiarize himself with the music. Sam realized part of the problem was his young singer's lack of musical training and knowledge. He insisted on regular rehearsals with the combo, so Elvis would go straight from his shift at Crown to either the Sun studios or the club where they were performing. Before long, he was about to drop from the grueling schedule. Something had to give, but the prospect of making a commitment either way terrified Elvis.

Even though he was paid a modest fee for performing, and was assured by Phillips that he was on his way to a solid singing career, Elvis clung to the job at Crown, part of him convinced his moment of glory would blow away any day. Driving the truck was a sure thing. If he gave it up, there'd be no more waiting for the future to happen. It would be time to succeed or fail and find out once and for all if he had what it took. Elvis finally took the decisive step the day Phillips gave him his first royalty check for two hundred dollars. That kind of money-making potential was all the incentive he needed to stop playing it safe.

The first thing Elvis bought was a dress and nice pair of shoes for Gladys—possibly the nicest shoes she'd ever owned. She kept them in a plastic bag beside her bed and looked at them every time she walked by the door. More than anything, those shoes symbolized where the family had come from and where Elvis hoped to take them.

Vernon thought it was a waste of money to buy shoes Gladys wouldn't wear—her feet were too swollen—but Elvis dismissed those concerns with a shrug, too pleased with himself over giving Gladys something Vernon had never been able to. Gladys just enjoyed having nice things to show off.

"You look like you're all dressed up to go to a party," I complimented her.

"You like it? I keep tellin' Elvis not to spend any more money on his old mama, but he don' listen," she said, sounding almost coy. "D'you see—Elvis got us a phone now, too."

"Too bad we ain't got anyplace to go or friends to call," Vernon sighed, dressed in his usual overalls.

Elvis stuck his head out of the bathroom. "It's all for you, Mama."

"Oh, stop flatterin' me or I'll take you serious."

Gladys sat down, her hand over her heart. "The

good Lord's surely lookin' after us—even if Elvis turned his back on church. You still go to church, doncha, Earl?''

"Yes, ma'am." Though not necessarily out of free will.

Elvis came out, ready to go. "I tol' you, Mama, I'll start going again when I ain't so busy."

"Nobody's too busy for God."

"B'tween rehearsin' and singin', I need Sunday mornings to sleep. You don' want me droppin' or gettin' too sick to sing, do you?"

"Course not, honey. But there's services later."

Elvis sidestepped that suggestion.

" 'Sides, I ain't too busy for God, I'm too busy for church. Don' get sour, Mama—you and Jesse pray for me today, okay?"

Gladys fretted that Elvis was playing with his soul by turning his back on church. Regardless of what Elvis said, Gladys knew avoiding church was the same thing as avoiding God. Without that guidance, she worried, Elvis would stumble down a reckless path and not find his way back out. For all the insecurities that hounded him, she could see that Elvis feared the wrong things. She had lived long enough to know we are our own worst enemies. The only way she knew to protect him was to be there to watch out for him, but she felt him slipping away.

Gladys sadly watched him get ready. "You gonna be out late again? Your daddy falls asleep with the birds. . . . I hate bein' alone."

"Prob'ly, Mama—it's business. Don' wait up—no sense both of us bein' ragged."

He kissed her good night. "I'll make it up t'you."

"Don' you go buyin' me no more pretty things, now," she called as we walked down the steps.

Elvis smiled as we got into his car. "That means she wants at least *two* presents."

Elvis sang and whistled, smiling at every girl we passed. He had good reason to be in such a lighthearted mood. In July of 1954, "That's All Right,

Mama'' was number three in the local country and western sales charts and went on to become number one in the Memphis area, despite the reluctance of many deejays to play the record on white stations. Because it sounded ''Negro,'' they assumed Elvis was black, so his exposure was confined to the Memphis area.

Despite his arguments to the contrary, Elvis Presley was a budding country star. On the strength of the record's popularity in Memphis, Phillips managed to get an audition for Elvis at the Grand Ol' Opry, assuring him it was just a formality and he was a shoo-in to be invited to perform. Even though he himself wasn't keen on country and western, Elvis knew how important an appearance on the Opry could be for his career, and his head was already swimming with visions of immediate, national stardom. To his mind, this was it.

Elvis asked me to go along and keep him company and was relaxed and supremely confident, almost cocky, on the drive to Nashville. His musicians, Bill Black and Scotty Moore, and their equipment followed in a car behind us, and the abbreviated caravan sped with positive purpose toward the shrine of country music.

''This right here is it, boy,'' Elvis shouted out the window as we neared Nashville. He was all wound up, and the words and pent-up frustrations spilled out.

''This could really be *it*. No more drivin' a truck, no more projects, no more bein' spit on by people thinkin' they're better. I tol' you all along I'd show 'em, didn' I? *Didn't I?*

''You shoulda seen Mama's face when I tol' her. She 'bout died and went to heaven. I knew I could make her prouda me if I only got halfa chance. Now I'm takin' care of her as good as Jesse would of—she don' hafta be so sorry he ain't here. I bet he's as surprised as she is. I tol' you I'd show *ever'body*.

''Wait'll those stuffed shirts at the Opry sees us— we're gonna turn 'em on their *ears.*''

And so it went all the way until we pulled in the parking lot behind the Opry, which wasn't the grand spectacle Elvis had been expecting.

"I seen barns that look better," he joked, slightly disappointed.

He led us to the check-in area with a swagger, the lord gracing the peons with a royal visit. Once we finally found the stage manager, who stared at Elvis as if he were a new species, we were told the time of the audition and pointed toward the backstage area where we were to wait. While the musicians carried in their instruments, Elvis carried his wardrobe, an eye-shocking Beale Street special he planned to wear on the show that night.

"They'll remember me one way or 'nother, won't they?" he laughed, reading my mind. "Mr. Phillips says they ain't never heard or seen anyone like me. We're gonna change that."

He practiced with his band a short time, and exchanged a few pleasantries with a couple of other performers waiting their turn, mostly a friendly group named The Jordanaires. Elvis made jokes and exuded a relaxed assurance, only his constant movement and an unconscious tugging at his sideburns hinted at any nervousness as the time for the audition neared.

"Presley, you're next. Get set up," the stage manager called. "You got five minutes, so move it."

"Bossy, ain't he?" Elvis laughed, but the guy's tone got under his skin and there was an edge to his voice.

Elvis and his band moved onto the great stage, and he looked out at the biggest auditorium he'd ever seen. It truly was a grand building, and the decades of tradition it housed made Elvis feel suddenly small and insignificant, which in turn made him angry and determined to prove his worth. The stage manager impatiently paced near the wings where I stood, and his irritated sighs made Elvis flinch. The Opry official auditioning him, Mr. Denny, sat waiting with an unreadable expression on his face.

Elvis took a deep breath, gave his musicians a quick

nod, and turned to face his impassive audience. He sang "That's All Right, Mama" and "Blue Moon of Kentucky," the way nobody there had ever heard. In the confines of the building that is country and western, it was plain as day to see that Elvis was cut from a different cloth. With his unique riffs, and hips and knees swaying to the music, Elvis unwittingly proved his own point—he was no more classic country than Hank Williams was a jazz singer. The songs might have been country standards, but to the judge's finely tuned ears, they no doubt seemed blasphemy.

When he was finished, there was an almost eerie silence from Mr. Denny.

"Thank you very much, Mr. Presley. I'm sorry, but I don't think your act is quite right for the Opry at this time."

Elvis just stood there, unwilling to give up.

"I know we started a little slow, can' we try somethin' else?"

"That's not needed. We appreciate your visit, but maybe you ought to go back to driving that truck, son."

Elvis was stunned and turned to his musicians who avoided his eyes. They packed up quickly and quietly with undue concentration. The next set of performers coming on stage gave Elvis a wide berth, as he walked off, unable to not hang his head in shame. The burly stage manager laughed derisively as he passed.

"Boy, you get a reg-u-lar haircut and take some singin' lessons, and maybe you'll be good 'nough for the Opry, but I surely doubt it."

Elvis's face fell, and he visibly deflated under the verbal punch. The earlier swagger and cockiness were replaced by teary-eyed insecurity. Elvis couldn't meet the stage manager's mocking eyes and hurried off the stage. He was already in the car when I got there, waiting for me with the engine running. The musicians leaned in the door before I got in and made a sincere effort to cheer him up.

"The Opry's run by a stuffy old bunch—everyone

knows they like to make you kiss ass a bit before letting you on their show, don't worry about it. You'll make it next time," Scotty said.

"They don't like anybody who don't have a Nashville address, neither," Bill added.

Elvis nodded but didn't respond. As soon as I got in, he screeched away, the accelerator accurately gauging his humiliation. Most performers equate appreciation of their art with an acceptance of themselves as people, but it was magnified and exaggerated with Elvis. Embarrassment became humiliation, disappointment became despair. Every hurt and setback became catastrophic failure and a reason to quit.

Elvis was inconsolable, so upset he refused to go back and retrieve the unworn outfit he'd forgotten and left behind in the Opry waiting room.

"I don't care—let 'em burn it. Make 'em all happy and feel good 'bout themselves. Don' matter—ain't gonna need it anymore."

"Why not?"

"I don' know how I coulda let mysel' be so stupid, thinkin' I was gonna make somethin' special o'myself. Any time in my life I expected somethin' good t'happen, it just blows up in my face.

"D'you see the way that stagehand was laughin' at me? I musta looked the fool up there."

"You did not. It was as good as I've ever seen you."

Elvis snorted bitterly.

"That's fine for honky-tonks filled with drunks that don' know better, but it ain't good 'nough for anythin' better."

It was a long, uncomfortable drive home. Elvis's granite jaw loosened as we drove into Memphis, and tears suddenly flooded his cheeks.

"God, Earl, what am I gonna tell Mama? How'm I gonna tell her I ain't good 'nough? She's gonna be so disappointed in me. And what about ever'body I tol'—they're all gonna be laughin' at me behind my back. I'll never be able to face 'em anymore."

"Elvis, it's just one show. You didn' want to be a country western singer, anyway."

"Just one show. I ain't good 'nough, Earl. What am I s'pposed t'do—play the same Memphis clubs over and over 'til they're sicka me? That's okay for now, but I gotta think about my future, and how can I take care of Mama like that? 'Sides, Mr. Phillips ain't gonna wait on me forever.

"I wouldn' blame 'im if he dropped me now—then where'll we be? I won' be able to get my job back at Crown, I shoulda never given it up in the first place. Now we're gonna be right back where we were—no place."

Elvis parked his car a block away from home, in front of a deserted, condemned building. He got out, slamming the door behind him and walked into the debris-strewn area. I followed at a respectful distance, knowing nothing I could say would help. Elvis picked up a large board and suddenly began smashing it violently into the ground, cursing and crying. He swung the board wildly until it was reduced to splinters, then sank to his knees, choking on the dust and the taste of despair.

Sam Phillips shrugged off Elvis's abysmal showing at the Opry and spent considerable time assuring Elvis he didn't need the Opry. Elvis was convinced his dream was dead but agreed to keep going for the time being, having nothing better to do.

In addition to the regular rounds of clubs, Phillips arranged for Elvis to appear for a week at the Louisiana Hayride, the same place he'd won an amateur contest just a few months earlier.

Elvis was excited at both the gig and going on the road. He'd never spent a week away from home before and was anticipating the anonymous freedom of being away from familiar places and faces, of not having Mama looking over his shoulder. Gladys, needless to say, was far from thrilled, but Elvis paid little attention to her fretting and was relieved when Vernon hushed her so he wouldn't have to.

On the drive to Louisiana, Elvis felt oddly removed from all he'd been through, as if it were really happening to someone else. It was hard for Elvis to comprehend all that had happened to him in the span of a few months. He'd gone from driving a truck to being on the radio, moved out of brawl-prone dives to more respectable clubs, had a record label behind him, and his name was known to thousands of people. He wanted to feel different inside, and tried to adopt an appropriate outer attitude. But inside, he felt as insecure as ever—certain he was going to fall flat on his face at any given moment and lose it all. He wasn't so much going forward as running scared at falling back. No Presley had ever been able to hang onto anything for very long, and that legacy filled him with unease.

Life on the road wasn't as exciting as Elvis expected. He still had trouble making friends with guys, although he had no trouble finding a willing woman in rough bars to share his bed. For the first time, he was able to spend the night with his conquests and discovered the joys of morning intimacy. The one-night stands he experienced in Louisiana didn't ease the loneliness he felt inside, but they fed his ravenous craving for sexual power.

In addition to performing, Elvis also did a few radio commercials. His halting and mushy speech drove the technicians crazy, but he was so thrilled at being on the radio like a real celebrity he didn't notice their irritation. He was justifiably proud, even if the broadcast was local. The only notoriety any Presley had prior to Elvis was of the negative variety.

Elvis called Gladys every day after his date from the previous night left, which often wasn't until the afternoon. She was overwhelmed at her baby's doing radio commercials—she had never dared to even dream of such an honor but was still having a hard time understanding what it meant or where it would lead. Elvis didn't know either, but he dared to let himself begin to dream again.

As Elvis became established in the Memphis club scene, Sam Phillips suggested he consider hiring a manager. Managers then usually did little more than arrange bookings and handle whatever promotional work there might be. Elvis hated talking business because he felt ignorant and incapable. He avoided putting himself in a position of ridicule and preferred to let others deal with contracts, figures, and money matters. Up to now, he had let Sam Phillips handle any business arrangements, but Phillips wasn't a manager. He had a record company to run and couldn't devote himself to Elvis.

More than anyone, it was Vernon who pushed Elvis to find additional business representation, urging him to find someone soon. An attorney might have made the most sense, but southerners have tremendous distrust of lawyers, convinced they are out to use the law to cheat you.

Phillips suggested Elvis and his parents meet with Bob Neal, a Memphis deejay who worked at WMPS. Neal was personable and unthreatening, a good old boy who came across like a friendly uncle. Vernon was unimpressed, but Elvis felt comfortable with Bob's easy-going ways, and Gladys was charmed by his gentle manners. In the autumn of 1954, Elvis turned himself over to Neal, even though he had no prior managing experience. Because Elvis was under age, Vernon and Gladys signed the agreement on his behalf, although neither side opted to have a lawyer present—a move Neal would come to regret.

The first thing on Neal's list of things to do was improve Elvis's image. He believed it was important to project a professional image and to live the part. He took Elvis to a car dealership and traded in his beat-up Cadillac for a brand-new Chevy, bought on credit. Elvis practically lived in the car for the first week—and certainly used it as a bedroom several times, ever mindful to make sure the seats were covered with towels.

Neal had no problem with Elvis's choice of clothes off-stage, but he thought the loud colors and wild patterns distracted from his performing on stage, and he suggested solids. White was too Pat Boone-ish for Elvis, but black suited him and enhanced his dark looks. Wearing all black added an air of brooding mystery that pleased him.

"They're my Outlaw of Love clothes," he laughed. "Women fall for the funniest things."

Elvis gave in to vanity with Bob's approval and had unsightly warts burned off his hands. Vernon thought it was a disgusting waste of money, but Neal defended Elvis, explaining a performer needs to feel confident if he's going to perform his best.

"People were always starin' at my ugly hands when I was singin'," Elvis said, showing me his bandaged hands. He felt good enough about himself to add, "Now, if they could do somethin' about my face."

In addition to playing Memphis clubs, Neal booked Elvis at fairs, store openings, school proms, outdoor concerts, and bars from Tennessee to Kentucky to Mississippi to Louisiana and back. Elvis enjoyed playing up his limited celebrity to the wide-eyed country girls he met at rural bookings.

He was especially attracted to fifteen- and sixteen-year-olds, but not for finding himself a good, simple, and pure steady. He was turned on at the prospect of converting a virgin into a bad girl. His obvious vulnerability attracted women, but he resisted letting anyone in. Like a sailor visiting foreign ports, Elvis left a trail of one-night stands in his wake.

Being the center of attention fed Elvis's fragile ego but caused its share of problems as well. More than once, his flirting got him into hot water and put him on dangerous ground. At one outdoor concert put on in conjunction with the opening of a new movie theater, Elvis flirted blatantly with a buxom blonde. He had never forgotten the advice he'd gotten way back at the Mississippi/Alabama State Fair—pick out someone and sing to them and pretend there's no one else in the room.

Later on, at a nearby bar, Elvis and his musicians were relaxing with a beer when a tense, hard-bodied farmer walked up to Elvis and grabbed his collar. His breath smelled of home-grown liquor as he leaned down.

"You got no right messin' with my girlfriend like that."

Elvis tried pushing his hand away. "Get offa me. I ain't messin' with no one."

"Not here, before. She ain't stopped talking about the way *you* sang to *her* since this afternoon. I can't for the life of me figure out what she sees in some funny-looking, skinny runt like you. Must of been too much sun."

Elvis wasn't one to back down from a fight, but this country boy was too big and strong to fool with.

"It's a trick—I jus' *look* like I'm singin' to 'em, but I ain't. I wouldn't know who your girlfrien' is even if she'd walk in right now. Maybe you should stop *her* from lookin' and talkin' 'bout other men 'sides yourself."

The farmer slowly straightened up, swayed as much by Elvis's down-home accent as his twisted logic. He let go but wasn't willing to skulk away.

"You leave my woman t'me, and you better watch yourself, regardless."

As soon as he walked out the door, Elvis let out a relieved sigh, and his drinking buddies broke into shouts of teasing laughter.

"That was a close one," Elvis admitted, smoothing out his crumpled shirt. "I guess you gotta watch women comin' and goin'."

"Ol' Bob would've turned pasty if we'd brought you back stitched up like a quilt."

"Forget Bob, it's my mama you gotta worry 'bout."

Other encounters weren't so easy. One afternoon at a country bar in Mississippi, Elvis cozied up to a woman who brazenly brushed his thigh with her fingertips under the table. He was fired up, but she teased him by wanting to finish her drink before leaving. Like a lot of women he met, she was attracted to the performer, with little interest in the man. Elvis resented it, even if he was using them in a similar way—but not enough to walk away. He'd get even later when they were alone.

She finally finished her drink, and as they got up to leave, an irate man grabbed her from behind and spun her around. When Elvis reached out for her, the man reared back and took a swing at Elvis.

"You son of a bitch, keep your filthy hands off my wife."

Elvis ducked and the punch grazed the side of his head. The man plowed into Elvis and they went flying over tables, arms flying about wildly, trying to land a blow. A crowd formed, urging them on, drowning out the pleading screams of the owner to stop. A bouncer finally pulled them apart and pulled Elvis to a far corner. His hair was everywhere, he had a bloody nose and was winded, but other than that, he was fine.

The bouncer poked him in the chest. "Ain't right to fool with Jimmy's wife."

"How was I s'posed to know she was married? She came on t'me, rubbin' me up with her hand."

"Shut up. A man's gotta protect what's his. Now who's gonna pay for the broken tables?"

"He started it, let him pay for it."

The bouncer shook his head. "I guess we'll let the sheriff figure it out. 'Course, fighting's against the law. I wouldn't be surprised if he threw the botha you in jail."

Elvis was familiar with country justice and knew he was beat. He reached in his pocket but only had a few dollars. "I'll pay, if I can call someone. I don' want no hard feelin's. I really didn' know she was married."

After his performance that night, Elvis insisted they leave for home right away. He was not interested in staying one more night in the area, half afraid the husband would come gunning for him. He was finding out the hard way that fame and notoriety had some down sides, and you had to be careful of angry boyfriends, jealous husbands, or plucky red-necks who'd love to prove you weren't anything special and bring you down a notch. Even among aquaintances back home, he sensed that very few people seemed genuinely happy for him. Instead, they seemed poised for him to fail. It was hard to completely enjoy any measure of success when you're always looking over your shoulder.

The only people he trusted, other than his family, were his audiences. When they clapped and whistled in appreciation of his music, *of him*, he found incentive in their acceptance and love.

Other incidents gnawed at Elvis. By January of 1955, his second record, "Good Rockin' Tonight," with "I Don't Care If the Sun Don't Shine" on the flip side, was released, with only modest success. The cool reception to his follow-up single chipped away at Elvis's confidence, and chilled his heart. He sank into a mild depression, worried he was stuck in quicksand.

"Bob keeps sayin' it takes a long time to make a name for yourself," he said in an exasperated voice, "but this is takin' forever and I don' have that kinda time.

"If I can only make 'nough money to get us our own home, that's all I want."

Personal appearances were still hit or miss. Elvis and his group, which now included a drummer, D.J. Fontana, were mostly a curiosity to the club patrons who preferred blue grass to the blues. Sometimes the curiosity wore off quickly. At the Lakecliff Club, the house had been packed when the combo started their set—and by the end, they were playing to a nearly deserted audience. The owner was so upset, he told them to skip their second set and clear out before they put him out of business for good.

A newspaper interview arranged by Neal with *The Memphis Press Scimitar* turned into another painful lesson of the price paid for being out there in the public eye. Had he been more savvy he would have coached Elvis, but Neal was too trusting and unknowledgeable, and the results were disastrous.

Elvis was nervous and eager to please the reporter assigned to write the interview by answering each question as honestly as he could. He was especially open about his mama. She was the number-one girl in his life, and he was dedicating his career to her. He thought she'd be delighted to see her name in the paper.

The article that came out was a small, uncomplimentary piece, with a mocking undercurrent. In the space of a few paragraphs the writer called Elvis a hillbilly cat, the Tennessee Tornado, the Memphis Flash, and Mrs. Presley's son. He poked fun at Elvis's closeness to his mama, implying he was a mama's boy, and insinuated Elvis was talented but simple.

The article shocked and stung Elvis. He took out his hurt on Bob.

"You shoulda never let me do that. I ain't *ever* talkin' to any more newspapers again. What'd I ever to do him? Or Mama? She's so upset she refuses to go outside. It hurt her to the bone."

"Elvis, sometimes writers take cheap shots to make a name for themselves. But it's just his opinion. Half the people who read it won't remember it by next week."

"What'd I do to make him treat me this way?"

"You can't take everything so hard or you'll make yourself crazy."

"It's not your mama that's cryin' all night," Elvis said in a weary voice. "If this is what bein' a singer means, I don' know—"

Elvis lost confidence in Neal after that, especially since his career had once again stalled. Despite his belief in Elvis's talent and sincere intentions, Neal was hampered by his lack of experience and limited time, as he was still a full-time deejay. Neal sensed Elvis's frustration and felt under intense pressure to do something dramatic, set ambitious new wheels in motion.

In March of 1955, Bob Neal took Elvis to New York to audition for Arthur Godfrey's *Talent Scouts* show, thinking it was a good way to get Elvis some much-desired national exposure. Bob took vacation time to drive up north with Elvis, who hated New York on sight. Too many people, moving too fast, paying too little attention to whether they knocked you over or not.

The production assistants running the rehearsals were brusque, rude, and talked too quickly. Elvis got flustered and gave a sub-par, awkward performance. Once again he was turned down, and once again he was discouraged—but not bitter. He had no use for New Yorkers, and their approval didn't matter to him then or later.

"New Yorkers're worse than the Opry," Elvis said. "They barely let me finish. You'da thought they were late for dinner. Can't imagine why anyone'd wanna waste their time in a place like that."

Still, Elvis was tired of playing the same clubs and worried Sam Phillips would lose interest. He was anxious to find new momentum but protected himself from disappointment by downplaying the importance of a singing career.

"Sometimes I wish I was back at Crown. If it weren't for Mama, I'd stop now."

"You don't want to stop singing," I said.

"I *can't* stop singin'. I once said somethin' to Mama 'bout it, and she looked so upset and worried—I can't disappoint her like that. She'd think I was a quitter. I couldn't live with that."

Elvis continued playing clubs, outdoor parks, fairs, and anything else Neal could find—and made a decent, if exhausting, living. As more people accepted his style, Elvis developed a small following, and began to recognize some of his more ardent fans, but paid little attention to the men in his audience. If he had, he might have noticed a heavy-set man who had taken a particular interest in his career.

Colonel Tom Parker had followed Elvis for months, but hardly considered himself a fan. He took care to stay in the clubs' dark shadows, not wanting to tip his hand too soon. Parker had made a modest name for himself managing Eddie Arnold, but was anxious to *make* a star, create a lasting place for himself in music history. He was a man who craved wealth and the trappings of success.

He was also a man who wasn't all he seemed. First, he wasn't a colonel, nor was his real name Tom Parker, nor was he even American. He was a clever, ambitious man who guarded his secrets closely while evading the Immigration Service and fulfilling his dream of being rich and famous—two goals seemingly at odds.

His time with Eddie Arnold and the measure of success they shared merely whetted his appetite. In Elvis, he saw a feast—a man who projected an ambiguous sexuality that if properly handled could draw both men and women. He viewed Elvis as a commodity to market and had put together a plan to do just that. He saw vividly what Sam Phillips and Bob Neal had both missed and knew he could catapult Elvis the way neither of them ever could.

Parker was smart enough to know how close-knit southern families were and was well aware of Elvis's special attachment to his mama—he'd done his homework. With them on his side, Elvis would be a snap.

Parker introduced himself to Vernon and Gladys at an upscale club. Gladys still refused to go to a bar, calling it distasteful for proper ladies, but clubs were another matter. She enjoyed the ladylike, colorful drinks and never got tired of watching Elvis sing. Vernon could take or leave the music but enjoyed the company of lively people—not to mention lovely ladies.

Parker came on very low-key, not wanting to scare them off with a hard-sell job. Vernon immediately took to the Colonel because they spoke the same language—money—and were both schemers. Where Parker plotted for wealth and success, Vernon devoted his energy toward avoiding work. Different goals, similar personalities.

When Parker shook Gladys's hand, her skin crawled at his touch. She distrusted his beady, cold eyes and didn't believe his warm words about Elvis. She instinctively knew Parker was a man who cared only for himself, and she was irritated at Vernon for being so friendly.

Parker waited until Vernon asked before revealing his profession. Vernon wasted no time in seeking out Parker's advice, and the Colonel skillfully steered Vernon into his back pocket.

"That boy of yours is just a few months away from being a big star—it must be very exciting."

"It was at first. Things are s'posed to be movin', but who knows. We'll prob'ly be sitting here five years from now."

"Not if you're willing to think big. If you keep thinkin' small, you'll stay small."

"That's what I keep tellin' him, but he don' listen. That manager got 'im all messed up."

"Vernon, Bob's doin' all he can. He's worked hard for Elvis."

Vernon grunted.

Parker casually mentioned he was in Memphis scouting new talent and setting up interviews with prospective clients. He hesitantly admitted he was so impressed with Elvis, he had already arranged to meet with Bob Neal and Sam Phillips to offer his services as a consultant. By the time Vernon introduced Elvis to Parker when he joined their table, Vernon was sold. Parker said hello briefly, then excused himself, saying he had another act to catch cross town.

Vernon was shocked that Elvis had no idea who Parker was.

"Daddy, I let Bob handle business and jus' show up where and when he tells me. That's why I'm payin' him fifteen percent."

"Ain't no way to run a career, boy. But maybe for once, Bob did somethin' right. Mr. Parker knows what *he's* doin'. Bob might learn a thing or two."

Elvis didn't admit it, but he wasn't too happy with Bob either. At this point, he was frustrated enough to consider almost anything, even paying for a consultant, whatever *that* was, although he didn't expect much to come from it. People were always promising things but seldom came through.

Parker came aboard as an advisor and was a pleasant surprise. He backed up his professed interest in Elvis with time and suggestions, many of which grated Bob Neal to no end. On the Colonel's strong recommendation, Elvis severed his association with the Louisiana Hayride, Bob's biggest coup, because the weekly drive was too time-consuming for a paycheck that was way too small. Bob was infuriated and turned to Elvis for support, but Elvis refused to get involved, partly because he figured he was paying them to handle business and partly because he was secretly relieved.

Elvis was tired of packing his car up for the same trip every weekend, but more than that, there was the little matter of an affair with a certain young lady that had gotten more serious than Elvis ever intended. She wasn't like the other girls he'd met who cruised the bars or hung around after performances. This girl he wouldn't have met at all if he hadn't driven by as she was on her way home. He recognized her from the audience and pulled over. They talked at the side of the road, Elvis attracted to her clean prettiness. She good-naturedly rebuffed his flirting but finally let him take her out for a burger. Although the evening ended with passionate kissing and touching, she refused to sleep with him that first weekend—but her smile held a seductive promise.

When they met up the following week, she wanted him as much as he wanted her. Except for his performance and calling Gladys, they spent all day in bed, making love and talking. Elvis was touched by her honesty and loneliness. She was older than him by a year and very unhappy at home, where she was stuck taking care of her younger brothers and sisters most of the time while her parents played cards with drinking buddies. To get time for herself, she'd lie and say she was visiting friends in a nearby town, although she usually took a bus to Memphis by herself and see a movie or just window shop. She thought most of the guys in her town crude bores and hadn't found anyone she'd want to wake up with every morning.

Elvis had never met anyone like her, so sweet and so passionate. He felt a kinship with her and even let himself feel warmth, but the very fact that she desired Elvis enough to sleep with him was a strike against her in the good, simple, and pure department. Also holding him back from becoming involved was his driving ambition. He didn't want any entanglements, because he was convinced it would hinder his budding career. He assumed she knew he was just passing through and thought they had an understanding. Elvis realized his mistake the night she told him she thought she was pregnant.

"You tol' me it was the wrong time o'the month for that," Elvis said in exasperation.

"I guess I was wrong. I'm not positive, but I'm hardly ever late. If you were so concerned, you shoulda used a rubber." She smiled, snuggling against him in his car, where they had just made love, parked down the street from her house. Elvis enjoyed the urgency and risk of having sex in a public place, but her announcement shattered his reverie.

Elvis was in a state of disbelief—he had never anticipated this—and gave a little laugh. She kissed him and held him tight, while he could only say, Oh, baby. She mistook his shocked expression and frozen smile for joy and climbed out of the car excited and happy. Elvis drove to his hotel, trying to figure out what to do, but the thoughts muddled in his head. What would Mama say . . . it'd kill her . . . why now . . . how could he support two more mouths . . . how could he keep singing . . . why did bad things *always* happen to him?

Elvis didn't answer his phone at all the next day and tried avoiding her after his performance the following night by slipping out the back. She was waiting for him, angry and crying, at his motel door when he finally got there, the smell of cheap perfume clinging to him.

Her tears softened him up and he comforted her until she wanted to know if he didn't want to marry her; then he panicked all over again.

"You gotta be crazy—I don' wanna get married. I *can't.*"

"You said you loved me," she wailed. "What am I s'posed to do about our baby?"

"You're not sure you are pregnant." Elvis pushed her away with a hard set to his face. " 'Sides, how would I even know it's *our* baby? If you whore around with me, Lord knows who else you whore around with when I ain't here. It could be anybody's kid, and I ain't takin' the rap for it."

She walked up to Elvis and slapped him hard across the face.

"My daddy always tol' me not to get involved with trash. I should have listened."

Fear and anger and panic boiled over. He grabbed her arm and dragged her to the door.

"At least I ain't no whore. You prob'ly ain't pregnant at all, jus' usin' it as an excuse to get me t'marry you. I'm sicka lyin', cheatin' women. Get the hell outta here."

He slammed the door behind her and turned the radio up full blast to drown out her crying outside the door. He hated himself for making her cry, but what else could he do? He couldn't stop now, not when he was so close. He lay on the bed with the pillow over his face, tears wetting the coarse cotton. He'd come so far and hadn't gone anywhere. He was still screwing up every way he turned.

He hadn't heard from her again, and more than once

he had to resist the urge to drive by her house. He wondered if she had been pregnant but was too afraid to find out. He justified his actions by convincing himself that she was just trying to use him to get away from her family. Elvis breathed a deep sigh of relief when his stint at the Louisiana Hayride was history.

Through his connections, Parker arranged bookings for Elvis at larger venues in the South, including an eight-day tour in Texas with Ferlin Husky. All the while, Parker was doing just enough to propel Elvis along, but keeping his full plan a secret. He wasn't about to share in the ultimate success with anyone. He was content to bide his time.

Thanks to Parker, Elvis's third single, "Baby, Let's Play House," was his first record to make the national country charts. Everybody celebrated the breakthrough, but the festivities were strained—there were too many cooks in the kitchen. The Colonel and Neal disagreed on virtually everything—where Elvis should be playing, what songs he should be singing, and most of all, what label he should be on.

Parker confided in Vernon with a shrug. "I'm trying to help the kid, but Neal's tying my hands. Tell Elvis I'll do my best, but I don't think I can do anything more for him at this rate. Getting on the national charts isn't that tough—but staying there is. I'd hate for Elvis to be a flash-in-the-pan because of an ignorant manager."

By the look of panic on Vernon's face, the Colonel knew it was time to make his next move. A shrewd businessman, Parker took Elvis, Gladys, and Vernon to a classy restaurant, tasteful but not too expensive—he didn't want to come across as extravagant. Just cultured. An expert name-dropper, he impressed them with stories about the likes of Carl Perkins, Hank Williams, and Jerry Lee Lewis. After dessert, Parker finally put his cards on the table. During his time with Arnold, he'd been able to develop solid national contacts. He knew how to deal with record companies and promised Elvis he could have him signed with a top label in a matter of weeks, because he knew the ins and outs of contract law and was personal friends with many music industry executives. He convinced them his contacts and knowledge of the way big business was played were two assets invaluable to a struggling performer like Elvis. He told them in a chilling voice that the difference between him and Bob Neal was the difference between success and failure, security or the return to poverty. Parker played on Elvis's most profound fears, and they proved to be his trump cards.

Back home, the Presleys had a long family conference. Vernon was all for Parker and said they never should have gone with Bob in the first place. Gladys was unable to explain her strong mistrust of Parker to Elvis, who wasn't a hundred percent sure himself. Change always filled Elvis with anxiety, and in this case, loyalties clouded the issue even more.

"I don' wanna be disrespectful to Bob or Mr. Phillips. I can't forget 'bout them."

"He's right, Vernon," Gladys agreed. "And at least we know we can trust Bob and Sam."

"It's about business, Mama, not who's likable. Son, Bob'll understand, he won't stand in your way. He did what he could, now it's time to move on. You'd be makin' a big mistake not givin' Parker a chance."

"But he also talked about droppin' Sun. I don' think I can do that to Mr. Phillips."

The discussion raged for hours, back and forth, a tortured process for Elvis, who wanted to do what was right but was driven by the desire to be *somebody*. When Vernon brought up legal and money matters, what it would take to buy out his Sun contract, Elvis threw himself down on the couch with disgust.

"I wish I understood half of what was going on."

"Which is why you *need* someone like Parker. He's the big time. None of us here are capable of handlin' it, but *he is*. And don't you forget it."

It was one of the few times Elvis let Vernon get so

involved in a decision, and Vernon finally convinced Elvis to make a change.

"I don't wanna keep playin' the same clubs for the next twenty years, Mama. I wanna see if I can do it, make somethin' of myself."

Vernon smiled. "Awright, then. I'll call Parker right now and tell 'im—then we'll call Bob."

Elvis met me later for a milkshake and some fries. He was still troubled by his decision and the uncertainty of it.

"I don't know if I'm doin' the right thing. Colonel Parker says I can make it really big, but to do that, I gotta leave Sun for a bigger record company. I feel worse 'bout that than I do for Bob. If it weren't for Mr. Phillips, I'd still be drivin' a truck.

"It's funny. I love singin', and when I'm up on stage, it feels *so* good, you can feel the good feelin' people are givin', but the rest of it can make you feel pretty bad."

Elvis signed with Parker, and within a few months the Colonel swung the deal that saw RCA buy out the remaining year of Elvis's Sun contract for $35,000—with a $5,000 bonus going to Elvis. He showed me the check and we just stared at it.

The money gave Elvis the freedom to start enjoying some luxuries—like buying his first complete outfit at Lansky Brothers and taking girls out on a fancy date. Some of his big nights out were disappointing. After trying two or three of Memphis's highly touted restaurants, Elvis decided he preferred the taste of *real* food served by people who didn't look down their noses at you if you used the wrong fork. He'd still take a girl to a nice place to impress her, but on his way home in the wee hours of the morning, he'd stop at an all-night diner for a greasy cheeseburger.

Elvis was most excited about the gift he got for all of them: He rented a furnished house on Getwell Drive and moved his family into their first real home. Gladys was so overwhelmed she got flushed and felt faint.

"Maybe we ought to go back t'other place," Elvis teased her.

In response, Gladys hugged Elvis for dear life, soaking his shirt with her tears. Even Vernon was misty-eyed when he walked into a clean-smelling, brightly lit, modest home in a neighborhood that had grass and trees. They were like kids let loose in a toy store, wide-eyed and unable to believe their good fortune. Elvis especially. But beneath the giddiness he felt an occasional flash of worry. For the first time in his life, Elvis actually had something to lose. It made him even more determined to work hard and do everything Parker said—after all, he had arranged for the bonus in the first place.

Vernon thought Parker was a gift from God, a wise sage who would lead them to the promised land of riches. Even sitting in her new home, Gladys still thought Parker was a hustler and someone to keep an eye on. Not even the gifts he continually sent her helped diminish her unease. Elvis didn't have strong feelings about him one way or another, he was just glad to have someone to handle confusing business matters and who could make him money.

"Hey, I'll stick with anyone who makes me rich."

Partly because of Gladys's dislike of Parker and partly because Elvis himself wasn't totally comfortable with his company, the relationship with Parker stayed very much business. He wasn't invited over for friendly dinners, nor did Elvis ever consider him a buddy. The only one who went out of his way to be chummy was Vernon, which was another strike against Parker as far as Elvis was concerned. But the bottom line was business—Elvis wanted to be famous and he wanted to have money, and he'd do almost anything to get that.

Elvis drove around town in his car like he owned the streets. He wanted to show off his good fortune to everyone he had ever felt insignificant next to, except it still didn't make him any more secure inside. But initially at least, it gave him pleasure to think he had something over other people. It made him feel like a big shot. And to cover his fear of losing that edge, he adopted a cocky demeanor.

Except around Gladys. He now knew she wouldn't tolerate a smart mouth or patronizing attitude no matter how much money he had in the bank, so at home, he was the same old Elvis. But when he was out, he became a swaggering Mr. Cool. When Gladys saw this side of him in performance, her face crinkled in concern and her hands worried the hem of her dress.

"It's all Parker's doin'," she told Vernon. "Elvis never acted like that before."

"Leave 'im be, Mama. Performers got to play to their audience," Vernon said, echoing Parker.

Parker *had* told Elvis he needed to sharpen his stage presence and develop an image, and to play up his sexuality and make both the men and women in the audience want him.

The erotic reference to men shocked Elvis, but it intrigued him at the same time. He'd never felt comfortable around men and had only begun to feel comfortable around women when he learned to "overpower" them with sex. The idea that he could control men the same way had never occurred to him, until Parker brought it up. Not by sleeping with them but by *daring* them not to notice his sexual smolder. And he found the thought of being wanted by a man oddly erotic, and it made him feel powerful and superior.

The only problem was that Elvis felt uncomfortable acting this out in front of his mama, so he began to gently discourage her from attending his performances at the nicer clubs, which were the only ones she'd attend.

"It's jus' the same ol' songs, again, Mama. 'Sides, I gotta talk to some businesspeople Parker's bringin', so I wouldn' be able to sit with you at all."

Gladys resisted at first, complaining that it was the only time she got to see him.

"I know, but I wanna keep us goin', don' I? It's jus'

for now. Once things get goin' good, we'll have lots of time together.''

Elvis did work hard at clubs and on the road dates Parker arranged, preparing for his first record with his new label. He couldn't afford any disasters—he might only get one chance, and if he blew it, he'd lose it all. The family was solely his responsibility. Since his signing and getting the bonus, both his parents quit working, citing health reasons, so the pressure was on.

It had only been a little more than two years since he had graduated from high school and started driving a truck, but it seemed a lifetime ago. Time had passed in a flash, with the nights on the road and in the clubs with the dozens of faceless women merging together into an indistinct flurry of images.

So much had changed in such a short period of time. Here he was on the verge of realizing a dream, and yet when he was alone, an unexplained melancholy would come over him. Sometimes he wondered about Dixie, hoping she knew what she was missing. But even that wish of measured revenge left him more empty than satisfied.

He felt curiously removed from a lot of the whirl-wind surrounding him, except when he was on stage performing. It wasn't just singing he loved—it was singing *for* someone. Even during rehearsals, he played to his musicians or whoever happened to be around. He fed off the response like a junkie off his fix.

Two years earlier, he'd thought that if he could make enough money singing so that his mama wouldn't have to work and they could move to a nicer place, he'd be happy. Success was supposed to change you and solve problems. But despite everything he'd achieved, he still felt the same inside. Sure, he was pleased and enjoyed the attention and notoriety, but when he was quiet and alone, he still felt an ache. An emptiness. He just hadn't accomplished *enough*. So he set his sights on making more money and being famous everywhere in the country, not just his region of the South. He was convinced *that* would make him happy and content.

He was counting on Parker to work his magic—that's why he was paying him almost half of what he was earning. Elvis was so busy looking ahead he was missing out on the present.

8

In January of 1956, after a lot of persuasive campaigning by Parker, *Cashbox* named Elvis the best new country and western artist of 1955. That same month, his first RCA single, "Heartbreak Hotel," zoomed to number one. Within a matter of a few weeks all hell broke loose, and the life he'd known before was gone forever.

A whirlwind of activity suddenly surrounded Elvis as the record company cranked the publicity machine into high gear to cash in on the popularity of "Heartbreak Hotel." While fans of all ages flocked to buy his records, he was a particular hit among teenagers and young adults—just as Parker had foreseen.

Parker had the instincts of a gambler and recognized that Elvis's career had stalled in the Memphis clubs and southern countryside simply because he was playing for the wrong audience. The Colonel kept his hunch to himself and continued the charade while Neal and Phillips were still actively involved. He knew Elvis would have a limited and brief career if he didn't break out in a drastically new direction, and he waited for the perfect time to launch his plan.

Elvis was neither true country nor a contemporary of the Doris Day-Eddie Fisher-Pat Boone style of music. He was a kid who spoke directly to his peers, and youth was the wave of the future. Others would come around in time, but it was the teens and just-out-of-teens that would usher Elvis in on a throne, due to more than sheer talent.

The fifties had been a decade of conservatism and repression. Uniformity and not rocking the boat were ideals to live by, but the social claustrophobia such a structured climate caused had the restless young in the country looking for their own identity. An identity as far removed from "I like Ike" as they could find. Someone like Elvis, whose unique singing and dancing style, tailored hair and bad-boy sexuality oozed rebellion and a break from the mundane. Elvis blew in on a breath of fresh air, and Parker was there to meet him and market him for all he was worth.

Elvis was an overnight sensation for most of the country and tumbled into the spotlight hardly prepared for its glare. Photo sessions were set up, and Elvis posed for hours under hot lights, trying to smolder for the camera on cue. Even though he was the music world's newest sensation, Elvis was intimidated by the impatient photographers who took roll after roll while Elvis tried to relax enough to get it right. He covered his nervousness with jokes and banter, but kept his shaking hands in his pockets. He finally asked for a radio to be turned on, and with music as his guide, he was able to strike the poses and catch the look.

Label publicists sat with Elvis trying to hammer out an acceptable, antiseptic biography. Vernon and Gladys were particularly worried that Vernon's unsavory past would surface, forcing Elvis to reluctantly confide in Parker about his family's prior troubles. The Colonel assured Elvis nobody would find out and filed it away for his own future use.

With requests for print interviews and TV appearances flooding in, Parker gave Elvis a crash course in how to meet the press and public. Whenever possible, he got a publication to agree to submit their questions first so he could coach Elvis on the answers. When a particular magazine or newspaper wouldn't agree, Parker would carefully remind Elvis to think over the question twice, speak slowly, but be friendly. To make sure all went smoothly, Parker hovered nearby, ready to interrupt if the direction of the interview took a dangerous turn. Elvis was grateful for Parker's protection and accepted the unspoken conclusion that without the Colonel, he would be lost.

Parker cleverly encouraged that dependency by playing on Elvis's obvious insecurities. He would explain a business matter or performance agreement in the most technical of terms, knowing full well it was confusing the hell out of him. When Elvis didn't understand, Parker would pat him on the back and tell him not to worry about it.

"I know it's too complicated for you—just let me handle it. You take care of the singing."

It's one thing not to like business matters, but it's another to be made to feel you're too ignorant to ever possibly understand. It made Elvis feel incapable, like a dumb little kid, which further eroded his already fragile self-confidence. Frustrated and convinced he'd never be smart enough to understand the business end of his career, he stopped trying. He turned it over to Parker completely, saying he didn't even want to hear any of it.

Instead, he immersed himself in the luxurious feeling of popularity and the excitement of being wanted by *everybody*— newspapers, magazines, national TV shows, even fancy nightclubs in Las Vegas. He fed off this public outpouring, especially from the fans who started surrounding him when he went out. Through it all, though, the best feeling was still being up on stage, singing to his people and basking in the love they sent back.

The Colonel understood media and he understood crowds. Newspapers were more apt to give preferential coverage to someone who created the biggest stir. Elvis's performances quickly gained notoriety after the release of "Heartbreak Hotel," because of the near-hysteria he caused among his fans. Parker ensured early crowd reaction by paying dozens of young girls money to start the screaming that would spread like wildfire through the audience.

Mob psychology is fascinating and predictable. Get one group yelling and pushing their way to the front, and everybody gets caught up in the swell. It wasn't honest, but it was brilliant strategy. Which is why Vernon swore me to secrecy.

"Elvis jus' don' understand business and he'd take it the wrong way. So'd his mama. But make no mistake, the Colonel knows jus' what he's doin'."

More than his singing, the Colonel was marketing Elvis's sensuality, which stirred the dormant fifties libido. His eyes held the promise of ecstasy, but at the same time, the vulnerability that was Elvis still shone through. The combination was irresistible. He was a consummate stage performer, and every member of that audience, man and woman, felt he was reaching out just to them. And they reached back.

Gladys was appalled at Elvis's provocative image and the reaction it caused. Even if she didn't see him perform much anymore, she was aware of the girls who were following him around, eyeing him with blatant invitation.

"They ain't got an ounce 'a shame, carryin' on like that in fronta him. It ain't decent," she said in disgust. "And it jus' ain't like Elvis, payin' attention t'trash like that. It's all Parker's doin'."

While Elvis left his image at the door when he was home, Gladys could still sense a change in him. There was a jauntiness she found troubling, because she associated it with insincerity. She dreaded the thought of Elvis turning into one of those smooth-talking musicmen with the shifty eyes. Like Parker. She was grateful for Elvis's sudden, mind-boggling success, but was afraid he had made a deal with the devil to get it.

She would have been convinced had she known what Elvis did when he was away from her on the road. The higher his song went on the national Top 40 charts, the bigger the selection of women. Even though Elvis was drawn to classy, sophisticated women, they were too intimidating to pursue. Instead, he turned his attention to the barflies and groupies, easy marks who were more open to suggestions, whether it be having sex in the car while parked on a public street or sharing his bed with another woman. Elvis first discovered the thrill of sleeping with two women while on tour in Texas and tried to repeat the experience any chance he got. It was exciting being watched by a third person and a turn-on to watch the two women together. It made him feel very aroused and very superior.

Parker didn't care about Elvis's sexual habits as long as he was discreet, but he disapproved of Elvis drawing attention to himself by staying in seedy areas.

"You're a star now. People are watching, so you need to *act* like a star," Parker warned. "Put up a good front in public, and you'll be free to do what you want in private. Just don't mix them up."

That was only one of his dual lives. The other was at home, where he was still under Gladys's watchful eye. The transformation from a sexy, libidinous singing star on the road to a mama's boy at home was stressful. At times he resented Gladys's constant supervision and questions, wishing for the freedom he felt away from her. But as soon as he entertained thoughts of being on his own, he was overcome by a stabbing guilt. How could he even consider shutting his mama out after all she'd sacrificed for him? So at home he reverted back to the dutiful son and kept his other life tucked away like a secret diary.

Elvis wasn't the only one with separate lives. Parker had been many things before re-creating himself as a music manager. The Colonel kept his past very much to himself, always fearful that the authorities might one day catch up with him.

Parker had been born Dries Van Kuijk in Breda, Holland. As a young man, Dries worked first as a dog catcher, then later as a barker for his uncle's traveling carnival. He found life on the road tiresome and entertained himself by hanging out with the freaks the carnival employed. He got a sort of malicious pleasure from the horrified looks of the townspeople when they saw him and his band of natural wonders strolling the streets. Seeing that the carny's life held little opportunity for advancement, Parker stowed away to America and entered the country illegally. He adopted the title and name of Colonel Tom Parker and set out to learn the music industry, where money was readily available for those clever enough to take it.

Parker had a genuine knack for promotion and management and slowly built a reputation, first with a number of smaller performers, then with bigger names like Eddie Arnold. As he became more established, he spent considerable time plotting to stay one step ahead of the Immigration Service; he never owned a credit card, bought everything with cash, overpaid his taxes so the IRS would have no reason to audit him, and he absolutely never left the United States. With no passport, he'd never get back in.

He was a compulsive conniver—perfect for wheeling and dealing with record companies, but dangerous on an individual level. Even though Bob Neal had a contract that ran until March of 1956, he had been dumped months before and got no share of the RCA money. As soon as Parker took over with Vernon and Elvis's blessing, Neal was history and knew better than to try and fight it. Parker could be vicious, and Bob Neal simply didn't have the stomach for it, which is why they each reached the respective level of success they did.

Ultimately, Elvis wouldn't stand a chance against Parker, either, but in the beginning all anyone could see was a future paved in gold as greed fueled ambition. Only one person silently prayed for things to slow down.

Gladys sensed Elvis was heading down a dangerous path, and the urge to hover over him was stronger than ever. She was honest enough to admit she wasn't smart enough to go head to head with big businessmen— neither was Elvis. They were suddenly at the mercy of strangers, and it scared her.

Gladys also resented having to share Elvis with so many others. She was painfully proud of him, but she desperately wanted her little boy back and the time they used to share together. For all the money and clothes and jewelry, she was lonelier and more neglected than she'd ever been in her life. She tried talking to Elvis about it, but he'd get exasperated and short with her, explaining it was *work*. Vernon didn't pay any attention to her, either, and the way he boasted about their money and good fortune smacked of sinful bragging. What none of them realized—not Elvis, not Vernon, not Parker—was that presents and gifts couldn't take the place of affection and time. Gladys's only comfort was the bottle, and she turned to it with a vengeance.

Elvis knew his mama missed his company, but he justified his neglect by telling himself he was doing it all for her. He'd slow down once he made it to the top. Then there'd be plenty of time to relax and spend all the time together she wanted. He saw how lonely she felt, but it wouldn't be forever—she just had to be patient.

Within weeks of bursting on the scene with "Heartbreak Hotel," Elvis was scheduled to appear on his first national TV show, Tommy and Jimmy Dorsey's *The Stage Show.* Instead of being excited, Elvis was apprehensive and reluctant to go.

"I don' do good in places like that," he told Parker, remembering the Opry and Godfrey fiascoes.

Parker patiently explained Elvis didn't need to try out, they were begging to have him on—and paying him for it.

That only relieved some of Elvis's anxieties. Because it was TV, he was very concerned what he would look like.

"On stage I know they're seein' me, but TV makes y'look funny. I don' wanna look like no rube in fronta all those people."

Elvis had wanted to wear one of his more colorful

jackets, but Vernon snatched it out of his hands, angering Elvis.

"Don' be grabbin' at my things. That jacket cost a lot of money."

"Then you wasted a lot of money. Looks like somethin' you'd wear in a circus."

"That's the style—ain't nothin' wrong with it."

"If you wear it on television you're gonna look like a clown. Parker says to wear black. You'll look better."

"Then let Parker tell me himself. He don' need to be sendin' messages through you."

"Elvis, watch your tongue," Gladys said unsteadily. "I can't stand all this bickerin'."

"Sorry, Mama, I'm jus' gettin' tired of bein' tol' what t'do 'bout ever'thing. I can' even wear what clothes I want."

Vernon tossed the jacket at Elvis. "Take it up with Parker, I'm only tellin' you what he said."

Elvis hung his jacket back up, a scowl lining his face. He was of a mind to do just that, go talk to Parker . . . but the urge faded quickly. Things were moving so well and so fast, it was hard to justify arguing with the Colonel. Besides, Parker always made him feel so stupid—it wasn't worth the effort.

Even though his appearance on *Stage Show* was well received, New York succeeded in taking some of the wind out of Elvis's sails.

"It's so big and people push right by you—nobody's friendly at all. Hell, if you say hello, they act like you're crazy. Can't find a decent cheeseburger in any of those restaurants, either."

Elvis was nervous and antsy in New York, uncomfortable with the cosmopolitan people and desperately homesick. This was one road he didn't want to stay on. He called Gladys every night, keeping her on the phone far longer than he did when he and his combo were playing the dusty clubs of the South. He was a fish out of water in New York and was convinced people were secretly making fun of him.

"If I hear one more person talk about my 'cute' accent, I'm gonna pop 'em," he said angrily. "Sometimes they'll play at bein' from the South, then laugh like it's funny. They know how to make you feel like dirt real quick."

Elvis was angrier at some reporters in a press conference who accused him of corrupting the morals of the nation's youth with his suggestive stage gyrations.

"It's not on purpose, that's just the way I sing best. I gotta feel the music ever'where. It's jus' singin', and that don' hurt anyone.

"As soon as kids get old 'nough, they'll settle down and start listenin' to other singers. I'm not doin' anything wrong . . . they just like my music."

Except for the actual act of singing, he enjoyed talking to the fans the best, signing autographs and posing for pictures with the "regular" people who loved him and his music. But the industry people he met made him feel inconsequential, and he disliked them for it. In public, Elvis buried his resentments and was gracious, accommodating, and polite, but back at the hotel he'd sulk. He knew he should be eternally grateful for being in this position, but success still didn't feel the way it was supposed to.

Elvis was expert at hiding his true emotions, particularly around people in authority. He'd swallow his bile and be a good boy to their face, then rage and sputter when they left. He was simply repeating and perfecting the way he had dealt with Vernon over the years.

In the spring of '56, Parker arranged for Elvis to appear in Las Vegas at the New Frontier Hotel. Even though he'd been traveling over a solid year, Las Vegas was something more than just another road show. It was the Big Time, the show place of the world where major performers showed off their talent. It told Elvis he had truly arrived, and scared him to death. Typically, his defense mechanisms transformed his excitement into complaints and worry. If he expected the worst, he wouldn't be disappointed when it happened.

"If I screwed up b'fore, I only had to worry 'bout the audience throwin' things at me. Now I gotta worry 'bout what the papers will say and whether I'll ever get to go on TV again," Elvis complained.

"I thought it was s'posed to get easier but it's gettin' worse. I hate havin' to read what people write 'bout me. I jus' *hate* it."

Las Vegas unsettled Elvis, but in a different way than New York had. At night Vegas was a spectacle to behold, but in the day it was run down, faded by the blistering sun, a mirage of an oasis.

Elvis was the new kid on the strip and hated the familiar feeling of being on the outside looking in. Not that the other performers he met weren't warm, but there was a professional distance, their egos challenged by the phenom. He tensed under their scrutiny as his insecurities bubbled to the surface. He wilted under the examination and retreated into himself and his room.

There was a lot about Vegas that appealed to Elvis and made him feel comfortable. He enjoyed the constant activity of the casinos, filled with people around the clock and the lively sound of money changing hands. The fashions of Vegas—sequined jackets and clingy materials in bright colors—matched his own loud preferences. On a more intimate level, the desert women were a relief after the "snooty" northern ladies of New York, whose class and sophistication had both attracted and intimidated him.

Elvis sneaked out on his own long after Parker assumed he was asleep. Wearing a hat to hide his telltale hair, he cruised the local bars to recharge his sagging batteries, the rowdy nightlife was comforting and familiar. He'd bring one or more women back to his hotel and keep room service jumping with orders of champagne for the ladies and oysters for himself. One night the shouts of pleasure got so loud that the front desk placed a discreet call to Elvis's room and politely asked for him to turn down the "radio." Elvis often had trouble sleeping and being awake at dawn made him melancholy, so the party would end before sunrise. After an all-night romp, he was worn out enough to fall immediately to sleep.

Elvis attracted a large audience at the casino, and although they were less vocal than his teenage fans, it was still a very successful appearance. Among the people watching Elvis with special interest was Hal Wallis, a Hollywood film producer. Wallis knew that many singers had made a successful and profitable transition to film, including Doris Day and Pat Boone. He suspected the camera would love Elvis, with his bedroom eyes and little-boy vulnerability. Wallis intended to be Elvis's ticket to the movies.

Parker greeted Wallis warmly but was noncommittal, letting the producer believe others had already made offers. For as good as Parker was, Wallis was better. He was clever enough and secure enough to let the Colonel believe it was he who had the upper hand. The bottom line was most important to Wallis. After all the lunging and parrying was over, Elvis flew to Los Angeles for a screen test, and was back in Vegas before dinnertime to catch the next train home.

"It's worse than posin' for pictures. There were too many people standin' 'round, and it got me nervous. It was kinda fun, I guess, but I'm sure Mr. Wallis was happy t'see me go. I don' think he could understand what I was sayin'," Elvis laughed.

He was happy to be back in Memphis and put the movies out of his mind, too wrapped up in the pride of buying his family their own home to think of much else. The house was on Audubon Drive, a quiet, middle-class neighborhood with nicely kept lawns; neat, freshly painted homes; and nervous neighbors who greeted the Presleys hesitantly.

Having a famous and controversial singer living next door worried the residents of Audubon Drive, especially when his family appeared to be something straight out of a Ma and Pa Kettle movie. Their first impressions were justified.

Elvis urged Gladys to show me around "her" house,

which was filled with new furniture that didn't match, in colors that hurt the eyes. Her true pride and joy, though, was the flower-trimmed backyard, and she had big plans for it.

"Mama's gonna fill it with chickens," Elvis said, not kidding.

Gladys grabbed Elvis's arm and pointed. "There's room back there for a decent-sized coop, and we can get one of them new egg catchers. Durin' the day they could have the run of the yard. We'll need a rooster, too. Oh, when can we get them, Elvis?"

Gladys loved her new home with all its luxuries, but she was also desperate to hold on to a familiar way of life. It was ignorance, not spite. The thought didn't occur to her that their neighbors might not appreciate being hooted out of bed at dawn by a cock's crowing. Nor did Elvis see anything wrong with having chickens and a rooster in the middle of a city.

"Will y'come with me, Elvis?"

Vernon walked outside. "Now, honey, Elvis has more t'do than gettin' chickens. It'll give you and I somethin' to do."

"I should be cleanin' the house instead of loafin'. It don' feel right."

"I told you, Mama, I'm gonna get us a maid. We can afford it. I don' want you to worry 'bout anything anymore."

Colonel Parker did the worrying for them all. He couldn't tell the Presleys what to do in their own home, but it was his job to avert any public disasters—and with Elvis and his kin, the potential was ever present. It was imperative the whole Presley family be prepared for the demands of success, no matter how inconvenient.

When the Colonel sat them down to give them pointers on dealing with the press, Vernon was amenable, but Gladys resented any intrusion by Parker and her feathers were immediately ruffled.

"If anybody from the papers asks you a question, give short answers—"

"How'm I s'posed to know how many words it'll take me?" Gladys asked.

"He's jus' sayin' not to go on like you do," Vernon said, angering Gladys.

"The Colonel's sayin' I talk too much?"

"Of course not, Gladys," Parker cut in. "Elvis is going to be a huge star, and we all need to help him any way wc can. I know you want to help."

" 'Course, I do, honey." Gladys reached out to Elvis, watching this scene uncomfortably from the doorway.

"I know, Mama."

Parker went on. "Always be prepared to have your picture taken when you're out with Elvis, too. You'll want to look your best whenever you're out, because you never know when a photographer will be nosing around. If one approaches you, smile and let him take the picture."

Gladys sat quietly for the rest of the meeting, but after Parker left, Gladys spoke her mind. "He's a bag of wind."

Vernon looked shocked. "Don't talk that way 'bout the Colonel. He's just tellin' us what's best for Elvis."

Gladys turned around and poked him in the chest with her finger. "I'm sicka hearing how ever'body knows best for Elvis. *I* know what's best for Elvis— I'm his mama."

Her violent reaction caught Vernon by surprise, and he answered quietly. "I mean in business. We need t'listen if we wanna make it easier on the boy."

Gladys sat down and wiped her forehead. "I don't wanna be worryin' every time I answer the door that I gotta be in my Sunday clothes. Or do I?"

"Won't kill you t'be presentable," Vernon said.

Elvis shot his father an angry look, then went over to Gladys and put his arm around her.

"You do whatever you want, Mama. This here's crazy. I don't want you unhappy—the whole reason I'm doin' all this is for you."

"He hates chickens, I could tell he didn' want me to get any," she said sulkily.

"He's from the city and don' understand people like us. And he don' take the time to explain things, either. The Colonel wasn't talkin' 'bout everyday. He just meant like at my performances, or if some writer comes over to talk."

Gladys buried her head on Elvis's shoulder, then took a deep breath. "Well, if that's all he meant, I can do that. I wanna do it for you. You know I wanna do everythin' for you. You jus' tell me."

She clung to Elvis so tight he grunted.

"You're gonna kill him yet," Vernon said, irritated.

By this time, I had started handling some of Elvis's personal business, like writing letters and organizing his fan mail. He was sitting at the table signing photographs when he suddenly remembered.

"Guess who stopped by last week? Red West. 'Member?"

I shook my head. "Don't know him."

"I didn't either," Elvis laughed. "We were in some classes together. He said hi sometimes, but we never talked."

"What'd he want—a job?"

Elvis looked a little irritated. "He stopped to say hello, just to be nice. Said he heard I was doing okay and wanted to give his best, that's all."

"If someone who never bothered to talk to you before suddenly shows up when you're famous, it means he wanted a job."

"Doing what?"

I shrugged. "Famous people always have other people doing things for them—doing their shopping, driving them around . . ."

"Nobody's drivin' my car but me."

"With the people you got knocking on your door, you should get Red to answer it for you."

"Oh, God, Mama was fit to be tied last night," Elvis said, looking around to make sure she wasn't within earshot. "Some girls were knockin' away at midnight. Pretty ones, too. I'd of asked them in and had double the fun if Mama hadn't woke up," he said.

"Elvis!"

"What?"

"You'd go to bed with two girls?"

Elvis gave a sexy smile for his answer. "Would and have. And I coulda had 'em last night if I'd wanted. Wait'll you start, then you'll understand."

That moment made me realize how much Elvis had changed, how his exposure to the world outside his home and neighborhood had sprung loose a wild side that would have otherwise been left dormant. Gladys's clinging possessiveness caused him to exert his independence and rebel against his mama in the only way he could. Away from the watchful eyes of Gladys, Elvis played out whatever sexual fantasies came to mind. It was the one thing his mama had no control over.

"Well, you shouldn't answer the door to everyone who has a mind to knock, regardless."

"You know I wouldn't do anything in the house— that'd be disrespectful."

"That's not what I meant. You're famous and need to start being more careful. And get a higher fence, so they just can't step over it like they do now."

"Be more careful of those girls? I can handle 'em. When they stop liftin' their skirts at me is when I'm gonna worry," he laughed.

"It's not girls—it's their boyfriends."

Elvis took the joke very seriously. "Maybe I *ought* to think about givin' Red somethin' to do. He's a big guy, maybe he could be a bodyguard when I'm out performin'."

Elvis was going to need a bodyguard at home, too. The people living on either side of the Presleys were very upset about the number of cars driving past, the noise, the crowds of girls encamped on the sidewalk, and the general disruption of homelife as they'd known it.

They were also appalled at what they saw when they

looked over their back fences—stacks of wood littered
the corner where Gladys intended to build her coop,
plus she had clothesline strung every which way so
she could hang her laundry out to dry, daily. This
neighborhood preferred not seeing drying underwear
spanning the entire backyard, high above the fence
sightline.

"It's going to bring down the value of our houses,"
one man shouted at Elvis in exasperation over the
phone.

Elvis wasn't about to compromise, or to tell Gladys
she had to change anything in her own house and yard.
He made matters worse by refusing to even discuss the
problems, nor was he about to alter his aversion of
confrontation. The hostility grew on both sides, and
soon the Presleys were the outcasts of a block that
couldn't have cared less if he was a star or not. No
longer whispering, they spoke cruel words loudly over
morning coffee and backyard hedges.

Elvis got so angry at hearing himself and his family
called white trash again, he stormed out to the backyard and broke several two-by-fours, littering the grass
even more. It was beyond him why anyone would be
upset.

"If I want it to look like a lumberyard, that's my
business. We got just as much right to be here. My
money's worth just as much as theirs, and I got more
of it.

"I won't have Mama cryin' and called bad names
again. If they don't like it, they can move. Or else I'll
buy up all their mortgages and kick 'em out. Goddam
jealous, that's all they are. Nobody wants y'to get
ahead."

In July of 1956, Elvis was riding atop the charts with
"Don't Be Cruel" and "Hound Dog." His popularity
was at fever pitch, and his first album was on its way
to selling a million copies, a feat never before accomplished. The money was rolling in, and it burned a
hole in Elvis's pocket. He bought a dozen more outfits

from Lanksy's but was happiest about the present he'd picked out for Gladys—a pink Cadillac.

"Won' she be somethin' special, drivin' 'round in that? Bet that'll burn the neighbor's butts."

"But your mama doesn't like to drive," I said.

"She ain't ever had a car like this before."

Elvis gave in to his desire to show off his wealth every chance he got now, in an attempt to prove his worth and value as a person to those who still considered him trash. In public, he was still polite and upbeat, but in private he would suffer through sharp mood swings, unable to understand why he was still having to fight bad opinions. Money and success had made a lot of things better, but he was disillusioned at the new troubles they caused. Sometimes he felt so worthless it was hard for him to remember how famous he was. Women were the best support for his sagging ego, and he would go out at night looking for someone to soothe his soul and release the building pressure.

But even this was more complicated now. Elvis was an idol, and he was news. He eyed the young girls who followed him with desire, but he had to be careful where he was seen and with whom, unless he wanted Gladys to read about it in the morning papers. He pouted at being unable to use his wealth and fame the way he wanted.

His attitude in the recording studio was changing as well. He wasn't as anxious to please and, knowing he was the star, often showed up late and unprepared. It gave him a feeling of power to keep people waiting and know they'd still be there when he arrived. However, when he got to the studio, he was full of downhome apologies and good humor, so his antics were forgiven.

Parker worked him hard during rehearsals, concentrating on stage presence and preparation. Elvis had a terrible memory and often forgot the words to a song, which could spell disaster on TV. When he'd muff his lines on stage at a live performance, Elvis covered up by dancing his wild gyrations. Half the time when he broke into the swiveling that made him famous, it was merely because he had forgotten the words, and dancing gave him time to gather his thoughts.

Other times, if the crowd was especially noisy and raucous, he'd just make up words as he went along.

"Sometimes I feel like a bucket full of holes," he laughed. "I look down and see all the faces and my mind goes blank."

Parker wanted Elvis relaxed but not *that* loose. He stressed the importance of being professional. It was fine to have fun—but in a disciplined way. The tutoring wore Elvis out, but he followed Parker's instructions and doggedly worked on memorization exercises and improving his stage presence. The last thing he wanted was to make a fool of himself in front of the fans who mattered so much to him.

Ironically, it was the small things that reminded Elvis he was really famous and gave him the most pleasure. Like when *Your Hit Parade* called to say that a singer would be performing "Hound Dog" on the show.

"You're kidding?" Elvis looked shocked. It was one of his favorite shows, and being honored by them was a special thrill.

When *Your Hit Parade* came on that night, we all gathered around the TV to watch. The singer was Gisele MacKenzie, and they had her singing to this long-faced, pathetic-looking hound dog. Midway through the song on live, national TV, the dog got bored and walked away.

Elvis howled with laughter. "That'll teach 'em to have anyone singin' my song 'cept me."

When he wasn't in the recording studio working on his singing or performing live on tour that summer, Elvis was now taking diction lessons at Parker's insistence. Elvis was about to take an important step in his career, and Parker knew there might not be any second chances if he blew it the first time around. Hal Wallis had made good on his word and signed Elvis to star in his first movie. Originally, it was going to be called *Reno Brothers,* but Paramount Studio changed it to *Love Me Tender* to capitalize on his latest hit single.

At first, Elvis resisted the idea of changing how he talked, angry at the implication he didn't speak well enough for the movies.

"If they don't like the way I am, then tell 'em to go to hell."

Parker was adamant. "The audience needs to understand you. Not everyone's from the South. We're not going to change you, we're just going to teach you how to talk for the movies."

This struck a sensitive nerve in Elvis, and he surprised Parker by arguing the point. "I'm tired of people always pointin' out what's wrong with me. I wanna sound how I sound. Screw 'em."

"Hollywood is what's going to make you the biggest star that's ever been, so stop being stubborn. You're also going to have an acting coach, so don't go planning too many nights out."

"I'd rather be out with people who like me than with someone tryin' to change who I am. I don' wanna sound like some northerner."

Parker eyed Elvis with an unblinking stare. "I'm sure your mama would be very upset to know you'd rather be out fooling with not one but two girls at a time like you did in Las Vegas, instead of being serious about your career. I'm sure she'd be *very* disappointed. It might break her heart, wouldn't it?"

The threat was brief and simple but to the point, and the argument was immediately over. After Parker left, Elvis went out in back, furious and frightened. He vented his frustration by throwing lawn chairs around.

"Nobody else has trouble listenin' to me. They already tell me what I can or can' say, what I can or can' wear on stage. Next they'll be tellin' me when I can take a crap."

He was too shaken to stay angry long, and a chill

settled over him. ''How in hell did he know? He must be spyin' on me. Goddam it, you can' trust *anybody*.''

Elvis grumbled and griped about all the preparation, but the news that he was going to be in a movie made him catch his breath. The significance of it overwhelmed and terrified him. He had no training as an actor and doubted a crash course would help much. Elvis also worried how he'd be accepted in Hollywood by its stars. In front of his musicians and instructors, Elvis covered his fear with bravado, but alone at night in bed, he hugged his pillow and prayed for Jesse to make everything alright.

With Parker a stern taskmaster, Elvis worked diligently to prepare himself for the next phase of his career. Elvis regarded the Colonel warily, and while they had never been buddies, a new coolness and distance separated them. When it was finally time to go, Elvis joked that he looked forward to going to California to work so he could get some rest.

Unless it was absolutely necessary, Elvis refused to get on an airplane, so we went to Los Angeles by train. Parker would fly out and meet us when we got there, Vernon and Gladys would follow in a couple of weeks, after Elvis settled in.

After the hectic last week and Gladys's frantic and tearful goodbyes, Elvis sank into his seat with a relieved sigh. He couldn't shake the worry that Parker would ''tell'' on him, and he hoped the trip would make it go away. As the train pulled out of the station, he immediately perked up, like a teenager whose parents have gone out for the night, leaving him with free run of the house.

''You don't know how nice it is not having someone look over your shoulder at ever'thin' you do. I can finally breathe again. I swear, once I make it to the top, I'm gonna retire, so nobody can tell me anything.''

Elvis was excited and jumpy, unable to sit still. He walked up and down the length of the train, then decided he was hungry and insisted I come with him to find food. Once in the dining car, he merely picked at his food. His main hunger was for a girl to pick up.

"Parker's been workin' me so hard I haven't had a date in weeks. No wonder I'm so wound up. Nothin' beats a woman for relievin' tension," he laughed.

Luckily for Paramount, there were no young or attractive women traveling on the train, and we spent most of the trip going over his script and practicing his pronunciation.

"Just like school, ain't it?" Elvis asked.

"Isn't it."

"If we weren't kin, I'd smack you," he said, shadow-boxing me.

It was good having a couple of days to ourselves and to be with Elvis away from fans and the pressure of being famous. Around a certain few people like me and his parents, he didn't have to live up to any image, so he didn't feel the need to try and impress us. He could relax and have fun without worrying someone was going to make fun of him or put him down. Seeing his old self again reminded me more than ever how so much about Elvis had changed, and how different he was now. He'd become so distrustful of people in such a short period of time—they either wanted to make him look bad or were laughing behind his back or jealous. He couldn't see it was his own insecurities that haunted him.

Most people who met Elvis assumed he was a cocky, self-assured young man reveling in his sudden fame. Obviously, Elvis was a much better actor than any critic would ever give him credit for. He was so adept at hiding his true feelings that it was inevitable they would erupt in an uncontrollable way at some point in time.

It was unbelievable to me that my cousin, who'd been so tongue-tied as a youngster, was going to be a movie star. I was happy for him but just a bit jealous, and I admitted it to him in the dark of our berth before going to sleep.

His voice carried a mixed message. "I won't lie, it's

nice havin' people fuss over you. Makes you feel special and important. But it's hard, too, 'cause half the
people are tellin' you what to do, and the other half is
waiting for you to look the fool.''

Elvis got a quick reputation as an all-American kid on
the Paramount lot his very first day there. When Hal
Wallis told Elvis to stop calling him Mr. Wallis, Elvis
just shook his head.

"I can't do that, sir. You're Mr. Wallis.''

If he hadn't been so sincere, everyone would have
made fun of him, but his innocent and guileless expression quieted the movie crew's cynicism.

Elvis wasn't very interested in the process of making movies. Although he admitted he was having fun
and enjoyed seeing himself on film, artistically he
thought it was pretty silly.

"But if they wanna pay me to play, I ain't gonna
argue—I mean, I won't argue.''

Much of Elvis's ease was due to his co-star, Deborah Pageant. She had gone out of her way to make
Elvis feel at home from his first day on the set. Deborah showed him around the lot and introduced him
to several people she knew. When the film started, she
assured Elvis it was okay if he didn't get it right the
first or fifth time and convinced him the point was to
enjoy himself. If he had fun, so would the audience.
Her good humor, lack of pretension, and quiet, easy
manner put Elvis at ease so naturally that by the end
of the first week, he was smitten with her.

"I think she's the one—I'm really in love this time,
Earl,'' Elvis said one day on the set. "Look at her. Isn't
she beautiful? I can't believe she likes me, too. She's
so . . .''

"Classy?''

"Yeah, classy, but not snooty. Special.''

Elvis and Deborah ate lunch together on the set and
spent several days together doing publicity photos for
the studios. He was so used to brash bar groupies that
he misread her subtle sexuality to mean she was vir-

ginal. Visions of romance replaced images of raw passion, and he pictured her in his home, sharing his life. When he sang to her in the movie, the feeling behind the words was genuine.

Vernon and Gladys blew into town like rumpled night and stark day. The size of Los Angeles immediately freaked Gladys out, and she refused to go sightseeing, choosing instead to stay right by Elvis on the set. Vernon was much more intrigued and adventuresome, and happily set off by himself, hiring cabs to take him all over, eating at the nicest restaurants. One thing for sure—Vernon had no trouble enjoying the fruits of Elvis's success.

Elvis did his best to cajole Gladys into being a tourist, but she wasn't having any. By the third day, his mama was driving Elvis a little crazy. He wanted her to enjoy her visit, but he didn't want to babysit and miss time on the set with Deborah. Gladys complicated matters further by taking an instant dislike to Pageant, mentally labeling her a Hollywood tramp and treating her accordingly. Her disapproval made him as angry, frustrated, and guilty as he had felt in high school. He dreaded disappointing Gladys but was tired of worrying about what other people wanted instead of what he wanted. It was easy to ignore her when she was home, but impossible when she was watching his every more. He wished she'd go home, then felt terrible when he saw her sad, vulnerable eyes staring at him with such love and pride.

The studio kept Elvis hopping from dawn to dusk. When he was done filming for the day, Elvis might go for more publicity photos, do an interview, or attend a function with Deborah. Even though he didn't like going to public functions, being with Deborah made it bearable. He couldn't be alone with her much because of their busy shooting and publicity schedule, and because Gladys was always close by. He talked to her on the phone every night, shutting himself in his bedroom so he didn't have to hear Gladys's pointed sighing.

Elvis tried to go sightseeing, but mobs of girls seemed to form wherever he went. Had he been alone, he would have enjoyed himself, but panting girls upset Gladys and forced them back to the hotel where he was bored out of his mind.

He couldn't even rant and rave freely, so he blamed his irritation on Hollywood instead of his mama's suffocating presence.

"If this is what bein' a movie star is like, they can keep it. What's the use of being famous if you have to stay locked up all the time? I had more fun when we were playin' Hernando's."

Like a spoiled child, Elvis drove room service crazy ordering cheeseburgers at all hours. For breakfast he insisted they make him a fried peanut-butter-and-banana sandwich, even though it meant the hotel had to send a runner out for peanut butter.

Parker dragged Elvis to a number of parties, some with Deborah, some alone. He didn't want Elvis linked to any one person and made sure he had his photograph taken with a lot of different starlets. Many people were anxious to meet Elvis, especially a young actress named Natalie Wood. She greeted Elvis shyly and they talked a long time. Elvis was attracted to her dark, pretty looks and innocent air and impressed that someone like her would seek him out. On a whim he invited her to Memphis, never believing she'd take him up on it.

His crush on Natalie blossomed simultaneously as his obsession with Deborah faded. His change of heart was colored by the realization his co-star didn't want him as a boyfriend or even a brief lover. He had only tried to kiss her, too respectful to suggest anything else, and had been shocked at her rebuff.

"She ain't . . . she's not what she pretended to be. She's just like all the others. They're one way to your face then another behind your back. I should of known someone like her would look down at me. Probably thinks she's better, or else why wouldn't she go with

me on a private date? It was jus' business for her—
she'd only be seen with me if the studio said to.''

''Why can't you just be friends?''

''You can't be friends with women, not like buddies. It don' work.''

Elvis's disenchantment with his perceived ways of
Hollywood grew as he absorbed barbs by local critics
ready to roast yet another singer trying to cash in at
the movies. Nicknames like Elvis the Pelvis and Swivel
Hips had eaten at him before, but this was worse.

''Don't show me any more papers,'' he seethed,
throwing them on the floor. ''And don't let Mama have
'em, either. It gets her too worked up.

''Who cares what these pencil pushers think? I don't
need 'em. They ain't the ones buying records. I have
more money than they'll ever see—who're they to talk
about me?''

He moved around the room quietly, not wanting to
wake his parents. When his anger subsided, the doubt
rose to the surface and its weight sank him to the floor.

''What if they're right, Earl? What if people stop
liking me and don't wanna hear me sing or hate the
movie? I don't wanna go back to the way we were
before. Everybody'd be laughing at me.

''All I wanna do is sing. That's what makes me feel
best. I wish I could just do that and forget everything
else.''

By the time the movie was finished, Elvis was ready
to go home to the familiar streets of Memphis. As we
neared the depot, his mood brightened and his body
visibly relaxed. The trip home had exhausted Gladys,
and she went straight to bed, and Vernon went out to
grab a bite to eat, giving Elvis some time to himself.
We jumped into his car and picked up some cheeseburgers at Leonard's, where Elvis rekindled an old flirtation with his favorite car hop. We ate while Elvis
cruised aimlessly, from Beale Street to the darkened
side roads on the outskirts of town. We flew down the
deserted back roads, the warm wind scented with night

smells blowing through the car. The open spaces gave
him room to breathe. He turned the radio up and sang
along with the same intensity he'd have for an audience. When "Hound Dog" came on, Elvis howled out
the window and drove the car in town to the music,
singing in a falsetto and laughing at himself.

We pulled up to his house well after midnight, but
a couple of persistent fans were still waiting, hoping
to get an autograph. The tension that had pinched his
brow the last days in California had blown away in the
sweet Tennessee night air. Elvis had been up for almost twenty-four hours, but he looked refreshed and
invigorated as he joked and talked to his faithful.

Memphis recharged Elvis and lightened his burden
of unfulfilled expectations. Throughout his career he
would always call Memphis home. It was his safety
valve and retreat, a place to salve the wounds and heal
the bruises of feeling knocked in the press and snubbed
by those who acted superior. Elvis was the biggest fish
in this pond, more accepted here than anywhere by
people who reminded him time and again why singing
was so important.

In Memphis he would always be second to none, the
king beloved by his minions.

9

In September, Parker pulled off his biggest coup to date—a booking on the Ed Sullivan show. What made it especially sweet was that Sullivan had previously announced he would *never* invite Elvis and his swiveling hips on the show. Viewer pressure made Sullivan eat his words, but he refused to admit complete defeat and would only let the cameramen shoot Elvis from the waist up, lest he corrupt the morals of young girls everywhere. Elvis's truncated performance became part of television history, and firmly established the boy from Memphis as the most popular performer in America. He was only twenty-three years old.

Elvis used to find it funny when he was warned about his personal safety, but a tense moment in the week following the Sullivan appearance scared him into reality and forced him to admit it was a serious matter after all.

Elvis returned home from a rehearsal session and noticed a crowd of fans in front of his house. He was tired, but he still enjoyed talking to fans and signing autographs and stepped out of his car and walked toward the group. A couple of young girls started screaming and made a mad rush toward Elvis—causing the other fans to do the same thing. He attempted to get back inside his car, but he wasn't quick enough, and they literally pinned Elvis against the hood. In their frenzy to get his autograph and touch him, the fans surged forward with pieces of paper and pens thrust into his face, everyone calling out "Elvis! Elvis!" Their combined weight crushed against him and scared the hell out of him when he found it hard to take complete breaths. He tried to push his way out from their grasp, but there were too many and his panic turned to terror.

Suddenly, the crowd began to let up and Elvis saw his dad and Uncle Vester, Vernon's brother who had married Gladys's sister Cletis, pulling kids away and restoring order. Elvis had never in his whole life been so happy to see his father. Vernon grabbed him by both arms and took him into the house, with Vester still holding the crowd back while lightly holding a menacing two-by-four.

"Boy, you're gonna get yerself killed one day unless you start rememberin' who y'are," Vernon told him. "Those fans of yours could love you t'death. We're lucky Vester was visitin', 'cause I don' think I coulda helped you alone."

Elvis couldn't stop shaking. Gladys was white as plaster, frightened by how suddenly the crowd got out of control. She sat with Elvis on the couch a long time, holding and rocking him, fiercely protective—upset over what happened, but vindicated having her child back even for this moment.

Elvis huddled in his mama's arms, thinking what if she had been with him. The fright might have literally given her a heart attack. The thought made him shudder, and he squeezed her in his arms. He'd die if anything happened to his mama.

Parker had warned him this would happen, but Elvis thought he was just talking to hear himself, as usual. But now Elvis realized he had to make some changes to protect both himself and his family. The first thing Elvis did was hire Red West to be his personal bodyguard. The necessity of it aside, Elvis felt very important needing a protector and went out of his way to let people know Red's function. He liked having someone around whose sole purpose was to cater to his needs, no questions asked. Although just Red was on payroll in the beginning, Elvis encouraged West to bring around buddies to tag along on excursions out. For the first time in his life, he had a group of male friends to pal around with, and he relished being the leader of the pack.

Elvis felt safe with Red, but he knew his living arrangements weren't suitable any more. Besides wanting a house with less public access, he craved more room so he could go outside and clear his mind; the days of taking walks in the neighborhood were over forever. Elvis also coveted stature. He wanted a home that made a statement about who he was and how far he'd come, a place where nobody—neighbors included—could interfere with his life. He found the home of his dreams at an estate named Graceland.

"So, what do you think?" Elvis asked.

He stopped his car on a beautiful street in an area called White Haven. I stared at the gated mansion in front of us—only presidents and governers lived in places like this, not the son of Mississippi sharecroppers.

"What's a matter? Cat got your tongue? Do you think Mama will like it or is it too much?"

"How couldn't she like it? How could *anybody* not like it?"

"It's called Graceland. Don't know why."

He drove on to the grounds, up the stately, tree-lined driveway, and parked near the pillared front entrance. We got out of the car, and I followed Elvis inside.

"It's got fourteen rooms, a big ol' kitchen, and a nice-sized backyard where Mama can finally get those chickens of hers. Ain't nobody gonna tell us what to do here."

He was right. There were no close neighbors, and anyone would have to climb on a ladder to see in over the tall fence and hedges that lined the property's perimeter.

"Guess the girls won't be able to step over that," I said.

"Remember that little house by the front gate? It's for a security guard. Parker thought it was a good idea to have one to keep an eye on everything."

"It's beautiful, Elvis."

"It's better than anything I ever pictured for Mama. No matter what happens, she ain't ever goin' back to livin' in any cramped apartment again. I made sure of that. This is ours no matter what."

We walked through every room, twice. Elvis pointed out which would be his bedroom, the music room, the guest rooms—all subject to Gladys's approval, of course.

He stopped and laughed. "I must sound like the starched collar who sold me this place. I jus' can't believe it's really ours. We're gonna be happy here, Earl. There's room for everyone."

"Half of Tupelo would fit."

"Maybe we should look up Orville Bean, ask him for dinner. Can't you see 'im? He'd choke on his cotton balls." Elvis laughed with satisfied revenge.

"God, what I wouldn't give to see that. Him and everyone else down there. I hope they realize it's me. Wouldn't be as much fun if they didn't."

Elvis and Gladys spent several full days in some of the city's most expensive stores picking out furniture, wallpaper, and paint for their new home. Gladys was in her glory—not because of the house, but because of the time Elvis was spending with her. But once the shopping was done and they were settled in their new home, Elvis turned his time and attention elsewhere, and she sank back into melancholy. The only difference was she now drank in beautiful surroundings.

Elvis was constantly on the go. When he wasn't taking off for an appearance in Miami at the Fountainebleau Hotel or on the Dorsey Brothers show or in Vegas or in Hollywood to discuss his next film project, he was rehearsing and recording. Once his business obligations for the day were done, Elvis concentrated on enjoying himself. On the road, he would cruise clubs with Red for women, letting Red do most of the instigating so as not to draw attention to himself with the local press.

At home in Memphis, Elvis lived out a fantasy adolescence. He rented out movie theaters to watch private showings so he could enjoy himself without having to deal with a steady stream of fans, and he paid the owner of his favorite amusement arcade to stay open after hours for him to play pinball and other games of chance until dawn.

At least once a week when he was in town, Elvis would rent out the Rainbow Roller Rink for seventy-five dollars a night. Elvis would tell Red to get together a nice-sized group and we would skate sometimes 'til dawn. Inevitably, Elvis would announce it was time for roller derby, but it was more a war than a game. We'd choose up sides, and he'd be out there leading the attack, acting more like a kid than he had as a kid. After hours of hurtling at each other, we'd all be exhausted and ready to quit, but not Elvis.

"You bunch of sissies, I'm only gettin' started."

"You also didn't get up 'til noon—give us a break," I'd pant.

"Come on. Red, Earl, you're on my team this time. Let's go, I wanna get my money's worth."

So up we'd stand and roll back into battle. These games got so physical that people would walk away with broken fingers and a body full of bruises. Elvis didn't care who went through the roller rink wall, as long as his team won the point. I'm surprised nobody was ever fatally hurt.

On all these excursions, Elvis was surrounded by a small group of buddies who began to wear their hair and to dress like him, although at this point, the only constant face was Red's.

Even dates were group activities. If Elvis had a prearranged date, Red and one or two other guys would bring their own dates along, and they'd have dinner, then usually go to a private movie showing or the arcade after hours. The limo would drop off everyone but Red, Elvis, and his date. If the girl had an apartment of her own, Red would wait downstairs until Elvis came back down. He always went home by dawn, knowing Gladys would be listening for him.

More often than not, the girl was still living at home, because Elvis was most attracted to teenage beauties. Graceland was out of the question, because his mama was there, and Elvis didn't want to risk going to a hotel in his hometown and be recognized. Instead, they'd drive to a secluded spot, or if the girl was game, just park on a street and make love in the back of the limo while Red and the driver stood guard outside, shooting the breeze and trying to ignore the car's shaking and the sounds of passion escaping from behind the rolled-up windows.

Once at Graceland, Elvis never strayed out of the house unaccompanied. Safety aside, a group of buddies acted as a buffer. For as much as he loved attention, Elvis hated feeling he was under scrutiny, and he found the line between the two getting hazier as time went on. Eating in restaurants became an ordeal as other patrons stared at him constantly or whispered about him in hushed tones.

"I wish they'd just come over and say somethin' instead of just watchin' me like that."

In cases like this, when he was unsure whether those watching him were excited fans or disapproving critics, he would get nervous and edgy. Having an entourage around him helped alleviate the anxiety he felt.

Elvis sometimes felt overwhelmed by the pressure of etiquette. Learning why you were given two forks and two glasses at a table setting was bad enough, but remembering not to put your elbows on the table, or tuck the napkin into your shirt collar, or wad your napkin into a ball on your plate when you were done eating was plain boring. But Parker harped on him about it and shamed him into paying attention by reminding him people would think he was an uncouth hillbilly. It was an effort to remember everything, and as a result, at home he rebelled and made it a point to be as "uncouth" as he wanted to be.

Shopping had always been a favorite pastime, and now that he had money, Elvis indulged himself often. Buying jewelry and clothes and gifts for himself and others gave him satisfaction. He enjoyed feeling generous and being able to afford it bolstered his ego.

"Look what I got you boys," Elvis would say to whomever Red had with him that day, dumping out the contents of an armful of bags on the car seat. Silver belt buckles, gold necklaces, hats, jackets, and rings, rings, rings would be doled out. "Take your pick."

There'd be a mad scramble for the trinkets, with the guys falling all over themselves to thank Elvis and tell him how generous he was and what a great pal—while Elvis smiled, looking terribly pleased with himself.

At that time and age, I saw nothing wrong with accepting the gifts Elvis gave me, but my parents hated it.

"Earl, it's not right wearing so many rings. It's plain showing off," my mother told me angrily. "You can give 'em money, but you'll never give 'em class."

"But, Ma, it would hurt Elvis's feelings if I didn't wear what he bought me. He'd think I didn't like it or appreciate it."

"Just like a Presley, can't help but spend money as fast as it comes in."

While Elvis was a compulsive spender, God forbid he think that you *expected* it from him. Especially later on in his life. It was okay as long as he wanted to do it, but don't presume it—or in some cases, even ask for it. If he suspected someone was taking advantage of him, he suddenly felt burdened and angry about it.

After Elvis found out he was going to be on Ed Sullivan, he called a lot of relatives, wanting them to watch and see how big a star he'd become. When Jesse told him he didn't have a television, Elvis got off the phone and told me to have one sent to them.

Vernon was doubly irritated: first that Elvis was

spending the money, and secondly that he was spending it on Jesse, who hadn't given any of them the time of day for years.

"Boy, ain't no need to go buyin' things jus' 'cause you got a few dollars in your pocket."

"I *want* them to have it, and don' tell me how to spend *my* money."

"Watch your mouth!" Gladys came from nowhere. "If being such a big deal makes you forget ever'thin' I taught you, I don' think I like it. You ain't gonna make any of us proud—not me, your daddy, or Jesse—with talk like that."

Elvis apologized and sent the television anyway. But on another occasion, one of Gladys's distant kin called asking for a loan to help pay off some bills that had accumulated. Elvis refused to take the call and slammed the door to his bedroom shut so Gladys couldn't hear him.

"If I start sayin' yes to one, they'll all expect me to support them. They'll come beggin' until they dry me up, and I'm as bad off as they are."

Elvis lied and told Gladys he had to see what Parker said, since he had just spent over $100,000 to buy Graceland. In all honesty, Gladys wasn't too upset. The only relative she asked Elvis to help was her sister married to Vernon's brother, and Elvis put that family up in a near-by duplex after they moved to Memphis. A couple of his first cousins on the Smith side came up and worked around Graceland as gardeners and handymen. Gladys believed in helping family but understood Elvis's reluctance and shared in it. First, she didn't really feel comfortable telling Elvis how to spend his money. He was the one working so hard for it. Plus, she had never forgotten that when she was so horribly alone and scared when Vernon was sent to prison, few of the people now asking for help had been there for them.

Like a new-age god, Elvis picked and chose who he would help and who he'd refuse; who he would lavish with gifts and who he would forbid Red to bring back again because they had made the mistake of not being grateful enough for Elvis's generosity. Elvis was not one to give his buddies a second chance. He didn't have to—there was a waiting list of guys who wanted to be his friends now, and his evenings out were well populated.

Elvis preferred the cover of night, the darkness enabling him to move around with slightly greater freedom. But staying up until all hours of the night meant he often didn't go to bed until it was nearly dawn. Parker accommodated him by arranging for his rehearsals and recording session to be held later in the day, so Elvis got into the habit of sleeping until past noon. Of all the things that worried Gladys, his night prowling and late sleeping filled her with the greatest apprehension. Darkness was associated with the devil for a good reason—it shielded under its blanket actions that would be shameful seen in daylight.

With all his material success, Elvis was still unable to shrug off those critics and detractors who branded him a fad or dangerous. Any time he would read a negative review or editorial, he would storm into his room and sulk or, if his parents weren't around, curse and rage at the faceless writer who had so insulted him. One day, Vernon walked in and caught Elvis pounding on the door in frustration. He stopped dead when he saw his father, who shook his head in amusement.

"Boy, who cares what any of 'em think? Ever hear the expression laughin' all the way to the bank? To hell with 'em."

After Vernon left, Elvis sat down in a chair. "He don' understand. I'm so tired of answerin' the same questions about how I sing, how I am on stage—defendin' everything I do when I don't mean to be doing anything. I just want 'em to treat me fair and to stop attackin' me."

Elvis hadn't had a steady girlfriend since Dixie. Deborah Pageant had been an unfulfilled flirtation, and

Natalie Wood had been little more than a fling. Much to his surprise and satisfaction, Natalie took him up on his offer and flew out to see him before he moved from the Audubon Drive house to Graceland. He showed Natalie his Memphis, with private roller skating parties, his merry band of men, and his adoring fans but was disappointed that she wasn't really impressed.

The fact that she was smitten with him wasn't enough, he needed to prove himself in her eyes. He knew Natalie was living in Hollywood and mingled with its brightest and best. He needed to measure up, and to feel in control. The best way he knew to control a woman was in bed, and although she was chaperoned, he didn't let that get in the way of his desire to add her to his list of conquests.

In later years, Elvis laughed when he heard stories about his allegedly platonic romance with Natalie. He bragged with glee about how one night he rented a movie theater and hired a limo to pick up everyone, except for Vernon and Gladys and the chaperone, who followed in a car behind. After the film was over and the last couple dropped off, Elvis and Natalie made love in the back of his limo, with the partition offering them privacy from the driver, who nonetheless discreetly avoided his rear-view mirror. He added that Natalie sneaked into his room that night, but the thought of having sex next door to his mother freaked him out, and he sent Natalie back to her room.

Elvis liked the pretty young actress, but the romance faded as soon as she got on the plane for Los Angeles. He disapproved of her coming into his room and trying to initiate sex under his mama's roof, and hadn't felt turned on to her the same way after. More than that, his roving eye had been caught by a local girl who was famous in her own right.

Anita Wood was the host of a local TV show, *Dance Party*. One afternoon while flipping through the channels, Elvis saw her and decided right then and there he had to go out with her.

"I gotta meet her, Earl. Call her for me, would you?"

"No, I will not. Asking a girl out is something you should do yourself."

"All I'm asking you to do is set it up. Oh, come on."

"Elvis, don't be rude."

"I'll just have to get Red or somebody to do it then."

"I'm sure they will—they don't seem to know better, either," I said, walking out.

Sure enough, one of his guys called. Evidently, Anita was quite flattered that Elvis Presley, who was now a movie star, too, wanted to take her out. She sweetly informed his spokesman that she already had a date for the evening in question, and no, she wouldn't break it—especially not for someone who couldn't call himself. If at some point in the future, Elvis wanted to call himself and try to arrange another time, she would love to hear from him. If not, he could go jump in the lake.

"Don't look so smug." Elvis threw a pillow at me after hearing her reply. "Some women think they're royalty or somethin'."

Regardless, Elvis did call, himself, soon after, and she quickly became his number-one girlfriend. Anita was great with Elvis. She liked him but wasn't in awe of his success, being a local celebrity herself—a former deejay, the current host of *Dance Party,* and an accomplished singer. They were a good pair. Although he saw her steadily, he refused to be exclusive with her and said up front they should both be free to see others.

Anita and I got to be very close, and I couldn't understand how Elvis couldn't be head over heels in love with her to the exclusion of all others.

"There's a lot of life Elvis needs to live before he's ready to settle down with one girl," she told me one night.

"In high school, Elvis would have killed for a girl like you."

"Well, neither of us is in high school anymore. Sometimes I think the older we get, the less sure we are of what we want."

She would have married Elvis had he asked, but she accepted the parameters of their relationship. Patience must have been one of her greatest virtues, although she sometimes came close to losing it over their lack of private time. Even when they spent an evening at her place alone, she was aware that Red was waiting downstairs for Elvis, at his insistence that he needed constant protection. But Anita wasn't another pick-up, and Elvis refrained from making vulgar comments about their sex life, the way he would with one-night stands.

Vernon liked Anita and thought Elvis should be grateful to find a lady of her caliber interested in him. He thought Elvis an idiot for not settling down immediately with her.

"Anita is one fine young lady, but he ain't never gonna keep a girl by dragging along ev'ry bum he calls a friend. If he don' watch out, I jus' might steal her away," he said with a wink.

With the pace Elvis was keeping, you'd think he was on the verge of exhaustion, but he was running on the fuel of a man possessed.

"It could all end tomorrow, and I don't wanna miss any of it. I'll have plenty of time to sleep when they forget who I am."

One of his newest means of getting around Memphis without attracting attention was by driving an old, black flatbed truck he found at a used-car lot. Wearing a pair of faded overalls—probably borrowed from Vernon—and a cap to hide his trademark hair, Elvis would drive and the rest of us, who by now included his cousin, Billy Smith, would climb in the back. We'd cruise around the outskirts of Memphis or go up and down Beale Street, sometimes all night.

On one of these drives that lasted into the next

morning, we passed by a roadside watermelon stand. A tired-looking farmer and his wife sat next to a huge pile of melons, while their kids played catch in the field behind them.

Elvis slammed on the brakes, nearly knocking a sleeping Billy off the flatbed.

"What's wrong?" I asked. "Did we hit something?" I didn't realize the *thud* had been Billy.

Elvis backed up the truck. "Earl, you got any money?"

Elvis often forgot to take his wallet and was always bumming money from everyone around him. Of course, he was good for it and paid up as soon as he got back to Graceland, often adding a twenty to show his appreciation.

We piled out of the truck, and Elvis told me to pay the people for the watermelons.

"How many should we get?"

"All of 'em."

"We can't take all of 'em."

"Why not?"

"There must be two dozen. What'll we do with them?"

"Eat 'em, or give 'em away. Don't matter. If we don't buy 'em, they'll probably just go bad, and these people's hard work will be for nothin'. Pay him and let's load up the truck."

At first the farmer thought we were playing a joke. Then he thought we were just plain crazy. But he finally took the money and shook his head while we tried to load all the melons onto the flatbed and secure them.

"Give him some extra, Earl," Elvis plucked some more bills from my hand. "Here, sir. Why don't you and the missus go buy cheeseburgers for you and your kids there."

"I can't take that," the farmer made a feeble protest. Elvis had handed him forty dollars.

"Sure you can, for your kids."

We drove back toward Graceland, only losing a few

melons on the way, when Elvis got his second brain-storm of the morning.

"I know what we can do with all these," he said, nodding toward the floor where a half dozen water-melons lay stacked beneath my feet.

"Yeah, sell 'em to get back my money," I said.

"Let's drop 'em off at that kids' place. The one over by where I used to live."

"You mean the city shelter?"

Elvis pulled the truck to a stop in front of the shel-ter. The officer on duty was shocked to see a group of scruffy, tired guys coming at him armed with water-melons. His jaw dropped when Elvis introduced him-self.

Although the rest of us were ready to drop, Elvis was as spry as if he'd just gotten up, and led the way in unloading the rest of the fruit. Driving home, Elvis looked peaceful and happy and I dozed off to the sound of him singing gospel songs.

Another night Elvis was driving a limo he had rented. The evening began at Chinault's restaurant, moved to the local arcade closed to the public during our stay, then was capped by a couple hours of cruis-ing the streets. He dropped off the others and went back to Graceland. Red had already gone to bed when Elvis decide he *had* to have an order of fries, so we went back out in search of an all-night diner.

We were barely two blocks from home when Elvis noticed we were being followed.

Elvis groaned. "There's a whole carload of them. Don' they ever sleep? I just want to eat in peace. I'm too tired to sign autographs right now."

Elvis found it hard to say no to a fan when asked directly, and he knew they'd either get him at the res-taurant or at home when he had to stop for the guard to open the gate.

"I guess I'm gonna have to lose 'em. Hang on."

Elvis made a sudden U-turn in the middle of traffic and almost flipped us over in the process—scaring the dickens out of me. Then he floored it, ran a red light, and didn't slow down until he was sure we were alone.

"Parker will have both our heads if you land in jail."

"Parker ain't the one who can't go anywhere for five minutes without people followin' him, either."

He wasn't being rude or disrespectful, just truthful. I never saw Elvis rude to any fan. He might have almost killed himself in an attempt to get away from them, but face to face he was always charming and polite. He respected them and relied on their love too much not to be.

Of course, not everyone in Memphis was an Elvis fan, as he discovered at a local gas station. Elvis had been tinkering with one of his cars and noticed it needed gas. I was over trying to organize his fan mail, so he called for me and we hopped in the convertible and drove to a service station a few blocks away.

As soon as he pulled up to the pump, right after him—out of nowhere—came a dozen cars of people who had recognized him—causing a major traffic jam on the lot. The owner took offense to the chaos on his property and asked Elvis to leave. Elvis apologized and got back in his car, which was surrounded by people. He started signing autographs. It was either that or run the people down.

The owner, not a patient fellow, came back. As Elvis stepped back out of the car to talk to him, the guy said, "I thought I told you to move," and hit Elvis.

Elvis hit him back, and a scuffle ensued that was finally broken up by the fans, who naturally all testified on Elvis's behalf when the police came. Ultimately, no charges were filed, but the owner came out on the short end of the stick. A massive boycott staged by Elvis's fans eventually put the guy out of business.

As 1957 came to a close and the holidays approached, Elvis looked forward to having the biggest Christmas celebration anyone could remember. He was determined to make up for all of the years his family gratefully accepted a basket of food from the county

welfare office as their sole present. He bought a huge
tree and hundreds of dollars' worth of lights and decorations, and turned Graceland into a Christmas pal-
ace. It was fun albeit overdone. Elvis splurged on gifts
for everyone, including himself. Naturally, Vernon
thought Elvis had gone too far.

"Christmas ain't a contest to see how much you can
buy. It's s'posed to be from the heart. And you ain't
s'posed to buy things for yourself, either. The more
he gets, the more he wants."

"He got a right to get himself some nice things,"
Gladys said. "He works hard for it."

"Well, he earns it, that's true enough. And at the
rate he spends it, he better keep on workin'."

"You know how mad he gets when you get on him
'bout that," Gladys warned.

"Who needs seventeen pairs of shoes? We have
more cars than people to drive 'em, and more rings
than fingers. I try to tell him to save some 'cause it
might not always be there, but he don't even hear me
talkin'."

Later, as I was readying to go home, Vernon stopped
me out on the front steps.

"Maybe *you* could talk to Elvis 'bout somethin',
Earl."

"You know nobody can tell Elvis much of anything."

" 'Specially not now. Acts like he's the president.
But his mama *is* worried about him. He stays out 'til
all hours and won't go to church no more. I tell her
he's jus' havin' fun, but I gotta agree with her 'bout
those fellows he goes out with."

"They're his friends," I said, even though I agreed
with Gladys, too. Fortunately, out of respect for
Gladys, only Red hung out inside Graceland, the others met up with Elvis elsewhere.

"Boy, you know hardly a one of them'd be 'round
if Elvis wasn't so free with his money. I try t'tell him
if you have to pay for people to be around, they ain't
your friends in the first place, but he don't listen. Just

gets that look and walks away like I'm talkin' through an empty hole in my head.

"Anyway, I was hopin' you might try to get him to go to church again once in a while with us. It'd mean a lot to his mama and give mc a little peace."

"I don't mean to be disrespectful, Uncle Vernon, but I don't know that's such a good idea. I'm sure the people at church would be fine, but as soon as his fans found out he was there, we'd have a riot on our hands."

"I hadn't thoughta that. Lord, some kind of life, ain't it? No wonder he's about to crack."

"Elvis is fine."

"Maybe so, maybe not. Too mucha somethin' can be as hard as too little, 'specially to someone like Elvis, who thinks he knows better than anyone."

Too much money and success a problem? I thought Vernon must be suffering from too many beers. Later, I would wish I had paid more attention to his simple logic.

The newest member of the Graceland household was Vernon's ma, Miss Minnie, who'd come up from West Point, Mississippi. Both Elvis and Vernon were concerned about her being alone as she got up in years, so they moved her into Graceland. Very tall, very thin, and very feisty, Miss Minnie was the prototype for Granny on the old TV series *The Beverly Hillbillies*.

Minnie helped with the cooking, even though we all tried to get her to take it easy.

"Don' want no handouts, 'specially from kin. I'll earn my keep if you don' mind."

Minnie adored Elvis. He could do no wrong in her eyes. Right behind Gladys, she was his greatest admirer, and very protective. One day I walked into Graceland to see Elvis.

"Miss Minnie, where's Elvis?"

"Upstairs, sleeping."

"I should have known—it's only one in the afternoon."

"I reckon he was out workin' late las' night, so

don't you go wakin' him up. Give the boy some peace. He left a note for you by the phone over there.''

I opened the envelope, and in it was a handwritten note, plus a bunch of telephone messages.

It read: "Earl, I need help. You seem pretty good talking to the press and everyone. Okay?''

This was as official as we ever got about my handling his publicity.

Christmas morning was unbelievable. First of all, in honor of the occasion, Elvis was up and dressed before noon. There were so many presents around the tree, we could barely get into the room. Elvis jumped around, a lacquered-hair Santa, piling presents in front of us all, including his parents, Miss Minnie, Uncle Vester and Aunt Cletis, Red, Anita, Billy, and Alberta, the maid. Every time he came upon a present someone had gotten him, he laughed and excitedly added it to his own pile. He had also wrapped several gifts he had bought himself so others could be surprised.

Elvis made everyone wait until all the presents were distributed before letting any be opened. He tore off the wrapping paper of his gifts like a greedy child, his face flushed and his mood light-hearted and excited.

Elvis had planned the day down to the last minute, and it was wonderful. We roasted chestnuts in the fireplace, sang Christmas carols, played tag football, drank champagne, and stuffed ourselves on a turkey dinner with all the trimmings and then some.

Maybe more than anything else, his freedom and ability to stage such an extravagant celebration symbolized to Elvis the depth of his achievement. It made him feel accomplished and secure. This was how he expected his life to be forever—surrounded by his family and friends in lavish luxury with not a care in the world. He had no way of knowing it would be his last fully happy holiday.

In those early years at Graceland, Elvis was a gracious and accommodating host. He greeted politicians, music industry officials, other entertainers, and friends of friends, all of whom had gone out of their way to meet the phenomenon. Half the time Elvis had no idea who he was meeting, but he treated them all with good humor and enthusiasm. Parker worried constantly that Elvis or his parents would make a gaffe and cause a public embarrassment, but that particular fear never materialized. Through it all, Elvis really seemed to enjoy being the man of the hour, and his humor was probably at its best then.

I remember once when a friend of my sister came to Graceland to meet Elvis. This girl was so wound up and nervous, she had me a wreck. When Elvis strolled into the room, I went to introduce them.

"Sherry, here's uh, you know—" For the life of me, I couldn't come up with Elvis's name.

Elvis laughed, stepped forward and held out his hand. "Hi, I'm Elvis Presley. Pleased to meet your acquaintance. You'll have to excuse Earl, here—his mind fails him on occasion."

And with that, he linked her arm in his and off they went to tour the house, leaving me with egg on my face. Elvis never let me forget about the day I forgot who he was.

Sometimes, other entertainers brought out a competitive edge to Elvis. Elvis had Jerry Lee Lewis over a few times, and they periodically went for motorcycle rides together, but overall Elvis avoided him whenever possible. Jerry Lee might have been the star Elvis had become, save for the scandal that exploded when he married his thirteen-year-old cousin, in May 1958, and Elvis suspected Jerry Lee was terribly jealous of his success. Elvis also thought he was too egotistical, especially considering his career was in a shambles. Later on, Jerry Lee would try to get Elvis's goat by bad-mouthing him in the press, but Elvis just laughed it off, finding his Memphis neighbor pathetic.

Because he chose to live in his hometown even after he'd become a star, former classmates who suddenly considered Elvis an "old high school buddy" would ring the house from the security gate and ask to see Elvis. Vernon and I both thought he should tell 'em to go to hell, but Elvis insisted on inviting each and every one in, knowing full well he probably wouldn't even recognize them.

Taking a cue from the Great Gatsby, Elvis would give them a personal tour of the house, dressed to the nines in jewelry and name-dropping like crazy. He joked and laughed with them, offered his best liquor, and had the cook whip up some lunch while going out of his way to make sure they knew how much he was worth. When it was time to go, Elvis escorted them down to the gate where waiting fans clamored for autographs. His old classmates never failed to leave impressed and shocked that the weirdest kid in school had become *Elvis*.

But as soon as Elvis came back inside, he stormed up to his room cursing and in a fit of anger.

"When we were in school together, they made fun of me and wouldn't even want to sit next to me. Now they can't wait to tell everybody they got to talk to me. They call me their old friend but they don't like *me* any better, just that I'm famous. I'm still the same person—I can jus' afford to live in a bigger house, so now I'm good 'nough to talk to. They only wanna know me for my money. Probably want me to give them a loan. Two-faced hypocrites."

He would work himself into a rage, then be distant and distracted the rest of the afternoon, wallowing in the belief everyone was out to take advantage of him. About the only people he completely trusted not to take him for a ride were myself, Gladys, Miss Minnie, Red, and Alberta.

Alberta was the maid Gladys had hired while they were still on Audubon Drive. She was a wonderful black lady, too down-to-earth to be impressed, shocked, or bothered by much. She and Elvis hit it off immediately—she recognized his vulnerability and felt an instinct to mother him, he got a kick out of her honesty and knew she would treat him the same regardless of whether he was rich or poor. They also had a wonderful rapport and loved to get on each other. One night Alberta was serving the dinner Miss Minnie had prepared.

"Elvis, does you wanna roll?" she asked, standing over him.

Elvis stood up beside her and did one of his famous swivels. "Alberta, I'll rock and *you* roll."

"You best be watchin' your mouth, or you bet I'll roll you one."

Another time, Elvis was trying to show off yet another new car—this one a brand-new Rolls Royce.

"Alberta, did you see my fancy new car out front?"

Alberta walked over to the window, peered out, and came back shaking her head. "All I see is some big ol' hunk of junk blockin' the driveway."

Elvis pretended surprise. "Well, I guess they got to know what it is before they can be impressed."

"No, sir," Alberta answered. "They got to *care.*"

Some employers might have found that kind of banter disrespectful, but not Elvis. It was play, and he knew that Alberta genuinely cared for him. It was ironic that the more successful Elvis got, the more he sought out simple people—the kind he had left behind in Tupelo as a boy.

Elvis was on top of the world, but there were already warning signs that his paranoia was growing. After having very few friends or even friendly acquaintances growing up, Elvis was suspect of any new person in his life and ready to believe at the slightest provocation that they were only around him because they wanted something from him—money, prestige, or a job. Elvis could be stubborn and Elvis had a temper, but I never saw Elvis be downright unreasonable until an incident with Anita.

He had bought Anita a beautiful ring that she treasured. He picked it out himself, had the setting custom designed, and gave it to her with a great flourish. Her happiness made him happy, and it pleased him when she showed it off to Red and his other buddies.

A few weeks later on *Dance Party,* Anita was on the stage singing a song when the cameraman zoomed in for a close-up of her hand wearing the ring. Elvis had been watching on TV, and when he saw the ring filling the picture tube, he hit the roof. Vernon, Red, and I looked over to see what was the matter.

"Did you see that? I can't believe she did that." He started pacing the floor.

"Who did what, son?"

"Anita is on TV showing off that ring I got her. I can't believe the way people do. I thought she was different."

On TV, Anita was still singing, the ring visible on her finger.

"So what if she's wearing it? Isn't that why you gave it to her in the first place? Don't you want her to wear it?" I asked.

"Of course I do, but not to show off. The ring filled the whole picture. What'll people think?"

"That she got some smart fella who knows a good lady when he sees one to give her a present, prob'ly," Vernon said.

"I swear." Elvis flipped off the TV and slumped in the chair. "I swear, some people are only around because I have money."

"That's what I been tryin' to tell you," Vernon said. "But I wouldn' count Anita in with that group."

Elvis kept quiet, his silence like a loud roar impossible to dismiss.

"Elvis, she wasn't controlling the camera. I bet she don't even know what happened."

"She probably put him up to it, then. Women are sneaky like that. Earl, you're 'bout the only guy I know that don't know that."

"Why would she do that, Elvis?"

"So people might think it's an engagement ring or somethin'."

"Who cares?"

"I don't like people thinkin' somethin' that ain't so. It's Anita's way of trying to pressure me."

"Any man in his right mind'd kill to get that girl," Vernon said.

"Yeah, well, I'm too busy to get mixed up with anybody. Anita's just gonna have to get used to it."

By the summer of 1958, Elvis was too busy for much else besides work and an occasional hour's fling. He was in the recording studio nonstop until it was time to leave for Hollywood to star in his third film, *Kid Creole*. The novelty of making movies had already worn off, and on the whole Elvis was pretty bored, especially since no co-star had caught his eye for a set romance. Parker kept a close watch on Elvis, aware of his penchant for staying out all night. That was fine while performing in Vegas or doing studio work, but the film business started at the crack of dawn and he wanted Elvis fresh.

This visit, the studio put Elvis up at the Beverly Wilshire Hotel, a very posh but very stuffy establishment in the heart of swanky Beverly Hills. Elvis was anxious to finish the film so he could get back to Memphis and have a little fun. Those plans and a whole lot more were shot to hell the second Parker called to tell him he had just been drafted. Suddenly, the bottom of his world fell out.

Elvis prayed it was a joke but knew Parker never joked about anything. He half listened to Parker but was too panicked to really grasp what he was saying. After hanging up, Elvis paced the hotel suite, getting more agitated as the shock wore off and the reality set in. In a rush of frustration, Elvis yanked open the window and started throwing out pieces of furniture onto the parking lot below, crying and cursing his damnable fate.

"Why now, dear God, why now?" he repeated over and over.

When hotel security pounded on his door, Elvis quickly pulled it together and sweet-talked his way out of a potentially sticky mess. He apologized and told the guard to have the front desk add the damages to his bill. When they left him alone, Elvis lay down on the bed and began to cry.

Parker immediately called the draft board and got a deferment that enabled Elvis to finish his movie, then return to Memphis for a few weeks. When he got home, Graceland was abuzz with panicked activity. Vernon and Parker talked in earnest tones, Elvis looked numb, and Gladys sat in the corner teary-eyed.

Elvis moved over to Gladys and put an arm around her. "Get a-hold of yourself, Mama. At least we ain't at war," he said with more levity than he felt.

Elvis looked up at me. "This never occurred to me."

"Colonel, I don' understand why he jus' can't get a deferment or go to the Special Services. Anythin' that don't derail his career," Vernon repeated.

Parker shook his head and patiently explained again. "No. We can't have Elvis pull any favors. The country doesn't look favorably on boys who shirk their duty to the military. It'd be bad business in the long run."

More important to Parker, he wasn't about to do anything that might give the government cause to take the smallest of peeks into his background. If they raised a stink, he ran the risk of angering some pencil-pusher who might start snooping around. He simply couldn't take that chance. Elvis had no choice but to serve his time.

But Parker made arrangements to make it as pleasant as possible, considering the circumstances. The army had okayed for Elvis to live off base during boot camp in a rented house as long as he showed up for reveille on time. That news cheered Elvis up considerably, and he immediately decided his parents, Red, and myself would stay with him during his basic training.

"Maybe there's a roller rink we can rent sometimes," Elvis said, trying to look on the bright side. "Maybe I could do some performances down there, too. We always got good crowds in Texas."

Parker shook his head. "I already asked. The army

says your only career for the next two years is as a soldier. We don't want to push them or they could make you stay on the base by yourself in boot camp, right? Plus, I'm working on getting you a nice tour of duty, so let's just do as they say and not rock the boat.''

Parker had no more pull about assignment than Elvis, but no one even thought to question him. Now more than ever, the whole family looked to him for guidance.

''What if we do get in a war somewhere?'' Gladys said.

''We're done fighting for a while, Gladys,'' Parker said.

''But what if we *do?''*

''I don' care about that, Mama, what about my singin'? Who's gonna care about me one way or another in *two years?* I might as well quit now, so I don' have to be humiliated when I get out and have to go back playin' those clubs.''

Parker shook his head emphatically. ''Elvis, you have records that haven't been released and a movie in the can. We can stretch out the product we have. There'll be a certain dark period, but that will only double the demand for your records and movies once you get out of the service.''

''I don' want to take the chance if I don' have to.''

''Can't you do *anything?''* Gladys asked.

''No, he's got to go. His career will be here when he gets back. We'll get a lot of mileage out of this, Elvis. I promise. I haven't been wrong yet, have I?''

Elvis and his parents slumped in aching resignation, each lost in visions of their respective worst fears.

''Maybe I should do a quick record of 'When Johnny Comes Marching Home,' '' Elvis said unhappily.

Gladys started to cry—her baby was off to the army.

Part IV

ALL
SHOOK
UP

10

On the morning he was inducted, Elvis spent his last hours as a civilian sequestered in his room, doubled over with anxiety and shaking with the fear of change. He tried to calm himself by pacing, but it didn't help. Every movement was abrupt and pained. He slammed his bathroom door so hard the hinge cracked. He snapped at anyone who asked him a question and found fault with everything—his breakfast was too cold, his shoes were dirty, his clothes hadn't been ironed properly. Nothing was right with his world anymore. Carrying his suitcase, he walked down the stairs with the step of a condemned man. No matter how much Parker tried to reassure him, Elvis had a premonition life as he knew it was over forever—the good times would be little more than memories. And in fact he was right, but in a way he never anticipated.

Less than two weeks after Elvis was transferred to Fort Hood for his basic training, we had moved the base of operations from Graceland to an isolated house Vernon had found in the dusty burg of Killeen, Texas. The only differences in the daily routine were Elvis's early rising hours and a sudden drop in the grooming time necessary to get ready—his head now shorn to nubs.

"Don't you dare say a word," he warned everybody when we arrived. "And stop starin' at me."

"I can't help it, it reminds me of your baby pictures," I teased. "I'd almost forgotten what color your hair really was."

"Just wait 'til you get drafted."

"Not me—flat feet."

"Flat head more like it."

"I was thinking on the way down here that you should have saved the hair they cut off."

"Why—to sell it?" Elvis laughed. "Wouldn't that be just like Parker? The man's got a nose for makin' money like a coon dog after hare."

Vernon appeared out of nowhere, frowning. "You boys ought to know better than to be makin' fun of the Colonel. At least *he* knows the value of a dollar."

Elvis turned away and rolled his eyes, but let it drop. He had bigger problems to worry about than his father's nagging. Foremost on his mind this second was how he would survive two months in Killeen—a hot, humid, hell hole in the middle of nowhere with bugs the size of small poodles. If the bugs didn't get him, the surging mob of fans surrounding the house would. It must have taken the locals all of an hour to find out where Elvis was staying. They were quiet but determined, lining up before dawn to see Elvis on his way to reveille.

"There was no house around with a fence, huh, Uncle Vernon?" I asked, peering out the window at a group of strangers inching closer to the front door.

Vernon sighed and shook his head. "That real estate agent promised we'd have all the privacy in the world here 'cause of how far outta town it is. He must be the one with the big mouth—how else could everybody know? People just don't respect others' privacy no more," Vernon sighed again.

"When did they ever?" Elvis asked. "In Tupelo, our business was always poked into. No secrets there, either. Ain't no different wherever we go, 'cept at least now, people are nosin' around 'cause they like me. They're not hopin' to run us out of town," he said pointedly, still irked over Vernon's earlier remark.

Elvis had never been one to work out regularly, so

the first weeks of training left him sore and walking like an old man. He'd come home aching and dog tired, miserable at how quickly his life had changed again— this time for the worse. He'd eat dinner in sullen silence, then trudge off to bed, already dreading the alarm clock that rang in pitch blackness.

His mood improved a little once his body adapted to the rigors of army life. One evening Elvis was still up at nine o'clock, making an attempt at being sociable by playing cards with me and Red. Gladys gave a violent start that made us all jump.

"What's that?" she asked, clutching her dress at the neck.

Vernon listened. "Sounds like someone tapping at the back windows."

"I wish they'd just come knock on the door instead of creepin' around out back," Elvis said with a sigh. "Fans down here are so different. They won't come up to you but will prowl around your backyard."

"I'm afraid to go take my shower," Red said, an impish smile forming. "Might get interrupted by someone climbing through the window."

"Aw, just go ahead and show 'em what you got, that ought to get rid of 'em," Elvis whispered with a leer.

Gladys stared hard at him. "I heard that, young man. You better watch your mouth 'round your mama and Miss Minnie."

Elvis came over and hugged her. "I'm sorry. It's from being 'round those soldiers all day."

"I knew the army wouldn't be good for you. Teachin' you to talk terrible."

The noise sounded again, but nobody made a move to go check it out.

"It's probably the roaches walking across the floor on their way to the leftovers," Elvis said glumly and gave a little shudder. "One jumped on me the other day. I'd about to die. Jumped clear off the counter onto my leg and ran down."

"Maybe you should bring your gun home and we'll shoot them," Red suggested.

"You better not bring any guns in here," Gladys warned. "I just hate the thought of them teachin' you to be a killer."

"Like Jerry Lee."

Elvis laughed, wagging a finger at me. "No thanks, one's enough." He turned back to Gladys. "Mama, I'm not bein' taught to kill. Mostly I'm learnin' how to run through tires without fallin' flat on my face and humiliatin' myself in front of the guys. Everybody's always watchin' me at everythin' I do, 'cause they know who I am. They're jus' waitin' for me to mess up."

Gladys cupped his face. "Maybe it's not too late for Parker to get you into the entertainment side of it. Can' he try jus' once?"

"No, Mama, I don't want to get into it again with Parker. And I don't want everybody thinkin' I'm shirkin' my duty, although I don' know what difference it'll make. Nobody's gonna care anyway in two years. It ain't so bad—if you don't mind bein' in prison."

Elvis didn't want his mama in a constant state of worry, and he tried to make the best of the situation, but he couldn't pretend to himself that he was anything but distraught. Elvis hated the army, his career seemed like a misty memory, and he was depressed by his surroundings: drive anywhere and the sound of the tires crunching all sorts of bugs into the pavement overshadowed any conversation; the steamy weather made breathing difficult, and your clothes were perpetually sticky and damp; moist sheets were scented with mildew; bugs covered grocery items and burrowed inside the packaging as well.

Elvis couldn't let go of what he left behind. His body might be in Texas, but the rest of his being was still firmly planted in Memphis. When he woke up, his mind took him to Beale Street, and he imagined listening to the musicians playing their final set before heading for an early morning burger at his favorite all-night diner. In the middle of a grueling ten-mile run, Elvis would lose himself and the pain by transporting himself back to pretty young faces that had given him pleasure and succumbed to his wishes in the cramped quarters of his car. After dinner, when boredom threatened to drive him stir crazy, Elvis pined over his inability to go out to the Rainbow Roller Rink for a night of fun or to sit in a huge movie theater with some friends. Lying in bed trying to sleep, he tried to blank out images of Anita in the arms of another man; suddenly he was feeling very possessive of her and wishing their relationship was more exclusive. More than anything, he missed performing and feeling the warmth of the audience wash over him. His life source was slowly leaking out, and his hands were tied to refill it.

Elvis hated being told what to do under the best circumstances. In the army, his life had been wrenched away, and he had no choice but to give it up. He felt panicky and out of control. He couldn't even enlist the help of some of the sweet young things waiting by his front gate to relieve his tension and regain control over *something*, because his mama was here watching his every move. He needed the offerings of his fans more than ever but felt so isolated from them. The people holding vigil in Kileen weren't as comforting as the regulars back home at Graceland, but Elvis welcomed them gratefully all the same. They proved he was missed, loved, and still special. Elvis couldn't stand the thought of never hearing the cheers and screams of an audience again, and the fear his moment was over made his stomach sour and his heart burn sorrow. He needed that constant affirmation from his fans, because inside he still considered himself white trash. As long as he heard the applause, he knew the secret that he was a fake was safe a while longer. He covered his fears by lashing out in anger at the most convenient target.

"Goddam Parker, I know he could of fixed this if he wanted to. Other stars get to go in Special Services, but no, not me. I've got to join regular and be miserable for the next two years. Easy for him. He's home bein' comfortable. On my money.

"You know, Earl, Parker don't give a damn second thought to me. Just my singin', and how *he'll* make money from it. Daddy likes sayin' how well we done by Parker, but all I know is that he ain't done so bad for himself out of me, either. Now he's got a nice two-year vacation, while my career dies. What's it matter to him? I've made him so rich, he don't ever have to work again."

Elvis knew how much could change in two years. It was time enough for a new performer to take the country by storm and steal away his fans, time enough for Hollywood to find a new leading man, time enough to become yesterday's star. If he was home and performing, he could fight off the challengers, but with him holed away in the army, his career was as good as dead.

He had worked and prayed so hard to be special, it killed him to be swallowed up in an organization that insisted he be no different from the next guy. Elvis didn't want to disappear in a crowd again, but at the same time, he didn't want to stick out in a negative way as an outcast. Because the other soldiers knew who he was, Elvis felt under pressure to prove himself. He was the odd man out all over again. For as far as he'd come, he couldn't seem to escape the feelings that had haunted him for as long as he could remember.

Elvis wallowed emotionally in his predicament and, in his deepest depression, even took this turn of events as proof of his unworthiness to have lived instead of Jesse. Jesse wouldn't have brought the family so far only to lose it this way. He was superstitious and blamed himself. Bad things like this happened only because he deserved it. This emotional non sequitur—taking the blame for situations out of his control because he felt so unworthy and lacking—would prove Elvis's ultimate downfall when faced with the ultimate crisis.

No matter where we were in the Fort Hood area, the water smelled brackish and looked tainted, as if something was fermenting in the pipes that carried it. It was so bad that Elvis ordered bottled water but too late to prevent Gladys and me turning up sick. I felt weak, but was still able to function, returning the press calls and accommodating the fans who showed up with autographed glossies of Elvis.

Gladys was another story. Feeble and suddenly looking quite old, she could hardly drag herself from the bedroom to the kitchen for a morning cup of coffee before heading straight back to bed. Despite the stifling heat, chills wracked her body, but more alarming was her deathly, yellow-tinged skin color.

Gladys was frightened and the rest of us were terribly concerned, especially being so far away from home. After a family conference including Elvis, Vernon, Miss Minnie, and myself, we decided that Vernon and I would take Gladys back to Memphis to see a trusted physician, and to recuperate in the homier surroundings of Graceland.

"It's somethin' bad, ain't it?" Gladys asked when told of the plan.

Vernon grabbed her hand. "Nah, too hot in August here for anyone 'cept lizards anyway. We'll come back in September when it's a little cooler, and when you're feeling better."

"I hate leavin' you alone." Gladys looked at Elvis with tearfilled eyes.

"I'll by okay, Mama. I got Red and all the roaches for company, and Miss Minnie to keep me fat. I'll call you every day. I promise."

Elvis convinced himself it was heat exhaustion, and while concerned, he wasn't worried. In all honesty, he was secretly relieved Gladys was going home. Now he could get rid of some of his tension and boredom with the pretty young girls hanging outside his door.

Vernon kept his thoughts to himself and presented a calm and reassuring front, but he feared something was very wrong with Gladys.

"It ain't the sickness I'm so concerned with," he

told me as we were packing to go. "It's whether she got the strength to fight it, whatever it is."

"Have you talked to Elvis about it?"

"And get 'im all riled? You know better than that. There's no keepin' calm when it comes to his mama. If it were me, it'd be okay, but not his mama. Then we'd have two of 'em to take care of."

Gladys was getting worse with each passing day and spent the entire trip home on her back, whimpering and feverish. I'd never seen Vernon so attentive as he was then. Of course, I'd hardly ever seen Gladys and Vernon together for any length of time without Elvis around, either. He held her hand, kept her cool with damp towels on her forehead, and comforted her with quiet humor and strong arms. She responded back with a closeness I'd never seen them share. It was then that I realized how much Vernon had sacrificed because of her relationship with Elvis.

As soon as we got to Memphis we headed straight for the doctor, who diagnosed hepatitis as soon as he took one good look at her. He prescribed some medicine and promised it would make her a new woman, but just to be sure she got complete bed rest, he wanted to keep her in the hospital for a few days.

"Why do you need to do that?" Gladys asked. "I'd much rather be home. I promise I'll stay in bed."

"I want to make sure you have no reaction to the drugs. It's standard procedure. You'll be back home in a couple of days."

I called Elvis that evening with the good news. He was surprised that she was really sick but relieved she was already on the road to recovery. In the background was the sound of music and festive voices laughing and talking—the distinctive sounds of a party.

"What'd they do—call off boot camp?"

He laughed. "Red happened to bring over some nice young ladies, and we're just getting to know each other."

"That you just happened to notice were standing in front of the house."

"They said they wanted an autograph, so I told Red to invite them in. They're real pretty, Earl. Texas roses in full bloom."

"No doubt. Where's Miss Minnie?"

"In her room, sound asleep. Don't worry, we got the door closed and are bein' real quiet, if you know what I mean. It's been too long since I was with a woman."

"There'll be hell to pay if Miss Minnie catches you."

"She won't. The door's locked. Give me the number of the hospital so I can call Mama before it gets too late. And before the girls get lonely—I'm gonna have double the fun tonight."

With Gladys gone, Elvis carried on like a sailor on shore leave. He raced home every night from training, ate a quick meal, and was ready for an evening of fun. Red would invite a girl or two to come for a drive, or if the pickings were slim there, they'd drive to local hangouts where Red would scour for pretty faces. Elvis would hold court in the back seat, often not waiting for Red to find a place to park before pushing the girl down on the seat to satisfy his raging need. If he found two adventurous girls, Red would see a tangle of naked arms and legs grinding and straining in an acrobatic pleasure contest.

He stayed out until after midnight but sailed through the day on a boiling reserve of sexual energy. He found the girls among the most willing to please he had ever met and felt freer to pursue them, knowing he was just passing through. His mood was the best it had been since receiving his draft notice, and he silently prayed that Gladys not come back at all.

Back in Memphis, doctors puzzled over why Gladys wasn't responding to medication. They tried several different combinations only to see her condition worsen. Gladys was proving to be her own worst enemy. Although only forty-three, she was in very poor physical condition—overweight, terrible muscle tone, a weak heart, and bloated liver from years of alcohol abuse. More than that, Gladys lacked the spark vital for recovery. Vernon had to lift her up just so she could sip from a glass. Her soul appeared as weak and tired as her body and ready to take its leave.

The doctor didn't tell Vernon anything he hadn't already sensed. Vernon hadn't slept in days but was still thinking straight. Maybe Gladys was doing poorly because she was depressed at being separated from her baby son. A decision was quickly made to send for Elvis in hopes of boosting Gladys's spirits and reviving her will and fight.

Within a few hours, Elvis had been granted an emergency leave of absence and was on a plane for Memphis. We put out a calmly worded press release explaining Elvis's return to Memphis, downplaying his mama's illness.

We picked up Elvis at the airport and drove him directly to the hospital. Red and Miss Minnie had also flown back, but they went directly to Graceland. Elvis was white as a sheet and too stunned to say much of anything. At the hospital, tears welled up in Elvis's eyes when he walked into her room. Vernon hadn't been exaggerating: Gladys was a wisp of her former self. Not weight-wise, just in physical stamina and bearing.

"Mama, what're you still doin' here?" Elvis asked quietly. He sat on the bed and held her.

"Oh, honey, you didn't have t' come all the way from Texas to see a silly old woman," she said in a little voice. "But I'm glad you did."

She pushed him back an arm's length to get a better look. "You look so tired, look at those circles around your eyes."

Elvis hugged her again, looking guilt-stricken. "Now stop all your worryin' about me. I'm here to worry about *you* for once."

I went with Vernon to the cafeteria for a cup of coffee. He was so tired his hands shook as he held the paper cup, but his voice was still strong.

"She lives for that boy. If anyone can make her get better, it's Elvis. I hope it don't upset Elvis, seein' his mama like that. Neither of 'em takes it too well when the other's hurtin'.

"Have you ever seen anyone that color before?" Vernon asked. "Makes me nervous."

When we walked back into Gladys's room, exhaustion etched her face. Elvis paced in frustration. Gladys gave me a smile.

"Earl, I'm glad you're back. You take Elvis on home, now."

"I don't wanna go home. I'm stayin' with you."

"You need to get some rest."

"They got cots here."

"I don't want you here worryin' every time I sneeze. 'Tween your army trainin' and bein' on an airplane, you need some rest. I know how you feel 'bout flyin' and how much it takes outta you. Your daddy'll be here with me."

"But I wanna be with you, too. Why can' I?"

"You have been, and I expect you'll come keep me company tomorrow. I'll be too upset if I know you ain't gettin' rest."

"Mama, I don't feel right leavin'."

"And I don't feel right you stayin'. I'm tired, honey. All I want to do is sleep. If you're here, I'll want to stay awake. You don't have that much time here, so use tonight to enjoy yourself. Then come see me first thing tomorrow. I mean it, son. Don' make me hafta ask you again, okay?"

"You're sure?"

She nodded. "Come give me a kiss, then you kids get out of here."

It wasn't like Gladys to be so insistent about Elvis *not* spending time with her. Gladys said goodbye to Elvis, her eyes filled with intense emotion and premonition, staring at Elvis as if she knew she'd never see him again.

That night, Elvis decided we should all go to the movies. Anita was with him, but it wasn't meant to be an intimate reunion date. Elvis insisted Red and I go, and had Red call some of his buddies to join us as well. If Anita minded, she hid it quite well. She understood how upset Elvis was and knew he needed a lot of people around as a diversion.

Elvis tried to enjoy the movie but kept fidgeting—his mind kept drifting back to the hospital room. After the picture, we stopped at a diner for cheeseburgers then headed back to Graceland. It turned into a late evening. Elvis spend a couple of hours telling army horror stories before sneaking off with Anita for some private time. The rest of us listened to records, played pool, or just sipped on beers 'til we ran out of steam.

I left Graceland and got to my parents' house about three in the morning, but the phone rang before I could even take my shoes off. It was one of the guys who was still at Graceland.

"Earl, you better come quick. Elvis's mama is dead."

"Oh, my God, when?"

"Vernon just called to tell Elvis."

"Where's Elvis now?"

"He ran out of here, I think he's on his way to his uncle's."

Vernon and Elvis sat huddled together on Vester's couch, just destroyed. Relatives were mingling back and forth, trying to comfort them, but it was of little use. Elvis refused to meet anyone's eyes, focusing on a spot far away. He appeared to be in shock, and his hands were blue and cold as death itself.

"How could she be gone, Earl? How could she go without lettin' me say goodbye. Why didn't I stay, I knew I should've stayed."

"She didn't want you to, Elvis. She wouldn't want you to remember her sickly."

"You don't understand. What am I gonna do? I don't know what I'm gonna do."

Vernon's eyes were swollen and red, but he was composed. Elvis was inconsolable. At one point he turned and buried his face on his daddy's shoulder and just wept. The rest of us stood around, feeling completely helpless.

Elvis with manager Colonel Tom Parker signing autographs in the early 1960s.

Opposite: Elvis clowning around with drums on a movie set in the 1960s. *Above:* Elvis at a piano on a movie set in the early 1960s. *Right:* Elvis with a fan on the set of *Flaming Star* in 1960.

Opposite page: Rare publicity shots of Elvis. *Below:* Elvis relaxing between films in the late 1960s. *Right:* Elvis on a movie set in the late 1960s.

Below: Elvis performing in the 1968 comeback television special. *Opposite top:* Elvis at a small party shortly after his July 1969 performance at the International Hotel in Las Vegas. *Opposite bottom:* Vernon Presley and son at the party following Elvis's International Hotel performance.

Opposite: Elvis in rehearsal for a stage performance in Las Vegas. *Above:* Elvis at a press conference in Las Vegas in 1969. *Right:* Elvis in rehearsal in the early 1970s.

Above: Elvis moments before his July 1969 Las Vegas performance. *Right:* Elvis at a press conference shortly before his performance at Madison Square Garden in New York on June 9, 1972.

On tour in the mid 1970s.

Opposite: Elvis greeting fans shortly after leaving his helicopter when he arrived in Hawaii for the filming of *Elvis: Aloha from Hawaii* in January 1973. *Above:* Elvis on tour in the mid 1970s. *Right:* Elvis rehearsing for a performance in Nassau Coliseum in New York in July 1975.

Photos taken from backstage at Elvis's final performance, at Market Square Arena, Indianapolis, on June 26, 1977.

The boy who would be king.

The night turned to morning and by nine-thirty, Vester and Cletis looked completely drained and ready to fall asleep on their feet. We gathered up Elvis and drove back to Graceland, but Elvis got hysterical as we pulled into the driveway.

"I can't go in," Elvis said.

"Why not?" Vernon said.

"I just can't. There's too much Mama there. It was always her house, not ours. Please don't make me go in. Let me just sit here a while."

Vernon sat them both down on the steps and wrapped his arm around Elvis's shoulder as Elvis buried his head in his hands and started to cry again. Deep, wracking sobs that shook his whole body.

"It's my fault . . . ever'thin' is my fault . . . how could I do this . . ."

Out of nowhere a herd of photographers and reporters, who had stormed past the open front gate the security people neglected to close, ran toward us. I jumped up and ran to intercept them, arms waving like a wild man.

"Stop! *Please stop!*"

They did. I begged them to respect Elvis's privacy, and they were surprisingly courteous and respectful. Not one person attempted to photograph him or call out a question, and Elvis was too grief-stricken to pay any attention to them.

Vernon and Elvis were still on the stoop an hour later, in plain view of the curious onlookers who stood outside the now-closed front gate. Elvis might have stayed there all day if it weren't for Miss Minnie coming out to fetch them.

She reached down and cradled Elvis's face. "Come on, son, you can' stay out here all day. You need to rest, and we gotta make arrangements for your mama."

Elvis let Miss Minnie guide him inside. Once the door was closed to the outside world, she hugged him tightly.

"What am I gonna do?" he repeated for the hundredth time. "How am I gonna live without her? I killed her. . . . I killed my mama. . . ."

As news of Gladys's death hit the papers, TV, and radio, the crowds outside Graceland swelled to gigantic proportions. Some came out of respect for Elvis, most were just hoping for a chance to see the grieving idol. Inside, Elvis was standing near a window, staring out as Vernon attempted to make arrangements for Gladys's burial.

"I think she should be laid out here for a day for family, then we'll have the funeral the day after. How's that, Elvis?"

"I wanna put her in the music room. She always loved it in there, then I wanna let everyone who wants to come in and pay their respects."

"What do you mean by everyone?" I asked.

He gestured to the crowd out front. "Them."

Vernon, Red, and I all looked at one another.

"Elvis, we can't let all those people in here," I said gently.

"Yes, we can. It's in honor to Mama. Don' tell me what I can or can't do for Mama. That's what I want, and that's the way it's gonna be."

"It'd be dangerous—we could have a riot on our hands. You could be hurt."

"I don't care if I am. If people wanna come pay their respects to Mama, then I'm gonna let 'em."

Vernon spoke up. "Elvis, you always said Graceland was your mama's house."

"It is. All hers."

"Well, there won't be much of it left if we open the doors and invite the world in. They'll strip the place. You know your mama wouldn't want her house torn to pieces. That'd upset her."

Elvis looked over, tears running down his cheeks. "I just want them all to remember her."

The day dragged by. Elvis's grief came in waves, and when it hit, he'd sag against the wall or sink to the floor, weeping agonized tears. He got so hysterical when Vernon went upstairs to select the dress Gladys would be buried in he almost had to be sedated. Vernon looked ragged but was in charge. He sent Miss Minnie to make some food and called me over for a private word.

"I'll feel better if you stay with Elvis. I don't think he oughta be left alone, even for a minute. Not even to go to the bathroom. He's in a bad way, and I don' trust 'im."

Security was tight, and the security guard at the gate was under orders to get clearance for *everybody*. Elvis would have been furious had he known how many fans tried to get in under the guise of being his old high school buddy. If Vernon, Minnie, or I didn't know them, they were turned away politely.

When the guard called to say a woman named Dixie requested clearance, it took me a moment to realize who it was, because of the different last name. Dixie Locke was now a married mom, but was unable to stay away from Elvis in his time of need. She had come as soon as she heard the news, even though she was unsure at the reception she'd get.

"I tried calling but couldn't get through. I wasn't sure he'd even want to see me, but I had to come over and at least see if there was anything I could do to help."

Elvis was sitting in a chair next to Red and Anita when I brought Dixie into the room. He went right over to her and held on for dear life. Dixie and Elvis walked arm in arm to the other room, while Anita watched with sad understanding.

Anita had tried to comfort Elvis, but he shied away from her, overcome with guilt that he had been having sex instead of being at the hospital while his mama lay dying. Her touch only gave him pain instead of comfort. She intuitively knew their relationship had died the moment they heard the knock on the door last night. She was just the first casualty of Gladys's death.

It was a painful day for everyone inside Graceland. I went to the kitchen for coffee, and Alberta, eyes brimming with tears, filled my cup.

"I can' stand to see that boy torturin' himself. Mr. Elvis could never do 'nough for her, anybody with eyes could see that. He was tryin' to make up her life o' hurt, but ain't nobody can do that."

Alberta looked up nervously, suddenly feeling as if she spoke out of turn.

"I'm sorry. My mouth talks 'fore my mind can tell it to stop."

Alberta served sandwiches despite protests, but once the food was in front of us, everyone ate hungrily, except Elvis. Exhaustion and grief turned Elvis manic. He talked nonstop, unable to sit still and relax. Vernon called the doctor for sleeping pills before Elvis made himself sick and everyone else crazy.

While waiting for the prescription to arrive, Elvis announced he was going to sell Graceland, then decided to tear it down instead and build a monument to Gladys. He was also going to donate all his money to a hospital built in her name. Parker stopped by in the middle of this monologue and left as soon as he paid his respects. He might rule Elvis's career with an iron hand, but he was not included in family business and sensed his presence was not welcome at this moment.

It took forever for night to come, and when it did, I accompanied Elvis upstairs, determined to see that he got some rest. While he undressed, I pulled a chair next to his bed.

"What's that for?" he asked.

"That's where I'm going to sit until you go to sleep."

Elvis nodded and seemed to accept being watched over. He climbed into bed and took two sleeping pills, but before his head hit the pillow, he was sobbing again, and the words spilled out in anguished torment.

He would never forgive himself for all the times he left Gladys to go out carousing when he knew she just wanted his company. He thought they'd have plenty of time to be together once his life wasn't so crazy. He realized she was lonely, but he didn't *want* to take the time just then. All he wanted was some time to himself, when he wasn't responsible for other people. He loathed himself for that selfishness and howled in grief that he would never be able to make it up to her.

His relief at seeing her leave Texas now paralyzed him with guilt. He hated women for their hold over his loins that made him betray Gladys and wish her gone. He had prayed she wouldn't come back, and God punished him by granting that perverse prayer in the most horrible of ways. He had killed her with his selfishness and lust.

Elvis also harbored incredible anger at Gladys for not letting him stay at the hospital and for just leaving him alone in this world. She'd left him and gone to Jesse, who Elvis had always believed was her preferred son. All of his hard work was for nothing. No matter what he did, he could never get out from under the shadow of his brother. He simply wasn't good enough.

Alternating and conflicting emotions played havoc with Elvis's sorrow-filled mind. When the sleeping pills mercifully kicked in and knocked Elvis out, he slept a fitful sleep, tears intermittently streaming down his face.

The next forty-eight hours were a blur for Elvis. When he wasn't weeping, Elvis walked around like a zombie, his stupor interrupted by occasional flashes of temper.

The day after she died, Gladys was laid out in the music room, where a local minister was leading the family in some prayers. Elvis sat stony-faced during the service, refusing to join in.

Vernon leaned over and whispered, "Elvis, come on and pray with us."

"What for? God didn't do Mama any good in the end, did he? Next time I pray, it'll be to Mama and Jesse, not God."

The rest of the day was quiet, because Elvis sat in the music room well into the night, until we insisted it was time for bed. Once again he slept with the aid of pills, although when he woke he looked more exhausted than ever.

The day of the funeral was the worst of Elvis's life. It started out badly the moment the attendants came to transport Gladys's body back to the Memphis funeral home. As they wheeled the casket through the front door, Elvis broke free from Vernon's grasp and ran after it. He threw himself on top of the casket, crying hysterically.

"Don't leave me, Mama—why are you leaving me? I did everything for you, it was *all* for you. I never wanted it for myself. Please don't go. Give me another chance, just once more, *please*. I'll do better this time, I promise, just let me try."

The rest of us were too stunned and felt too helpless to move, but the parlor guys made the mistake of trying to pry him loose.

"Don't touch her!" Elvis screamed. When they made another move toward him, he started flailing at them, impotent punches landing only on air. I shouted at the attendants to stop and motioned for them to just wait until Elvis was ready to let go.

It seemed like an hour, but after only a few minutes Elvis wore himself out and his grip loosened. Vernon stepped forward and gently led Elvis away, nodding to the parlor guys to hurry up with their task before he could start again. Miss Minnie gathered Elvis up in her arms and stood there rocking him like a baby.

The number of people waiting at the funeral home was unbelievable. The police department had set up crowd control lines to keep the throng from storming the chapel where Gladys's service was to take place. I arrived with my family before Elvis and was shocked by the festive air of many in the crowd. Near the entrance, two excited girls were talking and primping in hand-held mirrors.

"Do you think Elvis will like this dress?" one asked the other. "I picked it out just for him. I read he *loves* pink and green."

Several fans held autograph books and hopeful faces. It was a nightmare. Luckily, Elvis was too distraught to notice. He sat through the service with his head bowed, avoiding the eyes of the other mourners, unwilling to share his grief. The ride to the cemetery was strained but calm. Elvis managed to keep his composure until it was time for the attendants to lower Gladys's casket into the grave. His body twitched, but Vernon grabbed his arm to keep him from making a lunge at the casket. Elvis was beside himself with panic and grief, babbling incoherently just loud enough to be heard by those around him. He lacked the strength to struggle against Vernon or to even shout.

"Don't leave me all alone. Oh please, Mama, give me more time to make you happy. I'll be better—I didn't mean to send you away forever. Oh don't leave, I need to hold your little hands and feet again—it was all for you, I did it all for you."

He talked to Gladys all the way into the ground until Vernon and Miss Minnie gently led him away. Elvis was so emotionally drained, they had to half carry him to the car. It was a relief to everyone when Elvis passed out, and Vernon left him there in the driveway for over an hour before waking him.

Graceland was like a morgue. Relatives and friends mingled together around the dining-room table where food had been set out, but few people had much of an appetite. It wasn't as much Gladys's passing as it was Elvis's inconsolable and frightening grief. It was so acute, people suspected then he might be scarred for life.

Elvis's mind ran itself in circles, unable to think clearly or even form proper sentences. He talked, fueled solely on adrenaline that eventually had to run out, but while waiting for that to happen, Elvis raced on and on.

"Daddy, we have to sell the house right away. It was Mama's house, not ours. I don't want to be in it without her. I don't care where I live as long as it ain't here.

"When I get back from the army I'm gonna move to California and do my singin' there, if I have any fans left who want to hear me. And if there ain't, I'll just find me a wife, get married and have kids.

"Oh, God, why didn't I have kids? Mama always wanted to be a grandma, and I let her down. I thought we'd have time for that."

This time, Vernon broke in. "Son, your mama *never* felt let down by you."

"Don' lie to me. I know what I know. She was just too good to say anything. If she hadn't of had to look after me, she could have bettered herself, but she never complained, just too good.

"I'm gonna give up singin', it don' mean anythin' to me now—it was all for Mama."

By nightfall, Elvis had cried himself out for the time being, and an uneasy peace settled over Graceland. Miss Minnie insisted we all eat and shooed everyone into the dining room. Red and I followed her into the kitchen to get some cold drinks.

"I wonder where Alberta went to," Miss Minnie said, while fixing a plate of leftovers. "It ain't like her to go off without saying so."

No one could blame her if she never came back. "She's been run ragged the last three days. Aunt Minnie, should I set the table?"

"Let's just eat on trays, Earl."

I went to get the folding trays out of the kitchen closet and nearly had a heart attack when I stumbled over a body. It was Alberta, sitting on the closet floor, fast asleep, looking literally dead to the world.

"Oh, no!" I said. "Not another one."

Red, Miss Minnie, and I burst out laughing, waking up Alberta with a start.

"Lord, you 'bout scared me to death," she said, trying to get up gracefully.

"That's what I was afraid of."

We were punch drunk and in desperate need for any levity. We couldn't stop laughing. Vernon and Elvis came in to see what all the noise was about. When we told them, even Elvis started laughing 'til tears streamed down his face.

We left Graceland early the next day for Texas, Elvis's leave officially over with the funeral. He was up early and ready to go before anyone else was awake. He was anxious to get back to boot camp, finding it preferable to the ghosts in Graceland. The doctor who had prescribed the first batch of sleeping pills had okayed a second in case Elvis had trouble sleeping. He tossed the bottle into his bag, and none of us gave it a second thought.

Elvis didn't want to fly back, deciding instead he'd like to have his own car in Texas. We pulled out of the driveway in two Cadillacs carrying Elvis, myself, Vernon, Red, and Miss Minnie. Already on that day there was a change in Elvis. We put his deadened eyes off to mourning, but it was more permanent than that. The Elvis we had all known was gone forever; he'd been buried with Gladys. From this point on, Elvis was on a collision course with tragedy.

It took twenty years, but the roller coaster ride had passed its highest point and was about to begin its long, slow, final descent.

No matter how much Elvis complained at home about the service, he was a model soldier, mostly because it was very important to him that the guys like and accept him. As soon as he got back, it suddenly became very important for him to make friends. Instead of being alone with his grief, he sought to diffuse it through distraction. He craved male companionship and wanted to surround himself with it.

Elvis used his downhome charm and privileges to attract a new following. Once a week he invited a handful of soldiers over for a home-cooked meal and their choice of expensive liquors, subtly showing off a small taste of the good life.

"Elvis is a real regular guy," one boy named Sam announced after several glasses of brandy. "He don't act nothing like a movie star. Hell, I bet nobody back home's ever gonna believe I saw Elvis Presley scrubbing down the toilet."

On the whole, Vernon didn't care for the guys Elvis

brought home most frequently. Elvis surrounded himself with guys he felt superior to and could control. Elvis felt completely out of control about most things in his life—Jesse dying, kids making fun of him, having to leave Tupelo, his mama dying, being drafted, even his career was in the hands of someone who told him what he could and couldn't do. So in situations where he did feel in control, he went overboard and to extremes, particularly with women and the guys he collected as buddies, men who lacked any real ambition or abilities. The one trait they did share was a willingness to do Elvis's bidding and contentment to take whatever handouts Elvis was offering. Typically, he doled out the presents regularly and basked in his sense of largesse. But for as well as he treated his army buddies, Elvis showed flashes of unaccountable meanness, bordering on cruelty, with a lot of people—myself included.

Elvis had never been the most emotionally balanced of people, and he stood precariously on an emotional ledge. Life had thrown strike after strike against him: His upbringing and family life were unstable, with a smothering mother and an irresponsible father; Gladys never encouraged him to be an independent thinker so he grew up habitually dependent on others for encouragement and approval; his self-worth was bruised and scarred because he was known as the son of a jail bird and white trash; although he had earned a high school diploma, his education was spotty and just a bare minimum. Beyond all that, he had a family background of ignorant, simple people, and he simply hadn't been given the emotional tools to deal with difficult situations as they arose. The main person in his life, the one he had looked to for emotional direction and moral parameters, had abruptly left him. He was on his own, his emotional balance badly shaken, and one foot already stepping off the ledge into the blackness beneath.

He was filled with sorrow and guilt that fused to express itself as anger and resentment, lashing out indiscriminately. Girls quickly because the easiest and most frequent targets. Anita came down to Texas a few weeks after the funeral, and her suspicion that their romance was over was confirmed. Elvis went out of his way to avoid spending time alone with her, except for late at night when he was ready for sex.

Anita didn't stay long, unwilling to be used in that way, and it was obvious as she packed that she was leaving his life for good. Elvis didn't come to the door to see her off, angry that she had rebuffed his advances the night before, so she walked over to him.

"I shouldn't say anything at all to you, 'cause you don't listen, but maybe it'll get through anyway. You got to stop blaming the world for everything bad that happens to you. Just because you're hurting and angry doesn't give you the right to be hurtful. I'm not saying it's deliberate. Sometimes, without knowing it, people hurt first to keep from being hurt themselves. That's a good way to end up alone."

"I don' have to worry about being alone," Elvis told her.

Anita looked at him, but let it drop and left.

As soon as the car door slammed, Elvis breathed a loud sigh of relief.

"Got that cat out of my hair," he joked with some buddies. "Time to go back on the prowl."

"Most guys would feel lucky to have her," I said quietly.

"Let 'em take her," he said loudly enough for the rest to hear. "I don't want her no more. All she wants to do is trap me into marryin' her. All she's interested in is being taken care of. To hell with her, and to hell with anyone who wants me to do something I don't want to."

The house at Killeen needed a revolving door for all the girls who passed through. Every week, Elvis would invite over at least two girls to be his special date of the evening. Elvis referred to them as his flavors-of-the-day, and they were discarded as such. Elvis would see a girl who caught his eye at a bar or standing out by his gate, and a date was arranged by Red or one of his army buddies. Approaching a girl himself indicated an interest and respect he simply didn't feel. Which is not to say he wasn't charming. He was, until they had satisfied his desires—then he cooled and his distant manner left the more naive ones in tears of shame or fury.

Elvis laughed about one girl who literally went for his throat.

"I jus' told her, you got no cause to get so upset if I don' wanna see you again. I didn' make you what you are. *Whooeee!* She tried to scratch my eyes out. I don' know how they can expect you to treat 'em like ladies if they spread their legs before you even ask."

I wouldn't say Elvis exactly flaunted his women, but his dad didn't care and pretended not to notice, and Miss Minnie went to bed early and minded her own business. Neither of them felt the right or need to know what Elvis was doing every second the way Gladys had, although Vernon had a good idea.

"He's gonna exhaust himself. Between his army training and what goes on here, he'll either be in the best shape of his life—or dead.

"Oh, don't look so surprised," Vernon laughed. "I'm not deaf. Elvis is so used to lookin' over his shoulder to make sure he ain't bein' watched, the last thing he needs is for me to bother him over a few girls. 'Sides, he's old enough to do as he wishes. It's like a bird learnin' to fly—once he gets used to it, he won't feel the need to keep flappin' his wings."

Elvis and Vernon got along better than they ever had, although Elvis did lash into him violently when he came home to find his father chatting to two young fans who had been hanging around all day. They were so star-struck they were thrilled to have their picture taken with Vernon, the *father of Elvis*.

Elvis took one look at his daddy laughing with the girls and stormed into the house, slamming the door so hard the windows rattled.

"Goddam dirty ol' man. How dare he be lookin' at

anyone so soon after Mama's . . . Mama joined Jesse. Lettin' those girls rub up against him that way . . . and it's me they want anyway, not an old man like him.''

He went into the bathroom and slammed the door behind him. When Elvis came out he was sullen but never said a word to Vernon. Instead, he had Red go out and bring the two girls in and the three of them flirted most of the evening, Elvis making a not-so-subtle point to his father. But Vernon was smart enough not to give the girls a second glance except for a passive goodnight on his way to bed. After a day or two, the tenseness between them passed, and they resumed their unfamiliar and tentative bond.

Nobody was immune to Elvis's moodiness and sharp tongue, myself included. Elvis came home every day for lunch, a group activity where we'd all sit down together and catch up on the events of the day. Toward the end of his training, Elvis invited a few officers to join him at home for lunch. He had Miss Minnie cook a fancy meal and asked us to dress up; he obviously wanted to impress his superiors and expected us to do our part.

When the officers came in, Elvis neglected to introduce me, ordering me to go fetch some sodas instead. I did it and kept my mouth shut.

Later, when he suggested, ''Why don't you help Miss Minnie clean up,'' I did.

Once the chores were done, I went to sit down with my coffee, but Elvis put a hand out to stop me.

''Maybe it'd be better if you waited in the other room 'til we're done. We can go over business then.''

I looked at Vernon, who averted his eyes, then back at Elvis, who seemed determined to prove what a big shot he was by embarrassing me and showing off his hired hand.

I excused myself and went into my room to call our friend Eddie, who had moved to Waco, Texas, from Memphis a while before. I told him I was returning home on business and asked if I could spend the night.

Waco was a hundred miles from Killeen, but it was the nearest place to get a train to Memphis.

Vernon looked up at me with shock when he saw me standing at the door with my suitcase. Vernon knew why without being told and tried to talk me out of it.

"He didn't mean nothin' by it—he's jus' bein' orn'ry. Tryin' to impress the brass."

"He can do it without me. I'm going to stay at Eddie's tonight and catch a train home in the morning."

Eddie met me at the station and I managed a cheerful face, not wanting to put him in the middle. We spent a quiet afternoon catching up, which helped keep my mind off how upset I was at Elvis.

More than anything, I felt betrayed. There was nobody in his life who had been as loyal a friend, who had stuck up for him when others laughed behind his back, who had accepted him as he was, as I had. He seemed hell-bent on pushing everyone away to prove just what an awful person he was. He was on the road to a self-fulfilling prophecy.

Late that night, right before bed, I heard a car pull up outside and doors slam—*bang, bang*—followed by someone pounding on the front door. It was Elvis, and he was mad.

He walked past Eddie without acknowledging his existence. "Earl, go get into the car."

"No, I won't."

"I'm not asking you, I'm telling you."

"I'm going home."

"You're getting in the car."

"You can't tell me what to do."

"Get in the car!" he shouted.

In his face I saw anger, and pleading. He was a stubborn little boy who was too afraid to admit affection by simply apologizing. He cared enough to drive an hour and a half to come get me, but didn't want to make himself vulnerable by saying he was wrong and sorry. It's ironic that Elvis went to such pains to hide his vulnerabilities in everyday life because that's partly what made him so appealing as a performer. That emotional and sensual need made you want to reach out to him in any way he'd let you. The charisma he oozed on stage was nothing compared to his magnetism in person, though. I felt my anger and resolve melt under his steady gaze and gave in to it.

"Let me get my luggage."

We drove home in silence, shooting down the highway at a hundred miles an hour. When we got back to the house, Elvis stopped outside the front door.

"Don't you *ever* leave me again like that," Elvis said. Then added, "Please."

A restlessness filled Elvis, and spending a quiet evening home was impossible. Boot camp got him in the habit of rising early, and on weekends he was the first one awake. Several times that fall he came in and woke me in the predawn hours, insisting I get up and go with him for a ride to check out the scenery.

The morning air was damp and cool as we cruised in his Lincoln Continental convertible. On the first of these early morning excursions, we drove with apparent aimlessness, down the back roads of Killeen and over the Texas highways in search of "the scenery"— ladies underwear.

"Early morning's the best time, 'cause that's when you can see women hangin' their private things out to dry," Elvis said, as he slowed down near an unfenced backyard filled with clothes on criss-crossing lines.

From the sound of it, he had obviously pursued this pastime before. He searched out panties with studied intensity, and when he found a pair he liked, his breath quickened and he squirmed in his seat.

"Look there, Earl. I like those ones with the lacy edges. Can't you just imagine what goes inside. I bet they belong to a natural redhead . . . a sweet young thing."

The fantasies that excited him the most centered around young girls in their early teens with firm, untainted flesh. Sometimes he verbalized images, but most of the time he kept his thoughts to himself, his face flushed like a naughty boy peeking through a partially open window.

This particular peculiarity took on other shapes. He often wanted his dates to act out roles and play pretend games—a schoolgirl bending over for a spanking and begging for mercy, as he first spanked her than entered her from behind, or having them act as if they were virgins willing to succumb to his every whim. These power games made him feel strong, superior, and *in control*—and reinforced his belief that no woman would ever measure up to his mama in purity and goodness. They were all basically whores.

During this time, another quirk presented itself. Elvis became obsessed with making sure no woman he slept with was a mother. The idea of having sex with a woman who had given birth repulsed him. He always asked, and if his date's anatomy happened to be "looser" than he thought it should be, he would freeze and order them to leave, convinced they had lied to him. At least with teenage girls, he felt more secure he wouldn't be pleasuring himself with a mother.

If therapy had been as socially acceptable then as it is now, Elvis might have been able to understand his sudden obsessions and work to resolve them. But shrinks were for crazy people, and Elvis was left to fend for himself—an insecure, ill-equipped man with no self-esteem to begin with. The emotional breakdown he suffered with the death of his mother never healed, it festered and began to rot away the person he used to be and might have been.

He never repeated his early morning laundry excursions outside of Texas—once back in Memphis he would move on to more elaborate diversions.

Elvis was wound as tight as a coil in Texas and looked everywhere for release and comfort. One weekend he flew in a Vegas showgirl (he had met her during a previous appearance there). Oddly enough, Elvis treated her better than the other girls he'd been with since coming back, but he spent more time talking to her than anything else. Maybe it was because she was world-weary and wise to the battle of the sexes, and she had no illusions that they shared a future. Elvis didn't need to hurt her—a lifetime of broken promises had beat him to it. They talked more than anything, and he found solace in her worn soul. The truest testimony of his benevolence was that he drove to the airport with her instead of getting Red to do it. I went along to keep him company on the drive back.

As we walked through the airport after seeing the dancer to her plane, it grew very quiet as people whispered to each other that Elvis Presley was there. The only sound was the heavy *click, click* of Elvis's shoes. The silence was eerie and carried a sudden sense of danger.

"Whatever you do, don't stop, don't even make eye contact," Elvis said in a low voice. "Keep walkin'." In his mind, he relived the crush of the crowd in front of Graceland. He was now surrounded by hundreds of people, and he was frightened.

"I hate this, I hate this. God, how I hate this," Elvis said, his head bent toward the ground. "Can't go anywhere anymore and have a little privacy."

Elvis was at odds with himself on almost every level. He was terrified of falling back into obscurity but wanted attention only at his convenience. His solution was to retreat out of the public arena and create his own sphere as much as possible.

Elvis would go to great expense in his quest for a little privacy. On one of his last weekends at camp, Elvis rented out an entire hotel floor in Dallas. He invited some acquaintances in Memphis down and paid their fare. He wanted a party even if he had to import it from another state. Nobody was particularly thrilled with the idea, but off we went—Red, Vernon, Miss Minnie, myself, and Elvis. The first night there all we did was sit in one big room watching TV and each other.

"Might as well have stayed home and saved the money," Vernon grumbled.

''I got tired of lookin' at the same four walls,'' Elvis said. ''It'll be better once everyone gets here.''

The next evening was certainly more crowded, but Elvis's mood was one of forced gaiety. Elvis never really liked parties, and although he tried to enjoy himself, it was obvious he was just going through manic motions. No matter how many layers of gloss Elvis tried to cover his sorrow with, that melancholy remained with him and cast a pall over him.

Vernon and Miss Minnie retired to their rooms at the far end of the hall early, and the party lasted well into the middle of the night. While others still danced or talked in small clusters, Elvis abruptly stood up and called to me across the room.

''Come on, Earl, let's go to bed.''

I felt my face heat up as I saw eyebrows raise in surprised arches. Elvis called me again, and I followed. This wasn't the first time he had insisted I go to bed with him. He said he found it difficult to sleep by himself anymore. He needed a body next to his— it didn't really matter whose.

He undressed then stretched out on the bed. ''I jus' didn' feel like takin' one of those girls to bed tonight. I wasn' up to a performance.''

His complaint then was tinged with weariness, but as the years passed, his belief that every girl he slept with expected him to be an expert lover who would send her into spasms of ecstasy ballooned into a raging fury. Whether it was real or imagined, he saw disappointment registered on women's faces after their lovemaking, and the silent put-down infuriated him and made him more bitter against the opposite sex. Sex turned into a weapon: Hurt and control women before they belittled you in an attempt to show themselves superior. He saw people laughing at him everywhere and lashed out. But no matter how famous or beautiful his conquest, he could never convince *himself* he was her equal.

I slipped into bed beside Elvis and he talked himself to sleep with wishes of being back at Graceland.

* * *

The last week of boot camp brought with it a flurry of activity inside the house at Killeen, with Elvis preparing to go overseas and the rest of us packing up for home. As a final gesture of largesse, Elvis wanted to buy gifts for the officers and some of his buddies. For as much as Elvis enjoyed buying presents for people who would be impressed by his generosity, he'd grown increasingly resentful of being seen as a gold mine.

"Everywhere I go, the price automatically triples as soon as I walk in the door," he complained. "But if I complain, I'll read in the paper the next day I'm a cheapskate. You know half the time the reporters know what I've done before I do it."

His irritation was exacerbated by anxiety and sadness. On the way home, Elvis got sad.

"Mama would have loved goin' to Germany, wouldn't she?" he asked, getting misty-eyed.

Actually, Gladys hated traveling, but it wasn't worth arguing about.

"At least Mama won' have to be humiliated by me losin' it all, since my singin' career's as good as done, thanks to Uncle Sam. Not that it matters anymore, with Mama gone. She took all the good things with her and left me with nothin'."

In late September of 1958 Elvis boarded a train for New York, then he was shipped to West Germany on the USS *Randall*. He watched the coastline shrink and cried as he saw his world sink below the horizon. Nothing would ever be right for him; he knew he'd never be whole again. He was resigned to play out the hand life dealt him, a powerless pawn of laughing fate.

11

Elvis arrived in Germany with his aching spirit resigned to his fate but was quickly and pleasantly surprised to discover his fame had preceded him. The German people were more respectful and less intrusive than American fans, and Elvis basked in the warmth of their approval without being blinded by the glare of his celebrity. Some of the less-intimidated soldiers sought out his company, and he cultivated a cocoon that kept him from being alone, even if it didn't ward off his emptiness. Army life was undemanding and left him with ample free time to sample the German culture, especially the *fraulein*. His first girlfriend was a buxom blonde lass named Magrite, but she was soon replaced by an even younger American beauty who became his last hope for salvation.

The first thing that struck Elvis about Priscilla Beaulieu was her eerie familiarity. It took him several minutes before he put a finger on it—she looked uncannily like faded photos he'd seen of Gladys as a young girl. She knew who Elvis was, the whole world knew by that point, but wasn't in awe of him or his celebrity. Being the daughter of an air force captain, Priscilla had traveled extensively, and as a result, she exuded a maturity that belied her fourteen years. Her subtle reserve intrigued Elvis; she wasn't like any other young girl he'd ever met.

Priscilla's age presented a few problems in Germany. While fans were respectful as far as keeping a polite distance, the press covered his every move. Elvis found privacy more difficult to obtain than in Memphis, where he could retreat behind the gates of Graceland. He once took Priscilla to a movie, and when they came out, a crowd of almost a hundred people stood quietly across the street, just to catch a glimpse of him.

A few of the local papers found out Priscilla's age and made subtle but pointed reference to her youth, and Elvis immediately worried that the negative tone would turn people against him. He tried to diffuse any potential gossip by going underground with their relationship, which had barely gotten past the hand-holding stage. They spent time together in out-of-the-way restaurants or in parks out in the countryside. Elvis had never been on a real picnic before, with a blanket and basket full of food, and the magic of the experience left him starry-eyed. He was living out a fantasy world, moving through a time and place that couldn't last.

Because they met toward the end of his enlistment, Elvis knew their time together was limited, and that made each moment particularly precious. But what made Priscilla more of an obsession was the growing notion that she was more than the spitting image of a young Gladys. Everything about Priscilla convinced him she actually embodied the spirit of his dead mama.

Unlike the girls he met in bars or picked out of the crowd at performances or from the throngs in front of Graceland, Priscilla didn't throw herself at Elvis, and her bearing commanded respect. She was well-schooled but unpretentious, with an unassuming but warm, sparkling personality.

Somehow, Jesse had answered his prayers and sent Gladys back to him in the person of Priscilla. He didn't pretend to understand how miracles worked, he only believed in their possibility. He was being given a second chance to prove himself. He immediately put Priscilla on a pedestal alongside the gilded image of his deceased mother, whose memory shone more brightly in his thoughts as each day passed. *In return, the only thing he expected back was a sense of wholeness and perfect, unconditional love.*

The illusion that Gladys lived on through Priscilla was at once erotically arousing, emotionally satisfying, and a fountainhead of guilt. Long-buried Oedipal desires scratched at the surface of his consciousness and threatened to come forth. Their presence caused Elvis enough anxiety to keep him from trying to break down Priscilla's defenses so he could sleep with her. She was too good, simple, and pure for that, and even *thoughts* of her flesh under his made Elvis shrink with shame. Theirs was a relationship that would transcend the dirty physical.

Elvis was so wrapped up in his own reverie that he was blind to events happening under his very nose. Vernon and Miss Minnie had joined Elvis a few weeks after he arrived in Germany as a support network. Vernon loved exploring new places and made friends easily with his good ol' boy demeanor. Among his best new pals were an army sergeant and his wife, who were originally from Alabama. They spent many a fun-filled evening out at local nausbiers enjoying beers between oom-pah-pahs.

Elvis portrayed his father as the grieving widower, which is what he thought he ought to be, and spoke sincerely about their loss. For however much Vernon missed Gladys, and they had been together over twenty years, his loss was minimal compared to Elvis's. Since the day her twin son died, Gladys had never been Vernon's emotional strength. They were financial partners for good and for bad, occasionally found physical release in each other's arms and shared in the day-to-day struggles, but they had not been emotional partners. They didn't even really share in the raising of their only child. Elvis had been firmly her domain, with Vernon relegated to the position of interested spectator. If anything, Gladys's death opened up a new world for Vernon—a chance to find someone who paid attention to *him*, who noticed whether or not he was there and cared. Vernon missed Gladys's presence because it was so familiar, but his heart had not gone into seclusion.

When the army sergeant got involved with a project that required longer hours, Vernon gladly helped him out by escorting his wife, Dee, to dinner so she wouldn't have to be home alone waiting. The same charm that made his dad, Jesse, such a lady-killer, belonged to Vernon—and he found himself hit with sadness when Dee said goodnight and shut the door. What Vernon didn't realize was that Dee felt the same emotion as she watched him walk away in the darkness.

After a particularly romantic evening, Vernon blurted out his feelings and was overwhelmed when Dee admitted she loved him, too. They conducted their romance with the utmost discretion and managed to keep it secret for several months before an American reporter happened upon them at a remote village restaurant and recognized the handsome older man as Elvis Presley's father.

I got a call at Graceland from one of the wire services asking for confirmation that Vernon planned to marry a woman he had met overseas as soon as she divorced her husband. I assured them the report was the result of someone's having consumed too many steins of beer, but called Vernon anyway, just to let him know what was going on. I had promised the wire service reporter I'd get him one of Vernon's quotable quotes on the mix-up.

"The press seems to think that you're going to get married, except the lady is already married. We need to think of a comment."

There was such a long silence, I thought a disgruntled operator had disconnected us.

"Earl, can you tell the press we're friends?"

"I can tell them anything. Is it the truth?"

Again, a silence.

"Does Elvis know, Uncle Vernon?"

''Not exactly. I wanted to wait.''

Vernon told me their story, and the emotion in his voice was genuine.

''You know, Uncle Vernon, the press is going to find out eventually, and we're both going to look foolish for having lied.''

''I ain't got a choice, son. I jus' don' wanna mess while we're here. It'll be bad 'nough back home.''

Despite his anxiety over Elvis's finding out in the beginning, Vernon never seemed overly concerned about the publicity. Because he was really in love.

Elvis was one of the last to know about his father and Dee, but until he found out, his world was looking momentarily up. The last letter he sent from Germany was a rambling musing about Priscilla and Gladys and Jesse and his anxiety about coming back to face the prospect of starting over.

''You'll love Priscilla, 'cause I know how much you loved Mama. She's a lot younger than me, and I worry people will consider me a cradle-snatcher,'' he wrote. ''Vernon and Miss Minnie like her, too. It's a shame I'll be leaving so soon, but I know I'll be seein' her again, even if it takes a couple of years for her to finish up school. Unless no one cares about my singing anymore, then I'll come back to visit her here.

''I hope Parker's been earning his keep while I been over here. Do you think anyone cares I'm coming back? Sometimes I think it's better if I just stay here and not bother. Except they don't have any good stores to buy clothes, so I *have* to come back to Memphis.''

His last week in Germany was filled with emotion and promise, but he left with the full assurance that he and Priscilla were being guided from above and their reunion was a fait accompli.

Elvis was officially discharged on May 5, 1960, but Vernon flew back to Memphis with Dee a couple of days ahead. Nobody knew she had officially left her husband for good until Vernon finally admitted their situation to Elvis as he was on his way out the door to the airport. Vernon expressed relief at Elvis's apparent calm acceptance of the news, but it was wishful thinking. Elvis had just been so shocked he had blanked out. As the news sank in, Elvis threw a tantrum of frightening proportions that brought his neighbors running outside. He hurled furniture at the walls and left holes in the walls with his fists. Vernon had betrayed Gladys and had betrayed him. The tentative bridge of trust they were developing crumbled like dust in the shockwaves that followed Vernon's announcement. Elvis was also angry that Vernon had spoiled an otherwise sweet farewell to Priscilla, and he knew in his heart he could never forgive Vernon if he went through with his plan to marry.

Vernon was either blind or stubborn about how Elvis would take to Dee. "I've no reason to think he doesn't like her just fine. You know Elvis, he never says much. He was too wrapped up in that teenager, anyway."

It was strange to see Vernon with another woman, holding hands, exchanging kisses, and being a lot more physically affectionate than he'd ever been with Gladys. He was so animated, truly like a kid in love.

Dee was a striking woman, blonde and about twenty years younger than he. It was plain that she loved him dearly. They fit together well, and everyone at Graceland couldn't help but be happy for them, Miss Minnie especially. But the joyous atmosphere was about to be tempered with Elvis's arrival home.

A party had been planned to celebrate Elvis's return, and to no one's surprise, Vernon and Dee opted not to attend. Instead, Vernon took her for a night out at some of Memphis's finer clubs, excited to show her the finer points of her new home.

"We're gonna paint the town red tonight, so don't wait up." They laughed, hugging each other.

Red went to pick Elvis up at the airport, and when they got back, I went outside to meet Elvis. He stepped out of the car slowly, drinking in his surroundings. He took deep breaths, filling his lungs with the familiar

scents of his home. We hugged a long time and it felt
so good to have him back.

"You've grown up," he said to me.

"I was always more grown up than you."

"Okay, then, you finally grew into your ears." He
punched me playfully, then took another breath and
walked inside. He reacquainted himself by walking
through every room. Except for the removal of Gladys's clothes and other personal belongings, nothing had
changed in two years.

Elvis was pleased we had a party planned, and it
gave him something to concentrate on besides the sudden flurry of demons in his imagination. It wasn't a
good sign of things to come when Elvis didn't ask after
Vernon not being at his party. In fact, he never brought
his father up once; he just seemed intent to have an
enjoyable time. In the home movies I took of that
welcome-home party, Elvis looks so handsome in a
crisp, white shirt. He even danced that night, looking
all arms and legs, but not caring. When Elvis cut the
cake Miss Minnie had baked, he nearly chopped his
tie in two, and as we all laughed, it appeared the old
Elvis was finally back. But once the guests left, his
mood turned dark, like another person had suddenly
appeared.

"Is Daddy with that whore of his?"

"Elvis!"

"Well, she is. You know she's only with him because of *my* money. Nothing more than a golddigger."
Elvis began pacing with agitation.

"She seems nice enough . . ."

*"Don't you dare take her side against me and
Mama,"* he yelled, then added with quiet menace. "Or
you can get out."

"I wasn't taking sides. Maybe you should talk to
him—"

"Ain't *nothin'* to discuss. If that old man wants to
make a fool of himself with a golddiggin' whore young
enough to be my sister, I can't stop him. But I don't

have to pretend it ain't what it is. Whole thing makes me too upset to talk about.''

Elvis pulled a small vial of pills out of his pocket and grabbed a nearby bottle of beer to drink two down.

"You sick?''

"I ain't sick, 'cept of cheatin' liars like Daddy. These are to help me relax so I can get to sleep. Doctor in Germany said it helps get over jet lag. What you lookin' at?''

I shrugged and picked up a pile of dishes. Now I understood why he had been relaxed enough to dance and have a halfway good time.

"You ought to be careful with pills. They can get funny.''

"Earl, I know what I'm doing,'' he said with an edge. "I've had people tellin' me what to do for the last two years, so stop naggin' at me, alright? These'll calm me down so I can rest.''

His first week back was hectic. Parker arrived to brief Elvis on the status of his career, and Elvis was shocked to see it so healthy—record sales were still strong, RCA had the next batch of songs for him to record ready to go, Vegas wanted him for some dates, and his next movie was a go. Elvis seemed dazed that his public hadn't forgotten him after all and grateful to Parker for his part, which the Colonel naturally played up to soaring heights.

For all his relief that he had survived a two-year layoff, Elvis expressed mild chagrin that he had no say in the songs he'd be recording or the movie he'd be starring in. Parker ignored the complaint and forged ahead with a complex accounting of other business transactions that left Elvis with a headache.

After Parker left, Elvis roamed the house restlessly. He'd been given at least a week to reacclimate and rest, and after less than twenty-four hours, he was getting cabin fever. Minus distractions, Elvis was out of sorts and disoriented, suffering from a combination of jet lag, edginess from his "nerve pills," and a renewed sense of loss.

Being back in his mama's house released a flood of repressed emotions and memories. Everywhere he turned there were still reminders of Gladys: her favorite chair, her bedroom and the pillow she slept on, the empty remains of a chicken coop in the backyard beside a garden plot now overgrown with weeds.

Walking through the house, he relived her death and the long days waiting for her burial. The recriminations he flung at himself from inside tormented his mind. He clutched her pillow and wept anguished tears. Not even the conviction that he had found his mama's spirit in Priscilla assuaged his pain from the past. His freshly opened wounds turned that happiness to melancholy. He still missed hearing her voice and seeing her sweet face. Nothing and nobody could ever completely fill the void, which made Priscilla's importance that much greater. Especially since he had as good as buried Vernon, too.

In typical fashion, to help ease his pain Elvis turned his energies toward the temporary release and sense of omnipotence that came with sex. Several nights Elvis sent Red running to find him a date, which followed a predictable pattern. Elvis would shower and get ready while Red accomplished his mission, but Elvis never made his entrance until the girl, or girls, were already waiting in the music room. Red would introduce everyone, and they would chat and listen to records. At some point, Red would discreetly find something else to do and leave. After some more drinks, Elvis would sing to his guests. After an intimate performance like that, it wasn't long before a girl'd be rubbing his thigh in appreciation and they would shortly beat a hasty retreat to his room upstairs. If there were two girls and one got uncomfortable with the prospect of sharing Elvis with another at the same time, he would try to convince them it would be fun, but failing that he gave them cab fare and said goodnight. Most of the time, though, the girls were willing. First of all, groupies are out for one thing, anyway.

Secondly, it was made pretty clear up front that Elvis wanted to ''party'' with two girls.

One night during that first week back, Elvis was thumbing through the script of the film he was set to do, *G.I. Blues*. He threw it down in disgust, amazed at how quick the studio was able to take advantage of any situation.

''I ain't out of the army a week and they wanna put me right back in,'' he sighed.

He got up, stretched, and stood staring at me. Red was off, and Elvis had suddenly gotten an urge for female companionship. He wanted me to go arrange a date for him with one of the girls milling around the front of Graceland. Since his return, the number of people hoping to catch their first glimpse of Elvis had been larger than ever.

Back in high school, I had set up Elvis with friends of my sister, a neighbor and some aquaintances from Leonard's, but in those days Elvis would be lucky to get a deep kiss goodnight. I felt funny procuring a sex partner for him and told him so.

Elvis laughed at my shyness. ''Earl, we gotta get you out of your shell and into the world. Girls come here because they *want* to be with me. They're creamin' their little lace panties at the thought of walkin' through that door. Why do you think they stand out there 'til all hours in any weather?

''They're dyin' to find out if I'm any good and brag to their friends. Since I feel up to a big performance tonight, I don' wanna disappoint them. You'll be doin' them a *favor*. They'll be very grateful.''

I reluctantly agreed, swayed by his logic and by my desire to please him. On my way out the door, he called after me.

''Bring back four—we're *all* gonna have fun. And make sure they're young ones.''

He was right. It didn't take very long to find some girls willing to spend an evening with Elvis Presley. I ushered them past the guard and into Graceland amid some vulgar but good-natured comments tossed at

them by a few guys who stood on the sidewalk. When
Elvis made his entrance, a couple of the girls gasped,
and the temperature of the room heated up immediately.

I turned to leave, but Elvis grabbed my arm and
pulled me back into the room, closing the door behind
us.

"I told you we were *all* gonna have a party. It's time
you learn what women are meant for."

He introduced me to the girls, none of whom were
over seventeen, and told them to be extra nice to me.
They were so thrilled to be in Graceland they happily
complied and flirted with me constantly. Elvis conducted the ebb and flow of the evening with the skill
of a maestro, from the first casual touches to playful
kisses to urgent gropings. I wondered which of the
four girls would be mine, but Elvis had other plans.

"Let's go to my room and have some real fun."

It took me a split second to realize he meant everyone—all six of us. The electricity in the room made it
impossible to refuse.

In his room, Elvis took off his shirt and threw it
over the lamp, casting a sultry glow across the bed.
He undressed completely then flopped back on his bed,
gently stroking himself.

"First one naked gets this first."

Three of the girls giggled and began to strip but one
hesitated, having second thoughts at being part of an
orgy. Elvis reached up and pulled her down to him
tenderly, kissing and caressing her while the rest of us
watched spellbound. While they kissed, he slowly un-
zipped her skirt and slid it off. He broke away but kept
his eyes fixed on hers while he pulled her sweater over
her head, murmuring about how beautiful her breasts
were. Once she was naked beside him, Elvis smiled
at the rest of us.

"Better hurry up or you'll miss all the fun."

We all fell into bed, grabbing, touching, kissing,
rubbing against the body nearest our own. A couple
of times I inadvertently ran my hand over Elvis's soft

skin and he responded with a moan of pleasure, his eyes closed, the image of the perfect woman dancing in his head.

The activity came in waves of passionate release followed by calm, before starting up again. At one point Elvis got up to go to the bathroom, and when he returned, he looked at the rest of us in bed and laughed.

"What a picture you make."

Climbing back into bed he got an idea and grabbed my arm excitedly.

"Earl, you still got that movie camera you had at my party?"

"Yeah, why?"

"Go get it."

"Elvis . . ."

"Oh, come on, we're gonna make a little home movie starring these girls, who are prettier than any movie actress I ever met."

I explained it was too dark, but Elvis said to set up the light like I had the other night. His face was flushed red, and with his tousled hair he looked like an excited schoolboy, and he wouldn't take no for an answer.

While I scrounged up the lights and cameras, Elvis and the girls entertained themselves, and he made sure to keep their glasses full of bubbly champagne and their hands busy on his body. The sounds of their pleasure spurred me to hurry up, because I wanted to be back in bed with them. But first, I had to play cameraman for Elvis's director. He started the movie by talking playfully to the camera, introducing the girls as his co-stars, then grabbing one of them and flipping her over so he was poised above her, his profile to the camera.

"Make sure to get all of this, Earl."

With his eyes never leaving the girl's face, Elvis lowered his body onto hers, stretching her arms above her head and pinning them under his strong arms. He pushed her legs open with his knees then slowly began to make love to her, the bright lights glaring off his sweaty back. After a few minutes he let her go and

rolled on his back, ordering two girls into position—
one straddling his waist, the other his shoulders.

He only let me stop when we had used all the film,
then he sent the girls home by midnight saying he
didn't want their mamas to worry.

Elvis didn't get up 'til the next afternoon, and when
he came into the kitchen, I felt my face turn red with
sudden embarrassment. He laughed when he saw my
color and came up from behind and wrapped his arms
around me.

"I tol' you we'd have a good time, didn' I?"

Before sitting down for "breakfast," Elvis casually
told me to go buy plenty of film—and not to make any
plans for later.

Every night for the rest of the week, I selected four
of the most forward girls I could find, and every night
I made home movies of Elvis in every conceivable
position with them. One of his favorite things was to
watch the girls have sex with each other. The faces
changed and each group got younger, until on the final
evening there were four fourteen-year-olds—although
their bodies were a decade older. The sexual activity
got less gentle and more vigorous with each passing
night. One girl made the mistake of pouting with a
sigh of disappointment when Elvis couldn't make love
to her after finishing with one of the others. When he
was ready, he pinned her down with forceful, almost
violent thrusting, angry at the imagined slur on his
virility and causing her to cry out.

I don't know who he paid off, but Elvis managed to
get the film developed with no problem and planned a
night at the movies with Red and a couple of his army
buddies, who had already showed up at his door and
been given jobs as your basic go-fers.

Elvis locked the music room door and told Red to
start the projector. Grainy images came into focus,
and Elvis led the hooting, the barnyard king strutting
his stuff. As each scene flickered on the screen, Elvis
gave running commentary about how "loose" or
"tight" each girl was, his shorthand for how experi-

enced he figured they were. His favorite was the young girl he swore had been a virgin, and he pointed out bloodstains on his sheets to back up his claim.

The movies were Elvis's latest pride and joy. He and his boys watched parts of them every day until he left for Miami to appear at the Fontainebleau Hotel with none other than Frank Sinatra, and he stashed the films in a drawer without giving them a second thought.

Sinatra treated him politely but carried himself with the bearing of a man who knows his position. Elvis was courteous and intimidated, despite Old Blue Eyes' warmth. More than anything, Elvis felt exhilarated to perform in front of an audience, and on stage he felt Sinatra's equal. The concert went well and Elvis left soon after, curious about Sinatra's special interest in his upcoming film. He foolishly thought that maybe Sinatra liked his work and the thought gave Elvis's ego a nice boost.

G.I. Blues was a mindless star vehicle that was memorable only for his co-star, the stunning Juliet Prowse. As he had done before, he went after a lady of class to prove himself worthy and equal, believing it would gain him acceptance in Hollywood. Their affair was heated and Juliet lavished attention on Elvis, although she preferred spending nights at home rather than out on the town. Elvis naturally shied away from parties or gatherings where he might feel out of place or awkward, so he was more than happy to acquiesce, but not for that reason alone.

Elvis returned to Graceland after the movie wrapped, and Juliet kept in constant touch. Nobody could understand why she always used a code name when she called, and Elvis just shrugged when asked and gave a half smile. He finally admitted what was going on at a rehearsal shortly before he was to leave for Vegas. Elvis wasn't Juliet's only beau of the moment—she was also the apple of another singer's blue eyes, Frank Sinatra. Elvis felt supremely smug and superior, sweeping a big shot like Sinatra's lady off her feet. The guys in his band and some of his entourage (who followed Elvis wherever he went) slapped him on the back, impressed with his latest conquest. In the middle of his story, a phone rang.

"Oh, oh, Elvis, it's probably Frank," someone wisecracked.

In the days after that, if there was a knock on the door or an unexpected phone call or whatever, oh, oh, it's probably Frank, became the running joke. Elvis laughed harder than anyone, tickled at having put one over on the Chairman of the Board.

Elvis and Prowse hooked up back in Vegas for a couple of days before she headed to Los Angeles for some business commitments. One evening Elvis was in his dressing room, cooling down after a performance, when a stagehand peeked in and told him Frank Sinatra was outside to see him. Elvis laughed, assuming one of the guys had put him up to it.

Elvis yelled without turning around. "Alright you guys, cut it out, I'm too tired to fool around."

He looked up into his mirror in time to see Frank Sinatra walk through the dressing room door, accompanied by two unpleasant companions. The conversation was extremely civil and very brief. Sinatra complimented him on his show, on the completion of his new film, and offered some free advice—if Elvis wanted to continue working in good health, he should make sure he wasn't stepping on the wrong toes. Without ever mentioning her name or losing his smile, Sinatra succeeded in making Juliet Prowse the biggest turn-off Elvis could imagine.

From that night on, Elvis completely broke off all contact with her and gave orders to everyone, even Miss Minnie, that he would not be taking her calls anymore and to simply say he was out. She attempted to reach him for several weeks then abruptly stopped—to his immense relief.

Although Vernon, Dee, and Elvis lived under the same roof, Graceland was large enough so they could comfortably stay out of one another's way. Elvis avoided contact as much as possible, not wanting to be reminded of his father's betrayal. As soon as her divorce was final, Vernon and Dee got married in Alabama, partly to get away from the Memphis press and partly because they both had relatives there. The ceremony was organized at the last minute, Vernon undecided where and how he wanted it. Elvis refused to go, saying he was too busy with work. He also forbid anyone else to go, except for Miss Minnie, the only person who saw Vernon walk down the aisle a second time.

The snub stung Vernon but didn't come as a surprise. In his heart, Vernon knew he was much better off without Elvis there, that way he could enjoy his own wedding and not have to deal with Elvis sulking in a corner or upsetting Dee with his accusing stares. Vernon sensed the hostility, but underestimated its depth, because Elvis only vented it fully behind his daddy's back.

To Vernon and Dee's faces, he was merely rude and uncommunicative—a spoiled child punishing those around him because he didn't get his way. Vernon would have been shocked had he known the full measure of disrespect Elvis harbored. While Vernon and Dee lived at Graceland, there were many uncomfortable evenings around the dinner table on nights when the whole group was present. Elvis would carry on conversations without making the slightest effort to include, or even look at, them. If Dee asked him a question, Elvis would give a short, abrupt answer or pretend not to hear what she said.

One night, we had just sat down to eat when Vernon and Dee stopped in to say goodbye on their way out. Elvis sat, not saying a word, as Miss Minnie served dinner. He waited until she walked back to the kitchen then suddenly bolted to his feet and walked around the table, picking up plate after plate and smashing each one into the wall. The room was covered with food, and everyone stayed stock still, not wanting to inflame him even more.

"Goddam them to hell," he yelled as the plates were

flying. "How *dare* he bring that bitch into Mama's house? He treated her like dirt when she was alive, and he's still doin' it. The son of a bitch's got no respect for anyone. He don't care about me and certainly not Mama. She ain't cold in the ground, and he goes and marries a money-grabbin' whore.

"He put on a big act in front of everyone, so they'd feel sorry for him and think he was so sad, but I'll betcha he was glad to be rid of her so he could find himself a young cat to stick it to. It makes me sick. If it wasn' outta respect for Mama, I'd throw 'em both out on the street and tell 'em to go get jobs.''

He considered Vernon's relationship with Dee—the hand-holding, the intimate glances, the late mornings "sleeping" in—as nothing short of treachery. It was plain disrespectful to Gladys's memory to have married so soon after her death. A one-night stand would have been acceptable, but not genuine love. He saw the new Mrs. Presley as an attempt to replace Gladys and that infuriated him.

Elvis might have felt better had he let off steam directly by having it out with Vernon man to man, but of course he didn't. The fact that Vernon had been Gladys's choice for husband prevented Elvis from responding in a more outward manner. Gladys had always let him know in no uncertain terms that disrespect toward his daddy upset her and wouldn't be tolerated. Kin was kin.

Elvis was full of paradoxes that pulled him in opposite directions. Despite his acute disapproval, once Vernon married her, Dee became extended family whether Elvis liked it or not. Vernon still had access to all the money he needed, and Elvis even had an apartment built for them behind Graceland later on.

"Better than them livin' here," he said, letting everyone else know how much he resented it.

Elvis never had the confidence or nerve to stand up to his father. He could only rant and rave behind his back and cut him out emotionally. He bad-mouthed Dee any chance he could, painting such a horrible picture, a stranger would be shocked to discover she was one of the sweetest people you'd ever want to meet.

Having eyes and ears everywhere, Parker was well aware of the rift that had opened between Vernon and Elvis. The Colonel liked Vernon and considered him an important ally but knew it was dangerous and unwelcome to interfere in family matters unless it somehow related to business. He doubted Elvis would make a stand against Vernon, but he never took chances on things getting out of hand, so he found a way to relate it to business during their next meeting. Without asking for reasons or explanations, Parker impassively counseled Elvis against the dangers of a family feud leaking out to the public and even joked that it wouldn't look very good in the papers if the father of the country's most popular singer went back to living in a shack in Mississippi.

Elvis bristled inside momentarily but at that moment had other aggravations on his mind that were bothering him more. Parker had brought over another script Hollywood wanted him to do and a recording schedule. Elvis had been unhappy with several selections RCA had chosen for him, and many of the new songs bothered him even more. He didn't mind doing some of what they wanted, he just wanted to pick a couple out himself. He had complained to Parker before without result and was in a pissy enough mood today to bring it up again.

"I thought we agreed I'd get to do some other things?"

"You don't tamper with success," Parker told him. "Maybe later."

"It's always later. I don' see why I have to keep waitin'. They're makin' enough money off me, the least they can do is let me sing a couple of songs that make me feel good."

"The time's not right. Wait until we get you firmly re-established."

"You said I never became *un*-established," Elvis argued.

"Stop being difficult, Elvis. I'll see what I can do, but there's no reason to run off half-cocked."

After Parker left, Elvis had a mini-tantrum, hating Parker's patronizing tone but stifled by its force.

"Nobody wants to hear what I wanna do. They only care how much money I make 'em, not whether I'm happy or not. Sometimes I think Parker forgets he works for me. I'm tired of fightin' the people who are *supposed* to be on my side."

Graceland was like Grand Central Station in the hectic months following Elvis's return. When Gladys was alive, it had been her house, and Elvis didn't let his buddies hang out there much. Now, in addition to myself, Vernon, Dee, and Miss Minnie, several of his entourage were living there as well. Vernon complained more than once, but Elvis would have it no other way.

"They keep me from bein' lonely."

His boys ran errands for Elvis, played matchmaker, kept him company 'til all hours—often after Elvis finished with a date and sent her home—but their most important function was to serve as audience and fan club.

He was still haunted by the specter of Gladys, which in turn made him dwell on her alter ego, Priscilla, ever more often. As he reminisced, fantasized, and romanticized their time together, Priscilla grew to a larger-than-life idol in his mind. She was young, untainted and moldable. He turned her into the perfect girl he imagined she could be, leaving no room for who she really was. He began to yearn for her terribly. He wrote her long missives and checked the mail every day for her replies. If he were out of town, he had the letters forwarded—all the while he was maintaining his carefree bachelor ways. He still pushed sexual feelings about Priscilla off to the side, keeping his guilt at bay.

Despite his busy schedule and the constant attention from the people around him, Elvis's loneliness and depression overwhelmed him any time he wasn't actively distracted by sex, work, or the constant attention of his group of followers. At night, he was restless and itchy to be on the move, but going out in public meant dealing with fans. For as much as he loved them, he'd get weary of being smothered. He was either isolated at home or would rent out a place and be isolated there.

"I wish I could go out to a movie with everybody else, or go bowlin' with a bunch of people and mix with strangers without them watchin' your every move."

"They love you," one of his boys said.

"I wish they loved me less."

"No, you don't, especially those little girls. I'll take 'em if you don't want 'em."

"I'll break your arms," he laughed, getting a reprieve from the blues that threatened to settle in.

But his life *was* confining. In the beginning it was exciting to be so sought after, but the novelty had worn off and it became an increasing burden. Shopping used to be one of the joys of his life, but if he wanted to browse now he had to go after hours. On more than one Christmas Eve, Elvis drove down to Lansky's in the middle of the night, risking life and limb, so he could shop in peace.

On the Fourth of July, Elvis bought hundreds and hundreds of dollars' worth of fireworks. In Tennessee, you could get roman candles, M-80s, cherry bombs, rockets, sparklers, and almost any other kind of explosive you can think of. We saved half of them to light after dark, but the rest were used in a less festive way. Reminiscent of earlier days at the roller rink, Elvis chose sides and we lined up like a football team— or maybe an army is a better description—on opposite ends of the back lawn. On the count of three we'd break for cover and shoot off the fireworks at each other. The rules were simple—if you were left standing and weren't on fire, you won. With roman candles exploding in your back and rockets with M-80s attached flying at you from across the yard, it was like guerilla warfare.

Elvis led the charge with daunting aggressiveness, like a boxer pummeling away at a body bag. It was also a relief from the boredom of feeling cooped up and a welcome thrill. Fewer and fewer things gave Elvis pleasure any more.

For someone who'd grown up so poor, you'd have thought he would forever appreciate the finer things in life, but it was as if he was mad because the material things weren't enough. They hadn't given him the sense of wholeness he expected, so he occasionally treated his things with disdain. In his room, expensive pieces of jewelry were flung all over, some of it twisted from being stepped on. And yet, let someone from the old days stop by, and he wore them like a badge.

In the fall of 1960, after he'd returned from yet another movie in Hollywood, Elvis was particularly irritable and moody. It was like living with two different people, or identical twins with opposite personalities. Elvis was still one of the most charming men you'd ever meet, when he wanted to be. It's just that he often didn't want to make the effort. The exception to that was with children. With them he was always good, kind, and considerate, no matter what else was going on his life.

Over the years stacks and stacks of letters poured in from families saying their child was sick or dying and that their greatest wish was to talk to Elvis. Or how a phone call would help a child battle back from this disease or that injury. It was heartbreaking, and having that kind of responsibility heaped on his shoulders put a lot of pressure on Elvis.

A couple of secretaries worked out of a spare room in Graceland, going through the mail. The majority of letters were requests for autographed photos, but there were scores from lovesick fans who wouldn't settle for anything less than Elvis himself. I remember one woman who kept writing to say she had left her husband so she and Elvis could be together and included the number of the hotel where she was staying. Those letters got tossed after we got done laughing, but we had a special system for letters concerning sick children. We'd send back a questionnaire to the parents with a return envelope, marked with a red line down the side. Those envelopes were the first to be opened on any given day.

The questionnaire asked the doctor's name, their phone number, the nature of the illness, and other pertinent information to make sure the letter wasn't a phony. People tried every trick in the book to meet Elvis, even lying about a child's health. Only about a fourth of the questionnaires were returned.

Obviously, the situation had to be serious, or else Elvis would have spent all his days on the phone. Of those that checked out, we had to make sure a call from Elvis wouldn't be so much of a shock to the child that it would involve Elvis in a liability suit. If the child was still in the hospital—often they had recovered by the time all the paperwork was done—Elvis would put in a phone call.

No way whatsoever did Elvis ever mind making the time for this. He actually looked forward to hearing the little voices on the other end light up. On more than one occasion, Elvis did more than just call. If he found out the parents weren't able to continue treatment because of money problems, or that other kids in the family were going without because of the medical bills, Elvis had me make arrangements to pick up the medical bills until the child recovered. This happened time and time again. The only stipulation was that it was to be kept a secret. And to my knowledge, not once did the press ever find out how many dozens of children Elvis cared for financially. He didn't even like talking about it to me, but it was obvious it made him feel good. It was a reminder of his basic good soul, no matter how badly he behaved otherwise.

The contrast between the public image of Elvis as a happy, carefree man on top of the world who had everything going his way and the moody, depressed man he could be at home was carefully orchestrated by Parker. In public, whether in Memphis, Hollywood, or

Vegas, at concerts or out among his fans, Elvis became the Elvis the public wanted to see.

"They listen to your music and watch your movies to forget their troubles, so you better keep your best face on if you expect them to stay interested and supportive," Parker preached.

He also warned Elvis that loving fans could quickly turn to vultures once they smelled blood.

"They don't care about your troubles, except for making themselves feel better. A lot of them love you, but a lot feel satisfaction when a star screws up, too. For as fast as they can make you number one, they can forget you just as easily. Never forget that."

The publicity machinery surrounding Elvis helped maintain a certain public image in a lot of little ways. If a celebrity or politician was visiting Memphis, I made sure a greeting, in Elvis's name, was sent to them along with an invitation to Graceland if he was in town.

While he would dutifully sign autographs, he didn't have time to do it all, so I signed half of them so no fan would be disappointed.

Once there was a tragic school fire where several children were killed and a telegram was sent from Elvis, even though he didn't know about it until the next day.

I never did anything I didn't think Elvis wouldn't do if he had the time or awareness, but there's no denying much of his public persona was created and maintained by others over the course of his career. And as the years went by, the public image of Elvis grew further and further removed from the man he became.

Everyone around Elvis put off his uncharacteristically hard edge to the stress of coming home after a long absence. As the months passed and he didn't return to the same person he was before leaving, we started looking for other answers and excuses—he was older, he was still grieving, he was just tired, he was working too hard, he wasn't busy enough, he slept too late, he didn't get enough rest, anything but believe he could actually be changing before our eyes.

Vernon thought the answer was simple.

"He just needs a good woman."

"He's got several dozen," I pointed out.

"I mean one to settle down with, have a family. He ain't gettin' any younger. You can't tomcat forever. Gets too lonely."

Vernon was right that Elvis was lonelier by the week. His countless one-night stands and brief affairs left him more and more despondent. More cynical and resentful. No girl he met, whether starlet, famous actress, or hometown girl, met his impossible expectations and qualifications. As soon as a lady exerted any spark of independence or showed any sign of intellectual or professional equality, she was dropped. Elvis wasn't secure enough in himself not to feel threatened by a true equal, which was another reason he gravitated toward young girls.

While Elvis had extraordinary appeal, not every woman swooned at his feet. Although the number of Hollywood ladies that said yes to Elvis far outnumbered the no's, he took each turndown as an indication that the woman thought he wasn't good enough.

"She acted like I was nothin' more than white trash."

Back in Memphis, there were girls everywhere, but none of them struck a chord with Elvis. Any local girl who succumbed to his insistent sexual charms was instantly discarded as loose.

With each failure, Priscilla's star grew ever brighter.

Priscilla would have been surprised to know that Elvis barely talked about her in the months after his return. He kept their correspondence pretty much to himself, and when he did refer to her, she was included with several other girls he reminisced about.

But as the end of the year approached, he began to dwell on Priscilla aloud, bringing her up in conversation out of the blue and speaking of her as if she were a fairy-tale princess. The girl he described *was* too good to be true, and his wishful, insistent fantasy doomed their relationship before it began. Time and distance had molded Priscilla into the perfect woman.

Elvis hit a real low point a couple of weeks before Christmas as shiny decorations covered Memphis streets and a holiday atmosphere brightened the city. All the festive cheer made Elvis miserable and grumpy about everything—Vernon being happy, Dee loving Vernon, being at Graceland for Christmas without his mama. . . . He was particularly agitated at not having any control over his music or movies, and his anger festered inside him like a cancer.

"I'm getting fed up with Parker bossin' me around and refusin' to take me seriously on this. I appreciate all he's done, but it's *my* career, not his."

He resolved to have it out with Parker and called to arrange a meeting later in the day. Once Elvis jumped on something, he couldn't rest until he had seen it through, plus he wanted to act while he felt angry and sure enough about it. Confronting Parker was scary, but he challenged himself to take control. Maybe he could rid himself of that ever-present shaky feeling if he stopped letting other people have the last word.

Parker showed up, his face impassive as always, and they went into the music room and shut the door. Their conversation didn't last very long, and when they came out, Elvis's face was pasty and his eyes curiously deadened—the look of a condemned man. Elvis had underestimated Parker and his ability to keep his piece of the Presley pie firmly in hand. It wasn't until years later that Elvis told me what transpired between them, and by then it was too late to undo the damage. But for now, we were all in the dark. When I asked if Parker was going to do what he wanted, Elvis shrugged.

"I don' know. I'm sick of talkin' about business. I jus' wanna go lay down."

I followed Elvis up to his room, but instead of resting, Elvis sat on the floor and rambled on from topic to topic well into the early morning hours. He wondered who he had been in his past lives and told me about a book he was reading on reincarnation.

"It's nice knowin' you don't die forever. I guess sometimes jus' pieces of you can come back, too. I tell you, Earl, I see so much of Mama in 'Scilla. . . ."

His otherworldly thoughts brought Gladys and Jesse to mind, and he remembered conversations he'd had with them.

"They come a lot at night in my sleep. I keep imaginin' what it'll be like when my time comes to join them. I wonder how it'll feel to look at Jesse and see myself. . . .

"I can't see 'em in the day, but I can hear them. And I can *feel* 'em when I'm talking to 'em. It gives me so much comfort to know they're here with me. You know, they say I won't have to wait long before I join them."

"Elvis, don't talk like that!"

"Why? I'm not afraid. When it's my time, I have a feelin' I'll be more than ready to go. I'll be sad at leavin' certain people behind, but happy at who I'll be goin' to meet. You worry too much. Eventually, we'll all be together."

"Elvis, you're only twenty-five."

"I feel a hundred twenty-five."

"If you're just biding time waiting to die, why not just quit? You act like nothing matters except being dead," I said, disgusted.

"I promised Mama I wouldn't. She came to me in a dream, cryin', and I made a vow I'd keep tryin' to make her and Jesse proud. If I gotta be here, I sure don't wanna be livin' in some old shack again. I'll leave that to our relations. If they had their way, I'd be supportin' the lot of them. Give one money and it's like flies to honey, I'm sick of their beggin'. I'm so tired of everyone usin' me for what they want.

"The only one who doesn't is Priscilla. I think she might be the right one, Earl. I feel it. She's not like anyone else. 'Scilla didn't care who I was or what I had. She's simple. There's just something about her. . . .

"I remember back in Tupelo hearin' Mama say that if we just had enough money, we could breathe easy and be happy. Daddy would laugh and say, yeah, ain't nothin' like a little money in the bank. Here I got more money than anyone I know, but how can I be happy? Mama's gone, Daddy's married some whore, I got people who say they're my friends but wouldn't give me the time of day if I was broke, and women who don't know their proper place beside a man.

"It'd be different if 'Scilla was here. I know she can make me happy."

"You hardly know her, besides the fact she lives in Germany."

"She could come stay here. There's plenty of room."

"Elvis, she's only fifteen. Even if she wanted to come over, her parents might not be so thrilled."

"We got along great!" He jumped up, pacing the room. "I could tell they liked me by the way they were so warm and invited me to dinner and all. I'm gonna do it, Earl. I'm gonna call Joe and invite 'Scilla to come visit. It's what I've been wantin' to do. I really need her right now."

"He might say no."

"No, he won't. It's already been settled. That book I'm readin' talks about things that are meant to be. The fact that I'm even readin' the book to know things are meant to be is a sign.

"It's destiny, Earl. 'Scilla is my destiny—and I'm hers."

Part V

LONG
LIVE
THE
KING

12

Priscilla's arrival had Graceland abuzz with activity, and on the surface it appeared Elvis was coming back from his long battle against the emotionally debilitating grief that beset him after Gladys's death. Had anybody dared to peek under the comforting outer layer of his impulsiveness in bringing over Priscilla, a darker truth would have reared its ugly head. The basis for Elvis's animation was more mania than happiness. Desperate to find a cure for the wracking lack of control he felt over his life, which had been exacerbated by the recent confrontation with Parker, Elvis viewed Priscilla not as a person but as a solution. He was losing his balance on the ledge over the abyss that yawned beneath him, and he counted on her to grab on and not let him slip off. Priscilla did her best but found it impossible to save Elvis from himself.

During the weeks of Priscilla's holiday visit, life at Graceland took a turn for the "normal." Elvis appeared to spurn his old habits. He lavished time and attention on Priscilla, not so much as looking in another girl's direction. He went to bed at a decent hour, and was the first one up and ready to start the day. He refrained from inviting over the regular assortment of hangers-on and kept the number of people in Graceland down to a minimum to devote his full concentration on her. Elvis went shopping for gifts, without once grumbling about prices being jacked up on his account or being angry at the crowds that followed him. He even found it in his heart to be more polite and less vicious toward Dee. It was like being with Scrooge the day after the night before Christmas, and we all basked in the light of Elvis's happiness.

Christmas of that year was a happy day, and Elvis only slipped into melancholy for a few brief periods over his mama, but shook them off by devoting himself to Priscilla, who endured the scrutiny of everyone with admirable grace. She was sweet, very pretty, very sexy, young, and *very* naive. But not simple in the way of Gladys. She had the innocent and idealistic outlook of a well-cared-for teenager. Elvis presented her as a princess, and she happily accepted the role, not knowing what a straitjacket it would become.

Elvis talked about her constantly. After he made sure to send her to bed at a proper hour, he would bend everyone's ear.

"Didn't I tell you, she's *perfect*. You won't find another woman like her. I tol' you everything'd be better with her around. She fits in like she was born to live here."

It was one of the few things Vernon and Elvis saw eye to eye on. Vernon made a constant fuss over Priscilla, and between the two of them, her head was spinning. One evening Elvis took Priscilla for a drive to look at Christmas decorations, while Vernon, Dee, and I stayed home and relaxed with a few beers. Vernon was slugging them down triple time and was soon waxing philosophic.

"Yeah, I think that little lady might be just the one to tame our young stallion. It's time he settled down and thought about havin' a family."

"Uncle Vernon, she's not even out of high school yet. It's a bit early to think about that."

"She's more grown up than you think—she's already seen half the world. She's got a quiet way 'bout her, but Priscilla ain't no pushover. She's a good match for Elvis. I thought so in Germany, and I 'specially think so now, seein' her here with him." Vernon laughed to himself. ''She's prob'ly more than he can handle—serve him right.''

One afternoon when Vernon and Priscilla were out shopping for gifts, Elvis was antsy waiting for her to get back. He dragged me into the music room and pulled me down on the piano bench next to him. He had learned to play a few chords and sat there listening to the ringing tones before he decided we were going to sing. We started with a few Christmas carols, but before long, we were going through his own catalogue, then on to some of his favorite gospel hymns. Elvis closed his eyes and really got into it, singing as hard as he did on stage in front of a thousand people. He was flying so high he would have probably sung all night if Miss Minnie hadn't made us come eat lunch.

'' 'Scilla makes me feel like singin' all the time. I don' know what it is about her. Wouldn' Mama jus' love her?''

For her part, Priscilla seemed as delighted just to be back in America as she was to be at Graceland with Elvis. She bought magazines and wanted to catch up on the latest trends and fashions, go to the movies, watch television, and go out and have real American shakes and burgers. Her enthusiasm was contagious, and we were all happy and grateful to have her with us. The house radiated a life that had been missing for years. We put up decorations, sang carols around the tree, and had an old-fashioned Christmas dinner with all the trimmings. None of us wanted it to end.

In retrospect, we all put too much on the shoulders of that young girl, had too high expectations of what she could do—but none more than Elvis. She was on a pedestal so high, Priscilla would soon be gasping for breath at the elevated altitude.

Since she was underage and too young to go to clubs, Elvis planned a small New Year's gathering. Even if she had been old enough, Elvis wouldn't have taken her out; he wanted this one all for himself. The mood was cheery but controlled as music played and everyone wore party hats. Several times that evening, a look bordering on sadness crossed Elvis's face momentarily, but he was determined to enjoy every minute of this celebration. When it struck midnight, revelers around Memphis crackled the night setting off firecrackers and firing guns to announce the new year. Elvis hugged Priscilla, and she turned her face up for a tender but passionless kiss. Elvis walked her over to the piano and led everyone in "Auld Lang Syne," taking me back to the night we sat in Agnes's kitchen, drinking shots of milk and eating fresh baked cookies. Who could have imagined we'd be here tonight? Elvis's voice was richer, deeper, and just as clear, but what brought tears was the added pain it carried.

The next day, sadness got the upper hand. Priscilla's holiday vacation was about to end, and the thought of her leaving drove Elvis to despair. He was in the music room autographing a stack of pictures. Elvis usually entertained himself by making up scenarios—funny but usually X-rated—about the fans he was writing to, but on this day he hardly said a word. Halfway through, he leaned back in the chair and slapped the desk with the palm of his hand.

"That's it—I just *cannot* let her go back. I've been thinkin' and thinkin' about it, and I got it all figured out. She's *not* leavin' me—she's gonna *stay* here."

"Elvis, she's got to go back. Her family's there, all her friends, and she's still in school. She's only fifteen."

"I'm her family now, too. You've seen how happy she is. She'd rather be with me than over there in some foreign country with weird food and people you can' understand. That's no place for a girl like her. I told you, I have it figured out. She can go to school here and make new friends. There's no reason why not."

"Her father might beg to differ with you."

"I'll just have to convince him otherwise, then. Can you get ahold of the operator and tell them I need to make a call to Germany as fast as possible. Tell them who it's for so they'll hurry, okay?"

While I waited on the phone, worrying how I was going to explain this one to the press if he somehow pulled it off, Elvis went to enlist the aid of an unlikely ally—his father.

Vernon was as adamant as Elvis that it could work, and they went to talk to Priscilla together. After weeks of peaceful cohabitation, Vernon was apprehensive of the mood Elvis would revert to if Priscilla left. Like everyone else, he believed Priscilla's mere presence would solve everything and make Graceland a home happily ever after.

With Vernon on the upstairs extension, Elvis talked to Joe Beaulieu for close to an hour, while Priscilla sat listening quietly but anxiously. The rest of us roamed the house, nervously waiting for an answer. A sense that the peace of Graceland was at stake gripped the entire household. After sometimes impassioned conversation, it had been miraculously arranged. Priscilla would move to Graceland as a guest of Vernon and Dee, who would take personal responsibility for chaperoning her.

Elvis picked up Priscilla and swung her in a joyous circle. The king had taken claim of his queen.

The "honeymoon" period was short-lived. During the holidays, Elvis had focused exclusively on Priscilla, a luxury afforded by a hiatus from career commitments and by the fact that he didn't yet possess her. Once her residency at Graceland was assured and Priscilla was under his domination, he turned his attentions elsewhere. Like a child who cries and cries for a toy, plays with it for an hour, then tosses it to the side, Elvis took Priscilla's presence for granted. And since he didn't and couldn't make love to her, he was now ready and needy for the next conquest.

Elvis enrolled Priscilla in an all-girls school, Immaculate Conception, wanting her well educated and sheltered from the attention of teenage boys. Under the guise of complying with Mr. Beaulieu's conditions, Elvis tightened a protective net around Priscilla that effectively made her a prisoner. In the beginning, Elvis personally dropped her off in the morning and picked her up at night whenever he was in town or not in the recording studio. He surprised her with lavish gifts and treated her with kind words and actions.

The only one not thrilled with Priscilla was Parker. While it might be less difficult to pass her off as a friend of the family for a temporary visit, convincing the country Elvis was the platonic host of a live-in fifteen-year-old girl would be almost impossible. The only saving grace was the number of people who lived at Graceland and the fact that Elvis kept her under close wraps and didn't flaunt her in public.

While she adjusted to her new home, Priscilla seemed content to spend time in Graceland, but as she acclimated to her surroundings, the natural restlessness of a teenager surfaced. Elvis sternly cautioned her against going out alone at any time, citing his concern for her safety.

"We're not like other people who can walk down a street. Life's different for us."

Starting in 1961, Parker veered Elvis away from touring as a singer and more toward being a Hollywood movie star, where you could make the most money in the shortest amount of time and with the least effort. His albums sold the same, regardless of whether he promoted them on the road or not, so he confined regular live performing to Las Vegas. As a result, Elvis spent a lot of time away from Memphis in California and Nevada. This was a catch Priscilla hadn't contemplated, and the realization they'd be apart upset her. When she first pouted about an upcoming separation, Elvis cuddled her and comforted her with loving murmurs.

"You *know* how bad I want you to come with me, but you've got school. It's important to me that you get your diploma. I'll be back soon, I promise."

What he neglected to mention was that he preferred her confined at Graceland. He assumed it prevented her from meeting any young men and allowed him the freedom to partake in his sexual activity unencumbered.

He assuaged her upset by promising she would come

with him during the summer, and they'd be together all the time after she graduated. He was so sincere, she melted and obediently dried her tears with brave resolve. When he came back from a trip, he doted on her for a day or two before getting distracted with a rehearsal or an evening with his boys. But even when summer came, conveniently for Elvis, his schedule rarely permitted Priscilla to travel with him, so they were apart quite often. Priscilla was a beautiful bird in a gilded cage. At that age, nobody should be cooped up in a big house all alone, secluded and barred from access to friends her own age. She was just as much a prisoner of his success and emotional shortcomings as he was.

Every time Elvis went to Hollywood to make a picture, the papers would link him to this or that actress or starlet, and for the most part, the stories were true. He didn't care if the women of the moment knew about each other, but he did care that Priscilla not know. He cancelled his subscription to the newspaper and *Variety,* but Priscilla doggedly scoured the school library to read the gossip. Word of his romances made Priscilla more petulant before each trip, creating an uncomfortable tension between them.

Elvis denied the stories to Priscilla and passed them off as Hollywood gossip. As with Gladys, Elvis called home every day, but in this case, it was mostly to make sure she was home. He'd laugh off her concern and patiently explain the ways of Hollywood.

"They just do that to sell more papers and more movie tickets, darlin', so don't think twice about it. You know it's you I love."

She was young and in love enough to accept what he said, because she desperately *wanted* to believe he wouldn't lie to her. All of us were under explicit orders to avoid talking to Priscilla as much as possible. He didn't want to take the chance that she would grill us about what Elvis did away from her. It was very clear that if anyone let on about anything, they would be out the door immediately.

"My private business is mine—she got no need to know. Who I see's of no concern to her, we have somethin' different goin'.

"I'm not lyin' when I say the stories help sell tickets. It's important my fans see me with lots of different girls. Parker says my fans would be upset if I stayed with one steady girlfriend. It's better I be available. And I have to keep doin' these movies, who knows how much longer they'll care anyway."

Elvis was able to keep the peace with his convincing explanations for a long time, but as Priscilla got older and wiser, she also got less trusting, and it took much more effort on Elvis's part to smooth over the bumps.

When he was younger, fresh out of high school, sex was a harmless sowing of oats, almost good-natured fun and experimentation. But the double standard that had been there produced mutant seeds and sprouted a crooked branch. Now his exploits carried so much baggage, hidden meanings and power struggles, sex was harmful not just to him but every woman he became intimate with, whether physically or emotionally—especially the girl he professed to love.

Even though there were several Smith cousins on the payroll, Elvis didn't socialize with them much, preferring the company of his entourage. The last time he visited my parents' house was before signing with Sun. My mother's harsh opinion of Elvis reflected old family beliefs that had their roots in the tired soil of Tupelo.

The idea of Elvis living with a teenager was more acceptable and less shameful that his apparent carousing. The day a Memphis paper ran a photo of Elvis escorting a Hollywood star to a premiere of his most recent film, my mother pushed it away with disgust.

"You know, your Uncle Vernon never once cheated on Gladys, not that anybody could have blamed him. But you know why? Because the family wouldn't put up with it. At least our side wouldn't of. Your daddy would have gone and given him a good talkin' to, told him to stop it or else be cut out.

"Problem with Elvis is that he surrounds himself

with people who're afraid to open their mouths. Money makes people forget their morals. You ought to remember that.''

''I don't have any money,'' I tried joking.

''You're just as bad as the rest of 'em. Afraid if Elvis gets mad at you, you won't get to go places with a movie star. Blood's thicker than that. You of all people should put him straight.''

''It's his life, how can I tell him what to do? Elvis doesn't listen to anybody but Parker. And that's just about business, and he acts like he hates him for that, too. No reason to yell at me—I'm not the one doing it.''

''If you allow it, you're just as guilty. Before you know it, your morals will be as bad as his. He's not a good influence, never was. A horse's color don't change just because it gets a more expensive barn.

''That boy's been plotting at how to get back at the world since he was a toddler. He didn't wanna be a singer for the joy of it, he wanted to be famous to rub others' noses in it. But money can't hide the fact that he's a Presley, through and through. It's in his blood.''

Ever mindful of Elvis's threats, if Priscilla ever asked or pumped us for information, we all emphatically denied that anything was going on between Elvis and whomever, no matter how difficult Elvis made it for us to do. Had Elvis been able to establish a fulfilling sexual relationship with Priscilla, he might have been less inclined to seek the flesh of others. He was greatly aroused by her and admitted they played ''games'' but stopped short of consummation. Instead, he'd tuck her in, have one of us procure a hasty date, and have it off in the back seat of the limo—half the time without leaving the driveway. These raw encounters highlighted the pureness of his relationship with Priscilla. He couldn't begin to understand the real reason he felt so guilty about wanting to sleep with her, so he explained his determination to hold off on their physical relationship until a proper time by saying that with Priscilla, it was sacred.

While Priscilla pined alone at Graceland, Elvis amused himself with the girls he had on call in Hollywood, Las Vegas, and Palm Springs. Not all these encounters went smoothly, and Elvis still felt the sting of rejection acutely.

One romance that ended before it started was with Rita Moreno. He made a date with her and promised her it would be a big, romance-filled night out. When Elvis showed up accompanied by four other guys, Rita took one look, told him he could go fly a kite—with his buddies—and went back inside the house.

Elvis occasionally got more entangled than he bargained for when he became the object of some aggressive lady's desire. One co-star who pursued him with single-minded vigor was Nancy Sinatra, the female lead of *Speedway*.

For once, Elvis made an attempt to stay clear of an involvement, mostly out of the fear he still had of her father. But Frank couldn't have cared less who Elvis slept with as long as it wasn't one of his ladies—Nancy he could have and with his blessings. For Elvis, the affair was a way to pass time, gratifying mostly because of how desperately he claimed she wanted him; he laughed at how he could get her to do anything he desired. But when the movie was over, he didn't give her another thought—until she showed up at Graceland a few weeks later, after he was no longer available for her calls.

Elvis took her into the music room, and he was forced to break it off face to face, all along terrified Priscilla would find out who was there and grill him on it. Nancy eventually left, but for months, Elvis said he had nightmares of Frank coming to get him.

Juggling his affairs and living a double life was more stressful with Priscilla than it had been with his mama. He was always looking for ways to keep Priscilla in her place at Graceland and keep his secret life secret. After she graduated from high school, Elvis insisted she enroll in finishing school, so she would be ready to face the public.

Between the newspaper reports of his flings and the extended periods of separation, Priscilla grew impatient with his frequent departures and began to complain that she never got to see him. While her worries about his fidelity made him tired, her added complaints about his entourage eventually sparked a more violent reaction.

Elvis believed he was giving Priscilla everything she could possible want—nice clothes, a beautiful place to live, servants to wait on her, expensive jewelry, and a future with him. He simply expected unconditional love in return. While the intensity of his feelings for Priscilla were just as strong, her increased complaints smacked of sheer betrayal, wounding and infuriating him.

"I hate being nagged and questioned to death. Ain't nothin' worse than a complainin' woman," he fumed after a run-in with Priscilla. " 'Specially a young one. Means they'll only get worse later on unless you teach her different now."

Equally as upsetting for Elvis was the return of the heavy broodiness and ache of hollowness in the pit of his stomach. He silently blamed it on Priscilla—if she'd just love him and not try to *control* him, he wouldn't feel this way. She was letting him down, and it made him angry and mean.

Although nobody thought much of it, Elvis was never without several prescriptions for sleeping pills and tranquilizers. We all assumed his agitation and edginess was the direct result of the pressures of being Elvis Presley, and if the doctors said it was okay, it was okay. But his reliance on the pills and the amount he took kept gradually increasing as his body gave in to the addiction, a silent weed overgrowing his soul. There were plenty of signs that a terrible transformation was taking place, but they were excused, overlooked, and ignored by us all. Nobody around Elvis is completely without stain, myself included.

One side effect were sudden flashes of temper, as if his brain would suddenly short circuit and fire off a tension-relieving torpedo. I was with Elvis in 1963 while he was filming *Fun in Acapulco*, shot, of course, in Hollywood. He rented a house on Bellagio Road in Bel Air, a posh area adjacent to Beverly Hills, and made it a depot of activity. Priscilla was back in Memphis being baby-sat by Vernon and Dee.

One late afternoon Elvis was shooting pool with several of his buddies, who now did travel everywhere with him. One of the guys had brought a girl he had met at a bar earlier that day back to the house. She had followed in her car, and was excited to be under the same roof as Elvis.

I don't recall her name, but I do remember that she was a great Elvis fan but was being very quiet and respectful. But Elvis was in one of his moods—edgy and inhospitable. When the girl was introduced, Elvis grunted a hello, then asked her to leave.

"We're in the middle of somethin' here, darlin'. Why don't you go wait in the other room."

She sat on a chair outside the pool room all alone for close to an hour. She was very nervous and uncomfortable and wanted to leave, but a car was blocking hers in the driveway. When she came back to the game room to ask if the car could be moved, Elvis stared at her.

"Can't you tell he's busy at the moment? We're in the middle of a game here."

"I'm sorry to interrupt, but I really need to get going."

Elvis hated being contradicted, especially by a woman.

"I told you he was busy!" he shouted, picking up the white cue ball and throwing it at her with all his might.

It hit her with a sickening *thud* directly above her left breast. The force of the blow knocked her down, and it was obvious she was badly hurt. For a moment we were all frozen, shocked at the unexpected and senseless violence. Only her cries of pain snapped us out of it, except for Elvis. He simply walked out of the room, looking disgusted.

We tended to the girl for quite a while, until she was

calmed down and capable of moving. Someone drove her home in her car, with another of Elvis's gang following behind in another car.

I found Elvis in his bedroom, reading as if nothing had happened. He looked up when I came in.

"Is she gone?"

"Yeah, they took her home."

Elvis nodded and went back to his book. I sat down on the bed. "She says she's going to sue you, Elvis."

"She won't."

"You hurt her pretty badly. She could have you arrested, Elvis. I don't think your fans, or Parker, would be very happy about that."

"Earl, she only wants one thing, and that's some of my money. I'll make sure she gets enough to keep her happy and quiet."

It had become Elvis's policy never to apologize. He hadn't uttered an I'm sorry since Gladys's funeral to anyone for anything. His way of saying he was sorry was to buy you a present or give you money. While not everyone can be so easily bought, he was right about the girl. She didn't sue or go to the press with the story. Maybe if she had, it would have forced Elvis to take stock of himself right then. To own up to how much he'd changed in the last five years. It had happened bit by bit, day after day so nobody noticed very much, especially not him.

Elvis put his book down with a sigh and walked across the room to retrieve a vial from the top dresser drawer.

"I got to get to sleep. The doctor says I'm under too much stress and need to take it easy. That dumb bitch got me all upset, and I have to be at the studio at the crack of dawn tomorrow."

As I got up to go, Elvis came over to me.

"Thanks for taking care of things. You'll make sure she's okay, won't you? I got too much on my mind."

Dominating his thoughts that year was the fear of becoming a footnote in music history. The British Invasion and four shaggy-haired youths from Liverpool were changing the face of music in America. Since he returned from the army, Elvis's appeal had steadily moved into the mainstream, pushed along with the help of his unthreatening movie image and his association with polyester-clad Vegas. With the sixties loosening the moral constraints, Elvis wasn't the controversial symbol of repressed youth. Although he wasn't yet thirty, Elvis's career had entered middle age, throwing him into an early mid-life crisis.

His records still sold well enough, his movies made money, and the casinos packed them in for performances, but he had lost his identity. On the road during his early days with RCA, Elvis was the leader of the pack, the Outlaw of Love in black. Now he was known mostly as a star of bad movies he bitterly referred to as travelogues. He occasionally got to have input on the songs he recorded, but the final decision still lay in others' hands, and Elvis blamed Parker for much of his predicament.

"It's no wonder nobody wants to come see my movies—each one's the same as the last. They're nothing but travelogues. Stupid scripts that have me singin' stupid songs," he said in disgust.

"I begged that old man to let me do somethin' different, but he won't 'cause he doesn't think I can do any better."

Elvis's impatience with Parker had boiled over several times—and on two different occasions after staying up all night and working himself into a rage, he actually fired the Colonel. The first time, Vernon got nearly hysterical.

"You gotta talk to 'im, Earl, you gotta pound some sense into his head. Elvis needs Parker. There's no way he can run hisself. Parker knows how to talk to those Hollywood people and understands legal things. Elvis will be lost—we'll lose everythin'. He's just actin' crazy. You know how Elvis gets into a temper over nothin'. Without Parker, Elvis would still be singin' in honky-tonks and driving a truck."

Vernon need not have gotten so worked up, because Parker simply laughed off the threat. Each time Elvis tried to make the break and take more control in his life, assume more responsibility, he eventually backed down out of fear and insecurity, under pressure from the mysterious hold Parker exerted over him.

"Why *can't* you tell him to go to hell? You can find another manager easy."

Elvis would shake his head and bury his face in his hands. "I jus' can't. You don' understand, Parker's got me by the balls. Ain't nothin' I can do."

So his surges of independence never lasted, they merely precipitated orgies of hedonistic indulgence, the one thing he felt complete control over. Elvis played a dangerous emotional game of disassociating his emotions from his body's actions, and he was careless with the feelings of others. In one instance, it came back to haunt him mercilessly.

Among the many admirers among fellow actors and performers who would often seek to meet him backstage or at Graceland was Nick Adams. Nick was the star of *The Rebel* TV series and Elvis was impressed Nick had sought him out. Elvis was familiar with the show because he loved to sing the theme and mimic Johnny Cash.

> *"Johnny Yuma, was the rebel*
> *He rode, through the West,*
> *Yes, Johnny Yuma was the rebel . . ."*

Adams and Elvis hit it off, and Nick was a persistent friend. He called and wrote regularly and flew to stay at Graceland a couple of times. He and Elvis would go motorcycle riding late at night and stay up 'til all hours talking about the pain of celebrity. They also shared a mutual enjoyment of prescription drugs.

Whenever Elvis flew into Hollywood, he made sure Nick knew, and Nick became a regular at whatever house Elvis was renting. Elvis still hated sleeping alone, and he grew close enough to Nick to ask him to stay over on nights he was feeling particularly blue but not up to a sexual confrontation with a woman.

Although Elvis still enjoyed sleeping with two or more women, he seldom did any more, because he found it difficult to achieve more than one erection a night, and maintaining it once he had it wasn't as easy, either. Besides just getting older, the pills he took most certainly affected his performance in bed, and he was ever sensitive of ridicule from his dates.

A few years later, in 1968, when it had been a long while since anyone remembered hearing from Nick, a phone call came with the news that he had died in his Coldwater Canyon home from an apparent drug overdose. Elvis's immediate reaction was to sit on the steps, frozen and mute, then his eyes welled with tears and his body shook, as he rocked himself back and forth, arms clutching his sides.

Elvis was devastated and suffered through it for days. He sequestered himself upstairs and could be heard crying through the closed door. Late at night, Elvis came into the office, where I was organizing mail and photos, wanting company. Everyone else was already asleep, and Elvis looked in desperate need of some himself. He admitted he felt better since taking some tranquilizers, which explained the ever-so-slight slur to his speech. He sat in a daze, unable to come to grips with Nick's death.

"I shoulda been a better friend to Nick, I let him down. I didn' know he was so unhappy. Maybe if I'd of talked to 'im, I coulda stopped him. I jus' had no idea—"

Elvis's voice cracked as guilt held his heart in a vise. He felt responsible for helping send Nick off the deep end and was punishing himself for it. Elvis talked about how close they had been, particularly after a couple of foursomes, and admitted he had "spurned" Nick's friendship later, saying he had needed "room to breathe," because Nick had wanted "too much, ya know?" but never confessed directly the extent of their involvement. Although when some pointed comments were made about the two of them years later by a disgruntled hand Elvis just fired, instead of punching his lights out, which we all expected, Elvis got a pained look on his face and just walked way.

Regardless of any intimacies, Nick didn't kill himself over Elvis—it turned out he had a lot of demons haunting him. But Elvis beat himself over Nick's death for a long time. Not outwardly—after several days he appeared fine—but inwardly. Ironically, it didn't make him stop the meaningless affairs; if anything, it seemed to add some fuel to his self-destructive fire. In his heart, Elvis more than ever felt he was no damn good.

Like Elvis, Nick was looking for a savior, and as Elvis would find out as his life went on, the only one who can save you is yourself. Also like Elvis, no one thing did Nick in, it was the combined weight of a lifetime. Nick's death offered a valuable lesson, but Elvis couldn't see the life-saving forest for the self-loathing trees.

By the middle of the decade, Elvis's career began to slump. Record sales were down, he hadn't had a hit on the charts in a while, and his movies weren't packing them in the way they used to, although they still made tidy profits for the studio. His fans were still loyal, but in a quieter way. It was the time of the Rolling Stones, the Beatles, and hippies. The national hysteria that surrounded his meteoric rise in the late fifties had dissipated. To the youngsters of the sixties, Elvis had become passé. Not exactly someone from their parents' generation, but certainly not a ground-breaker anymore. The social changes were coming so fast that legacies seemed short-lived.

In Hollywood, Las Vegas, and Palm Springs—the places he spent most of his time when not at home— people would point and stare if they saw him in public, but he wasn't followed by a caravan of adoring groupies anymore. It was a hard thing for Elvis to go through, because by this time, his self-worth was almost totally intertwined with his professional appeal. He needed the adoration of his fans to feel loved and valuable. That's why he still called Memphis home.

He was the local boy who'd done good, and they were fiercely proud, and in Memphis he was still king and couldn't walk down the street without attracting a mob. He was the biggest fish in that southern pond and wasn't about to give up his local status to be just another minnow out west.

Unwilling to expose himself to derision, he seldom accepted invitations to parties or premieres when in Hollywood.

"I know they laugh at me behind my back, 'cause I don' always talk right and dress the way I like. It don' matter if I did learn to talk like 'em or make more money than all of 'em put together, they still think they're better than me."

His need for public adoration made live performances increasingly important to him. He never held back on stage and always gave his all when performing, working his tail off to please the fans, so they would love him back. Singing to strangers in a darkened showroom or arena was the purest form of making love for Elvis, because it was the one time he was willing to completely surrender himself to another and expose his needs and vulnerability. People walking out after an Elvis concert swam in an afterglow of emotional intimacy.

When he wasn't on stage, Elvis fell back into the rut of proving his continued desirability and exerting power and control via the women he could attract, but he only found a measure of solace in pills that relaxed—and numbed—his mind.

Home life presented new pressures. While he grappled with figuring out his professional niche, Elvis felt he was being put under the gun concerning marriage. He accused Priscilla of trying to back him into a corner and Vernon for aiding and abetting her.

"A reporter asked me the other day what you was planning on doin' 'bout Priscilla," he said casually.

"What about her?" Elvis asked.

"She's been livin' here since she was a spit of a girl, and nobody's made too much of it out of respect, but people are beginnin' to wonder if you're ever gonna make it legal.''

"We ain't doing nothing *il*legal."

"Maybe you ain't, but that ain't how it looks, and you know it.''

"I don't care how it looks. I'm tired of people constantly poking their noses into my personal business.''

"Elvis, don't you think it's about time you two finally settled down? You ain't ever gonna find anyone better than Priscilla. If you wait too long, you'll lose her to someone with some sense.''

"No, I won't. We got plenty of time for all of that. I'm too busy, and my fans wouldn't like it.''

"You can't run your life worryin' 'bout what strangers think.''

"We all know *you* don't," Elvis countered.

Vernon just shrugged. "And I'm all the happier for it. Who cares what others think?''

"I care about what *I* think, and *I* don't think it's time to get married. 'Scilla knows I love her, so why can' she jus' let things rest for now? I don' understand what the goddam hurry is—we got the rest of our lives together.''

In the early days of his career, Elvis cultivated the notion that his career would suffer if he was "off the market.'' He believed a major part of his appeal was the fantasy that he was anyone's for the taking. With his career in danger of being permanently mired in "travelogue'' movies and middle-of-the-road songs, he didn't want to rock the boat further. Neither did he want to give up the image he had of himself as the Outlaw of Love, the restless spirit. Settling down as a husband would effectively and permanently close that chapter of his life when he felt the most alive and vital.

He was also afraid of the commitment of being an official husband and worried the constraints would get in the way of the time and attention he paid to his career. A sidebar to that was the matter of infidelity— if you weren't married it wasn't technically cheating.

Vernon dropped unsubtle hints about the joys of wedded bliss, but since he was married to Dee, that didn't do much to warm Elvis to the idea; it only served to make Elvis stop speaking to his father for a few days. When he was home, Elvis avoided the issue by spending as much time with his entourage as he did with Priscilla. For the most part, he still treated her like a china doll in front of others, even if she made him madder than hell with what he considered unreasonable complaints.

The constant presence of his gang became a bone of contention. Priscilla wasn't the only one who resented them. Vernon considered them all users and hangers-on. Their function was to be at Elvis's beck and call, acting as errand boys, party partners, occasional pimps, late-night companions, and whipping boards.

Except for Red, who'd been there from the beginning, Vernon couldn't understand why Elvis insisted on throwing away his money on them. Vernon and Elvis got into several heated arguments, and like any kid, the more Vernon objected, the more Elvis defended them. While Vernon's main gripe was financial, Priscilla let Elvis know she resented the time he devoted to them instead of her. He construed her loneliness as criticism, which infuriated him.

"That's the trouble with women—it's *impossible* to make 'em happy. She complains when I go off to work, but then complains even more when I get back. If she missed me so much, you think she'd be trying to give me a little peace. She jus' wants to have a say in everythin' I do. But like I told her, they're my friends, and there's nothing wrong with having your friends around."

"Maybe she just misses you—she's alone in that house a lot."

"I miss her, too. I tell her that all the time, but she don't hear what I'm sayin'. I don't make her feel bad about her friends. Women just like to complain. I guess I figured she was different, but maybe she's not."

The irony is that as much as Elvis yearned for a buddy network and paid through the nose to have one, he never trusted the guys who comprised his gang. He suspected each and every one would make a mad dash for the door if he went bankrupt, and because of that expectation, he often treated them cruelly, finding reasons to insult or embarrass. If Elvis got it in his head that one of the guys had made a cutting remark or committed some other sin, like greed, he would fire him at the snap of a finger; each knew there was a waiting list of guys to take his place. Even Red wasn't immune from Elvis's distrust, although he had always been a most faithful friend and employee.

Again, I feel compelled to say that the escalating drug dependency worked on his subconscious fears and insecurities and let them flourish in his cognitively impaired but conscious mind. In the same way we can scare ourselves to death crossing a lake in the pitch blackness of night, creating monsters out of waves and killers from shoreline bushes, the drugs whipped his imagination up into a frenzy.

Elvis attempted to mollify Priscilla and make peace by allowing her to come visit him in Hollywood during the filming of yet another forgettable movie. Priscilla was delighted to be out of Graceland and in California with Elvis, but her happiness turned bitter as Elvis couldn't refrain from testing her patience to its limits. He left her alone and still saw other women, even though Priscilla was waiting for him at home. The trip turned into a disaster, and the bad feelings on both sides erupted into a terrible fight.

The argument started with Priscilla accusing Elvis of running around behind her back, humiliating her. Guilty as sin, Elvis responded with fury that she dare question him about anything he did, and went into a rage. As if in a spell, he snapped.

"I am so tired of *everybody* tryin' to control my every move. I don't know why she torments me like this," Elvis said later. "I thought she loved me enough to be different, but I keep forgettin', I guess, she's jus' like other women. I wanted to strangle her to shut her up, and that's the truth."

Instead, he attacked her clothes.

''All those pretty things she loves wearing' so much, things *I* bought her, I jus' wanted to rip 'em to shreds to teach her a lesson.''

After he vented his fury on her clothes, Elvis grabbed Priscilla and threw her bodily out into the driveway, tossing the destroyed garments after her. Priscilla collapsed in the driveway, sobbing, confused as to what she had ever done to make him treat her this way. Elvis paced the front room, but as the sounds of Priscilla's cries filtered in, he ran outside and knelt down beside her, holding her, begging her forgiveness. He lifted her in his arms and took her inside, then came back and picked up the clothes littering the driveway himself.

It was like he was two different people, each fighting to overpower the other.

In 1966, Elvis was signed to do the movie *Viva Las Vegas* with Ann-Margret. She was a class act—talented, sexy, and a genuine person, not Hollywood at all. There was an immediate attraction between them, and as Elvis craved someone to get his mind off his dissatisfaction with his career and his anger at feeling railroaded into marrying Priscilla, it was inevitable they would have an affair.

Elvis and the red-haired beauty fell into a relationship that was passionate, intense—and volatile. In the beginning, Elvis was totally smitten and didn't care who knew it. Part of the initial appeal, as with the other actresses he'd dated, was her standing within the Hollywood community. Despite the number of films he'd made, despite his status as a superstar with movie fans around the world, Elvis never felt truly accepted in the movie community. Hedda Hopper, for example, ripped him to shreds in each movie review she gave, and Jackie Gleason, who Elvis had always admired, said publicly that Elvis was a mediocre talent that would not stand the test of time. Maybe through Ann-Margret he could finally gain acceptance. Plus her genuine sweetness drew Elvis to her. She was sexy without being a slut. She was with Elvis only because she truly cared, and he sensed she didn't care how much money he made or who he was.

Ann-Margret was the kind of woman who brought out the best and worst in Elvis. Wanting to impress her, needing to feel worthy of her attention, he turned on the charm and let his boyish, vulnerable side show and won her over with his sense of humor—always one of Elvis's better qualities but one few people saw. She was a very independent, self-assured woman—the type of female that frightened Elvis to death and made him feel inferior and threatened. That inner conflict made for lots of pain and emotional scenes, probably more on her part than his.

This was one of his more public affairs insofar as the amount of time they spent together and his "faithfulness" to her—during that time, she was the only woman he saw. It didn't take Priscilla long to find out, but there wasn't much she could do but ride it out while Elvis wrestled with his predicament.

Someone older or someone who didn't love Elvis as much would have told him to take a permanent hike, but not Priscilla. Then again, what else did she have to hang on to? He kept her isolated and dependent, so she wasn't in the best position to walk. And in his egocentricity, he naively never considered the possibility he was forcing her into the arms of other men.

Elvis vacillated between the two women for a long time. Ann-Margret affected Elvis, and he wasn't able to shake her the way he had other affairs. If he hadn't been so tied up with insecurities, he might have fallen for her all the way. Other than Priscilla and Dixie, Ann-Margret was a love of Elvis's life—but when they met he was carrying too much baggage, and he was too scared to change horses midstream. Priscilla was safe and more manageable, or so he thought, and much less scary.

The excuse he found to drop Ann-Margret was classic Elvis. A picture of the two of them appeared in a local Los Angeles paper, identifying them officially as an "item." When he saw it, he prowled the house, slamming doors and yelling.

"If Ann calls, I'm not here. Not today or any other day. And you can tell her I said that. She can go find someone else to use. She's nothing but a publicity-hungry cat. She arranged to have our picture taken and put in the paper. I told her that we had to be quiet about it, because I didn't want no trouble. She's tryin' to *force* me into choosin' between her and 'Scilla.

"I was fool enough to think she really liked me, but she's as bad as the rest of 'em. Usin' me for publicity to get her name in the paper."

Probably because I was such a fan of Ann-Margret's, I contradicted him.

"Elvis, she's already a star. Why would she do something like that?"

"She's a woman, and that's reason enough. She's tryin' to force me into marrying her or something by makin' people think she's the only woman in my life. I tol' her I had 'Scilla to consider."

It was a convenient excuse. Elvis had been in Hollywood long enough to know that half the publicity generated was at the urging of the studio or on the part of an enterprising photographer, but this scenario suited his needs. He didn't want to know the truth.

"It had to be her, and if I ask, she'll only lie about it. Now I'm gonna get cryin' and ten kinds of hell from 'Scilla. Then *she*'s gonna start in 'bout how I'm always gone and start badmouthin' you all.

"Christ, I wish she'd find someone else and leave me alone. I'm tired of getting it from all sides. Can't get peace anywhere. Not at home, not at work . . ."

Elvis paced around the room, slapping glasses off the tables and kicking furniture.

"Nobody gives a good goddam about the piss-poor songs they're making me do, or that every movie is more stupid than the last. No wonder I'm a laughing-stock. Sometimes I ask myself why I keep comin' back. I mean, what am I tryin' to prove? Parker sure can't tell me.

"I'm stuck doin' stupid movies and singin' stupid songs, but I won't be stuck with women who won't listen to what you tell them. You better tell Ann exactly that next time she calls."

Elvis got himself so worked up he needed to calm down with some Quaaludes, which had been prescribed by one of his doctors. Once their soothing effect took hold, he called Priscilla as if nothing out of the ordinary had happened. He'd deal with her upset later.

Despite his tirade, Elvis found it difficult to tear himself away from Ann and continued to see her over the next few months, but for all intents and purposes, the relationship died that afternoon, and it wouldn't be long before he'd finally make Priscilla his wife. The affair with Ann-Margret and the turmoil it caused within him propelled him to finally marry Priscilla—the one woman he still mistakenly thought he could mold into his perfect woman.

"Nobody I've ever met loves me as much as 'Scilla does. She knew from the beginnin' it'd be her—I always let her know that. I wouldn't let her be with anyone else, so it has to be me.

"Maybe that's what's been missin', and I didn't know it. Bein' married must make a lot of things different."

Elvis and Priscilla were married in the Las Vegas fishbowl instead of the privacy of Graceland—he had no intention of entering this rite of passage without the whole world watching. After the briefest of honeymoons, the only thing marriage changed was Priscilla's name, because Elvis wouldn't and couldn't give up his affairs. He felt suffocated by his personal and professional life, the only release being the high of a new conquest and the comfort of tension-killing drugs. Exactly nine months after his wedding date, Lisa Marie was born, but not even the little princess could stop her daddy's self-destruction.

13

Frustrated at his stagnating career, Elvis gathered his resources and told Parker he wanted to go on tour again, yearning to get that old feeling of the road back. Parker ran with the idea and announced it to the press as a "comeback tour"—a notion irritating Elvis to no end.

"I haven' been away, just doin' those stupid movies he insisted on. He's makin' it sound like I'm a has-been."

Parker convinced Elvis it was a publicity ploy, something to make people take special notice. The King was going to re-establish his place—not just as a singer, rock star, and movie idol—but as one of the great all-round entertainers *ever*. This appealed to Elvis so much he wanted to take it even further. He wanted to go on a world tour.

"When I left the army, I promised those folks I'd come back, and now's as good a time as any to do it. Then we could go on to England and Japan. . . ."

Parker wouldn't hear of it. Elvis argued himself blue in the face to no avail—he didn't know about Parker's illegal immigrant status and assumed it was just another case of the Colonel's controlling him. Elvis ranted, raved, pouted, and claimed this latest run-in with Parker left such a sour taste in his mouth about the tour that he was of a mind to cancel the whole thing. But once the rehearsals were arranged, Elvis felt that itch to perform and devoted his full energies to preparing a terrific show.

The one who suffered, of course, was Priscilla. Elvis was preoccupied and didn't see how she was languishing for his time and complete attention. Not even the news she was pregnant made him reach up and take her off the pedestal and bring her beside him. He simply didn't treat her like a real woman—for one, he never bragged about his sexual exploits with her the way he did about his affairs. In fact, he left the impression that while their sex life was warm, it wasn't exciting enough for him nor did he pursue it with much vigor. After waiting so many years for the proper time to consummate their relationship, he still was beset with the subconscious conflict of the Gladys/Priscilla idol he had constructed. He got plenty of sex elsewhere, what he craved was another mama to take care of him.

The comeback "tour" ended up being a much ballyhooed concert in Hawaii. Elvis received an enthusiastic reception but not much else came from it. The movie scripts sent to him were still mindless pap, his records weren't climbing to the top with a bullet, and knowing Las Vegas was still a stronghold only served to depress him more. He dealt with his frustration by lashing out at those around him, the way most of us do.

For those of us who had known Elvis as he once was, the new incarnation was painful to see and difficult to be around. When he was a child he had to be an adult, now as an adult, he was living out a prolonged adolescence. Understanding what fueled his torment didn't make it any more palatable, and it became increasingly harder to justify condoning it via my continued participation. There were always so many traumas and dramas—covering for Elvis with yet another girl, not that the affair itself gave him any happiness, but the danger and intrigue did; screening telephone calls; avoiding Priscilla lest she ask an embarrassing question; feeling the resentment of his

entourage because of the bond Elvis and I had; seeing
the pill bottles multiply on his nightstand; and watching Elvis compromise himself almost every step of the
way, thinking one thing and acting as if he thought
another.

The Stanley boys were a good example of that later
on. Elvis was always bailing them out of one mess
after another, resenting them for taking advantage of
him but at the same time feeling responsible for their
behavior. Elvis assumed that being raised in the com-
forts of Graceland and exposing the boys to a fast life
of women, pills, and free-flowing booze had corrupted
them. Every time he had to bail them out of jail, or
pay for a bar they had busted up, or pay off a bar
patron they had pummeled, Elvis swore it was the last
time and he was going to cut them off. But as soon as
he faced them in person, the edge taken off by some
pill, he felt guilty and welcomed them back into the
fold—with them unaware they were ever out.

Somewhere along the line, Elvis never learned it
was okay to get mad at people directly, that having it
out and working it through let off constructive steam.
Elvis feared that anger might lead to his rejection—a
thought that touched the center of his soul. The only
people he felt in control enough to confront and overpower were his hired boys. Since he paid their way,
he felt he owned them. The Stanley boys would have
been in the same boat, except that they were step-
brothers and carried the leverage of family ties, loose
as it was.

Elvis eventually got back in his own way when he
had an affair with Billy Stanley's wife. It was his way
of showing his contempt and resentment of Billy, plus
it served the purpose of reaffirming Elvis's appeal.

Beyond all that, Elvis lived a lifestyle that was difficult to keep up with. When he was home, he stayed
up till all hours, able to sleep late into the afternoon
the next day, but for those of us who had work to do,
it took tremendous stamina to overcome the lack of
sleep.

Everything put together was taking a tremendous toll on me. My health suffered as did my enjoyment of doing Elvis's publicity, and finally one day, I woke up and admitted to myself what I'd been trying to avoid: I needed a break from the whirlwind that was Elvis Presley, Star. It was time to move on. But Elvis wasn't just someone I worked for. He was family and a best friend, someone who knew as much about me as I did about him. Even if I went off the payroll, I could never completely leave Elvis.

Remembering the incident in Texas, I was apprehensive, but when I told him what I had decided, he gave me a long look, smiled and grabbed my shoulder. There was no big emotional scene, just a quiet conversation tinged with a little sadness and nostalgia. I could tell he'd been expecting it. When he found out I wanted to move to Los Angeles, he immediately offered to get me a job at Paramount, then sat staring out the window.

"I was wonderin' how long it would take for California to get you. You always did have a thing about Hollywood, way back to Tupelo. God, remember those movie magazines of yours?" he chuckled. "You read those things 'til the pages wore out. Probably still would if you weren't so afraid of running across a picture of me with someone."

"I've run interference for you with so many girlfriends, I might as well move to California and try out for their football team."

"Remember that time I forgot and made two dates for the same night?" He laughed out loud. "I about killed you. I know you were tryin' to teach me a lesson tellin' the one I couldn't make it because I'd gotten a bad case of hemorrhoids from wearing my pants too tight."

"You wanted to tear my head off."

"I would have, but you ran in to Miss Minnie. You lost me a good date that way. How could I see a girl after she's heard something like that. She'd take one look at me and crack up."

Elvis wiped the tears from his eyes and sighed.

"We've had some times over the years, haven't we? God, ever'thin's changing. You're goin' off, hippies are takin' over, and I'm gonna be a daddy. I used to figure I'd have kids by now—course, there are those claiming I do."

"Please, don't remind me."

"I do want to be a daddy—I think I'll be a good daddy. Havin' a baby's gonna change ever'thin'."

Elvis doted and spoiled his little daughter beyond imagining. She was perfect and his spitting image. For a while, just looking at her overwhelmed him with emotion and chased away his torment. But as the newness wore off, the powerful hold of his drug dependency tightened its grip. Deep inside, Elvis was living a self-fulfilling prophecy that he would be left alone because he did his best to drive people away.

He had always placed all his eggs in any one given basket: If he was rich enough, he'd be happy; if he only had Priscilla to take care of him, he'd be happy; marriage would make everything perfect between him and Priscilla, and he'd be happy; being a daddy would change the world, and he'd be happy. Except money hadn't changed his background; Priscilla fell short of the unreasonable image he had created; she betrayed his trust by complaining and standing up for herself, proving she didn't love him unconditionally; Lisa Marie was precious, but Elvis was too needy to experience the true riches of having a child; his career had been a disappointment, and he felt used and taken by everyone around him.

Gladys had taught him well by convincing him he was the source of her happiness and fulfillment, driving home the belief you find such intangibles from others, instead of realizing it first must come from within. Everything he had expected to fill the emptiness that yawned inside him had failed him. He was angry at the world but held himself in greater disdain—if he'd been worthy enough, his expectations would have been met. He turned ever more self-indulgent as his self-pity consumed him.

The most shocking side-effect was his sudden lack of vanity about his appearance. It was a combination of drug abuse and self-punishment, and indicated a certain amount of surrender—he was on the verge of giving up altogether. It also kept him from being wooed by Hollywood.

Of course, Elvis maintained he could lose the weight any time he wanted by upping the number of karate lessons he took a week, and claimed he was just relaxing and enjoying the fruits of his years of hard labor.

Lisa Marie provided Elvis with the perfect excuse to leave Priscilla behind. Ignoring her objections to the isolation, Elvis paid little attention to her.

"Why don't you take up hobbies or learn to cook," he told her. "You know how crazy it gets when I'm working. I don't want her flying all over the place so I have to worry 'bout her. I feel better knowin' you're home, and that's where I want you to be."

The double standard within him was so fixed, it didn't occur to him that Priscilla might get lonely enough to have affairs of her own, which in fact she did. In the same way that Gladys and poverty had robbed Elvis of his childhood, Elvis stole Priscilla's adolescence by shutting her up in Graceland. The time had come for Priscilla to try out her wings, and her actions put everyone in a dangerous muddle.

While Priscilla strove to create her own emotional life, Elvis plodded through his. He grew increasingly paranoid about the press and developed a phobia that people were literally out to get him. For protection, he began carrying a gun, loving the sense of power it gave him.

His paranoia wasn't relegated to the press and faceless would-be assassins. Anyone around him was suspect, as was chillingly proven when he summarily fired Red. Jealousies abounded among the men in Elvis's entourage, with power plays and cliques the norm—plant a seed and watch it grow. Red was loyal through and through and not devious enough to watch his own back. Somebody, somewhere along the line, put a bug in Elvis's ear that led him to decide Red was just using him. Betrayal and treachery would not be tolerated, and Elvis cut him off, just like that. He refused to give a reason and got into a heated argument with Vernon that ended with Elvis reminding him who held the purse strings.

Even Red was at a loss as to why Elvis cut him off so abruptly, but once Elvis let go, there was no coming back. Red went the way of so many others.

On the road during his personal appearances, his weakness for the ladies was as evident as ever. During a performance, it wasn't unusual for Elvis to single out a girl he found particularly appealing. During intermission he'd point her out to one of his guys and instruct him to meet the girl in the lobby and bring her backstage after the show. In 1971, Elvis was appearing at the Sahara Club in Tahoe and saw a girl who knocked him off his feet.

The girl in the audience—let me call her Mary, but that was not her name—was with her mother. She wore minimal makeup but was very pretty. Elvis made lots of eye contact with Mary, was very flirty and sang half of his show directly to her.

Immediately after the show she was escorted—minus her mother—back to Elvis's hotel suite. She stayed with him throughout the rest of his Tahoe engagement, and he liked her so much that he risked taking her with him to his home in Palm Springs.

The Palm Springs house was a bit on the tacky side, because it was used primarily for romantic rendezvous. Elvis, Mary, and his guys settled in for a few days of R & R, and the party began as soon as Elvis called Priscilla to say goodnight.

Elvis's usage of prescription drugs had branched out to include more than just sleeping pills—painkillers and depressants of various types were taken carelessly, including Hycodan, a narcotic. Elvis took some to get "loosened up" and gave Mary some as well. They retired to his room, and the guys with Elvis thought no more about it.

The next day, Elvis was later than usual getting up. One of his group knocked on the bedroom door for several minutes and, when there was no answer, walked in. Elvis was groggy, trying to respond to the knocking. Mary was lying very still, unconscious. They tried waking her up, and when she wouldn't, they panicked.

Some of the guys insisted an ambulance be called immediately, but the others were afraid. Thank God, good sense won out. The paramedics were called while they dragged Elvis out of bed and threw him into a cold shower to clear out the cobwebs. By the time the medics got there, Elvis was dressed and alert. Aware of what was going on, and informed of Mary's precarious state, Elvis wasn't overly concerned. He stayed in the back room reading until the ambulance left, then sent out for pizza.

Mary remained in intensive care for several days, lingering between life and death. Elvis never once went to see her, he never once called. Mary pulled through, and when she was released, there was a return ticket to Lake Tahoe waiting for her. He made it a point not to be available for any communication with her after that.

The shy, polite, fun-loving kid was long gone, replaced by a walking drug store. If anyone ever dared to caution him, Elvis would laugh.

"I am careful—to make sure I don't run out. It's doctor's orders, cousin. I need to stay loose and relaxed, or my blood pressure gets too high. It helps me forget my troubles.

"Work, family, marriage—you name it. 'Bout the only thing I can count on is when I'm on stage. I know those people out there love me just the way I am. Everybody else seems bent on giving me a hard time.

"Lisa now, she's an angel—too bad she can't give her mama lessons. All we seem to do is fight. Nothin' I do makes her happy anymore. I don't know what she wants."

Probably just a more normal life and less abuse would have sufficed. Elvis got careless and less discreet with his affairs, tormenting Priscilla by flaunting his other women. Obviously, he wanted her to know, to punish her for failing him and to test the strength of her professed love. Once he *accidentally* forgot to destroy a note sent by one of his flings.

"If it weren't for 'Scilla, I'd of had it framed," he said. "The boys and I nearly wet our pants when we read it. It said, I'll never forget last night and she signed it, Lizard Tongue. And it was," he laughed. "I ain't never felt nothin' like it in my life. Of course, when 'Scilla found it, she ripped it to shreds."

He ducked Priscilla's accusation of infidelity by swearing the letter was from a crazy fan who sent it after a concert. He deluded himself into believing Priscilla bought that story and was over her anger and humiliation.

He ran out of alibis the night Priscilla caught him red-handed in Palm Springs. She drove down to the sleepy desert resort with a girlfriend from Los Angeles and barged into the house. Some of Elvis's guys tried to stop her or call out a warning, but she was on fire and not to be messed with, and she burst into the bedroom. Elvis responded with his own fury, incensed that Priscilla *dare* check up on him, the illogic of his argument exasperating. They screamed at each other, hurling slurs and accusations at one another. The incident didn't immediately break them up, but it slashed an irreparable tear in the fabric of their relationship.

In January of 1972, Elvis was appearing at the Hilton in Las Vegas when he was introduced to a top-notch karate instructor from Hawaii named Mike Stone. They had met once before when Elvis was performing in the islands, but they got a chance to get to know one another during this appearance on the Strip. Elvis and Mike hit it off and became fast buddies. Elvis hired Mike that very night to be his personal karate instructor—and made arrangements for Stone to give Priscilla lessons as well.

"Maybe if she has somethin' to do, she won't always be on my back about not bein' there," he said snidely.

Elvis trusted Priscilla, partly because he kept her pretty well isolated, partly because his sexual ego wouldn't dream of her infidelity, and partly because she was simple and pure and not driven by thoughts of the flesh—or so he convinced himself. It never occurred to him that Priscilla would be unfaithful. He once joked about it.

"Nah, I've ruined her for any other man. Once you've had the best, you're hooked. And all the girls tell me I'm the best. 'Scilla ain' like that, anyway. Never has been—that's why I picked her in the first place."

On the few occasions that Elvis let Priscilla and Lisa Marie travel with him, it wasn't unusual for Mike Stone to show up and give them instruction. In California, Elvis owned a house in exclusive Holmby Hills, and it was from one of the maids there that word first got out that Priscilla and Mike Stone were having an affair. In the past, everybody looked away, but this time, something nudged Vernon and made him especially nervous. He couldn't blame Priscilla—he'd been after Elvis for years with dire warnings that he was going to lose his pretty, vivacious wife if he didn't take better care of her. But Elvis was still his son, and he sensed how close to the edge he was.

"Maybe she'll end it before there's any trouble. It'll kill Elvis, even if he does deserve it. That girl's been through hell."

Vernon's prayers were not answered. Later that year, Priscilla showed up unannounced in Las Vegas. Right before he was to go on and perform, she told him she was leaving and that there was another man. Then she left him to wallow in his disbelief and *his* humiliation. Elvis was in a state of shock but never considered cancelling the show, and that night he gave one of his most affecting performances ever. He bled for his fans—had he shown Priscilla half as much, they'd have still been together.

That night, I got a 3:00 A.M. phone call.

"Earl, another man's taken my 'Scilla. She told me she's leavin'."

I pretended to sound shocked, and asked who it was.

"She wouldn't say, but when I find out I'll kill him. I mean it—I can't stand the thought of another man laying his filthy hands on her. I'll kill him—I'll have it cut off."

Elvis went on and on, sometimes yelling, sometimes crying. "What did I do? I gave her *everythin'* any woman could ever want. She had pretty things and a maid to take care of the house, I encouraged her to learn things and invite people over. . . .

"She said she was lonely, but there was always people with us. And I can't be home all the time—I got to work. My career's important to me. I know people don't buy my records like they used to and I don' do movies much, but the fans that I do got, I gotta keep them happy. They're all I got now.

"Everyone is always leavin' me. I suppose it's only a matter of time before my fans do, too.

"Goddam that Mike Stone. I'm gonna have him killed. I am—I've already got someone working on arrangin' it. He'll be sorry he ever thought about touching my wife."

The last threat wasn't idle. Elvis *had* ordered someone to arrange a hit on Stone. I know because they told me. This person was terrified—he couldn't arrange a killing, but he was afraid of what Elvis would do to him if he didn't. He needed the money Elvis paid him to live on and had no other marketable talents. He'd never come close to pulling down at a real job what he earned with Elvis.

"He's crazy, Earl, you can see it in his eyes. Especially when we're in Las Vegas, that's all he can ever talk about. He shot up the TV when *The Streets of San Francisco* came on because one of the cops is named Mike Stone. He calms down at home, but here he's just nuts."

If Elvis really wanted to have someone killed, he

knew enough people in Vegas to have it arranged himself. Although Elvis had probably forgotten how to do anything for himself by this time. Still, I didn't think he meant it deep down—I *refused* to believe it. Elvis might be out of control, but he was still a good person deep down inside. That side had been buried by his disillusionment, isolation and pain, but it was still there.

I suggested we call Elvis's bluff. If he was ready to go ahead with a killing, the police would be called instead.

When the flunkie told Elvis a hitman was ready and in the wings waiting, Elvis stared at him a long time, then gave a little laugh.

"Aw, the hell with it, let's forget about it for now."

Throughout the period between their separation and the divorce, Elvis never gave up hope that Priscilla would come back to him. He called her constantly, tried to win her over with shared memories and a belief they were each other's destiny, but she wouldn't be swayed.

Elvis took his anger and frustration at Priscilla's rejection out on whoever happened to be in his path. He almost caused a riot at one concert by throwing his expensive rings into the crowd and coaxing the ladies to come get them. Several people were injured by the sudden crowd rush, and Elvis was forced to pay a lot of money to avoid being sued for even more.

He nearly caused a racial incident by insulting his black back-up singers on stage by telling the audience they had "catfish on their breath."

He developed an intense dislike and resentment of other entertainers—almost every other entertainer. Robert Goulet was a favorite target, as was Pat Boone. One time when Elvis was in Vegas, Goulet came on the TV during dinner. Elvis picked up a gun and shot the TV—causing it to explode, glass flying everywhere—then calmly put the gun back down and continued eating.

He pulled a gun on Jimmy Dean, after the easygoing country singer joked about how long he had to wait for security to clear him back stage.

Nothing he did changed the fact that he had lost Priscilla, and they were divorced in California during the fall of 1973. I was with Elvis on the day they went to court, and his moods were swinging wildly between depression and fury.

At one point, he reached out and held her hand, begging her not to go through with it. He couldn't believe she was really leaving. Outside the courtroom, reality began to sink in and Elvis shook with fury. He reached into his pocket, grabbed a handful of cash, and threw it at her.

"That's all she ever wanted from me, anyway. I gave her everything but it wasn't enough. Nothin' ever been enough."

Elvis was able to delude himself he wasn't a drug abuser because his pills and liquids were prescription medicines, doled out by doctors in response to Elvis's complaints of stress and insomnia. When he traveled, his suitcases were loaded with dozens of little orange bottles filled with a myriad of pills, and his medicine cabinets at home were a cornucopia of pharmaceuticals.

When Elvis was under the influence of whatever drug was his favorite at the moment, you could expect the unexpected. One afternoon Elvis and a couple of his buddies went to have some prescriptions refilled at his favorite pharmacy. Elvis was upbeat, almost manic, that day and in the mood for company. The pharmacist, who was a big fan, loved showing off to his customers that Elvis Presley was a friend—so much so that on a couple of occasions the pharmacist let Elvis don his coat and hand out prescriptions to startled customers. Elvis would laugh like a little kid at the double-takes he got and would stand behind the counter for hours, entranced at being in the company of thousands of pills.

It seemed like harmless fun, but the joke masked a mind and soul that was racing out of control. In public situations like that, Elvis was usually expert at hiding the turmoil beneath the surface, but periodically his mood would abruptly turn black, stunning those who were unaware of his chemically induced emotional swings and causing Elvis to hurry home and shut himself in his room, often for days or weeks on end.

The drugs Elvis took to calm him actually exacerbated his feelings of vulnerability and insecurity. His greatest fear was being poor, and Elvis dwelt upon it constantly. On more than one occasion, he took handfuls of jewels and cash into the backyard of Graceland and buried them—little treasures to call upon should he suddenly find himself penniless. Certain members of his entourage would watch Elvis digging in the dark, a pathetic figure trying to ward off his worst nightmare. They didn't try to stop him, because on one hand, they knew how violent Elvis could become if you got in his way, and on the other, they knew full well the odds were great that Elvis would remember nothing of his handiwork by the time he woke up the following afternoon. Once they were convinced he had forgotten his buried treasure, they would dig it up and split the stash among themselves, secretly laughing behind Elvis's back. It's no wonder he used to say he never felt he could truly trust anyone.

Elvis's last chance at salvation came during 1975 in the unlikely form of Barbra Streisand. She and Jon Peters flew to Las Vegas and asked Elvis to co-star in the re-make of *A Star Is Born*. Elvis couldn't believe it—the chance to work with a real actress in a real movie, not some "travelogue" where the only thing that changes is the scenery. Playing a broken-down rock star appealed to him—it wasn't just a role, it was his life. He could pour everything into it.

As far as he was concerned, it was a done deal and he was already making plans. He arranged to take acting lessons and told the cook to take it easy on the fried foods, although his bloated appearance suited the character.

He turned the negotiations over to Parker with more than a little smugness.

"Won't he have a small calf to find out Barbra Streisand, an Academy Award winner, wants me? Wait 'til I tell Daddy and Miss Minnie. This is what I've been waitin' for.''

Elvis was so sure he had the role sewn up, he checked himself into a Memphis hospital under an assumed name—and under the cover of darkness—to get a facelift. The vanity of it all wasn't lost on him, but he didn't care—visions of a career rebirth danced merrily in his head.

''Jus' don' make me laugh,'' his muffled voice came across the phone line. ''My face feels like someone packed it in cement. God, I look like a mummy. Maybe I should try out for a monster movie instead.''

Elvis was so busy luxuriating in his own emotions, he failed to notice Parker's lack of enthusiasm. The Colonel was used to calling the shots and was insulted that Streisand approached Elvis directly. He wasn't about to relinquish control at this late date, nor was he willing to have Elvis prove him wrong. Parker had spent the last decade telling Elvis he wasn't good enough to make it without Parker. His favorite putdown was ''I do everything but go out and sing for him.''

Nor was he about to let some woman go over his head. Parker had all the money he could ever spend, but he wouldn't give up his power without a fierce struggle. The biggest shame is that Barbra's people bent over backwards, but Parker easily managed to find deal breakers—billing and money. He wanted Elvis's name, and Elvis's name only, above the title and a million dollars.

Parker told Elvis that Streisand changed her mind, and decided to go with the more popular Kris Kristofferson. Elvis was crushed and holed up in his room for a full week.

Elvis didn't discover the truth until after the movie had been made, when a studio lawyer came to visit him backstage in Vegas. When he confronted Parker, Parker shrugged.

''You don't need Streisand. I'll find you something

better where you don't have to share the screen with a scene stealer.''

Elvis was furious and beside himself with despair. He almost hit Vernon for siding with Parker yet again.

"This was the chance of a lifetime. I can afford to work for free if I want. Goddam it, it's my career, not yours.''

"The Colonel's always known best. You'll see. If it weren't for him—"

"Shut up! Jus' shut up!''

Parker was dealing with simple people and he knew it. Elvis never made another movie.

His lost chance at returning to the top touched him to the very core of his soul. It festered and poked at him, not letting him rest. No amount of drugs or women could completely erase the horrible knowledge that he had let it happen by a deal he'd made with the devil years ago. In a last moment of lucidity, Elvis gathered himself up and realized if he didn't make a break now, he never would. He had spent his adult years going through a painful adolescence, and he was ready to assume responsibility for his life. Besides not wanting to fade away into a has-been, he wanted Lisa Marie to be proud of him. It was time to come clean and to stop running scared.

He put himself on the line and told several people he was going to fire Parker, and that if Parker wanted to try and ruin him, so be it. He didn't have much left to lose as it was. He also confessed to the secret that had hung over his head like the sword of Damocles. In the liberal atmosphere of the seventies it was hard to believe what Parker had used to control Elvis for the last seventeen years—a week's worth of home movies of Elvis in bed with underage groupies.

Elvis said that Parker somehow found the tapes—or had paid one of his early hired hands or household staff to keep a special eye on Elvis. He never knew who. But Parker knew as soon as Gladys died, he'd need to find a new leverage. The day Elvis intended to lay the law down to Parker about the direction he wanted to take his career, Parker countered with checkmate. With the Jerry Lee Lewis scandal fresh in everyone's mind, Parker convinced Elvis his career wouldn't be worth spit if those tapes made their way into the hands of the press. He had him by the balls and would twist them any time Elvis displayed a surge of independence.

But confession is good for the soul, and Elvis felt a weight lift off his shoulders. Years of being professionally submissive couldn't be erased in a day or even a month. He had built up his strength for the confrontation, but in his mind the decision was made.

The phone woke me in the middle of the night, and I knew immediately it must be Elvis.

"Hey, whatcha doing?" he asked.

"What do you think?" I laughed. "How's it going on your end. Everybody alright?"

"Oh, yeah. Dad and Miss Minnie are on my tail just like always," he said with affection. "I got me a new girl."

"Yeah, I know, you wrote to me about her."

"That's right—I forget things sometimes."

"You okay?"

"I'm just tired. There's nothing wrong. I'm starting to take up exercise. I need to get back in shape."

"You must be in love," I joked. He laughed.

"Not that much. No, I'm gonna go back on tour. We're going up to Maine first, then travel all over, just like the old days. Let the rest of the world know I'm still alive. But I gotta lose some weight first. I started a few days ago and should be in great shape in a month or so—if I live through it.

"Then before we leave, I'm gonna kick Parker out on his ass. If nobody wants to come see me sing, that's their problem. I'll be there even if it's just for one person.

"What's worse than the exercise is not eatin'. I'm so tired all the time, sometimes I don't think I can make it, but then I remember Lisa Marie and hear

Mama or Jesse remindin' me I made a promise. I'm gonna make 'em all proud.''

It was the last time I heard his voice.

A slight breeze cooled the night air and I shivered, bringing me out of my reverie. Who can say if Elvis would have had the wherewithal to follow through on his plans? Drug addiction is insidious and a mean opponent to the strongest of competitors. All I knew was that Elvis wanted to try, he realized he didn't want to die, he didn't want to give up without a fight. He just realized too late. Climbing out of a seventeen-year hole was asking a lot, but Elvis found it in himself to want to try. He sought redemption, but the years of abuse had the final say and shut his body down before he had a chance to wage his toughest battle.

Like Van Gogh, whose visions resulted in both beautiful paintings and the loss of an ear, the very qualities that made him a performer for the ages also worked to destroy him. Greatness is seldom achieved without great sacrifice, and in Elvis's case, he was the sacrificial lamb.

As I sat there, trying to come to terms with my sense of loss, I thought about the legacy Elvis had left behind and realized that as long as his fans played his records and remembered his talent, Elvis would live on forever. The seediness of his final years that have been covered ad nauseam elsewhere should be tempered with the knowledge of what brought him to that point. The Elvis of the seventies is not the Elvis that deserves to be remembered.

While it's true that the very success he dreamed would set him free became a prison that was his ultimate downfall, we shouldn't pity Elvis. He accomplished more goals, experienced more success, left more of a mark, touched more lives and *lived* more than ten average men.

He was like a nova, a star so bright that it burns out quickly—but not before lighting up everything around it.

About the Author

Earl Greenwood, a second cousin to the late Elvis Presley, was with Elvis Presley in a personal and professional capacity—serving as his press agent for a time—throughout Presley's career. He lives in Los Angeles.

Kathleen Tracy is a writer who lives in California.

Buy them at your local
bookstore or use coupon
on next page for ordering.

There's an epidemic with 27 million victims. And no visible symptoms.

It's an epidemic of people who can't read.

Believe it or not, 27 million Americans are functionally illiterate, about one adult in five.

The solution to this problem is you... when you join the fight against illiteracy. So call the Coalition for Literacy at toll-free **1-800-228-8813** and volunteer.

Volunteer Against Illiteracy. The only degree you need is a degree of caring.